PRAISE FOR

Gettin' Kinda Itchie

In the 1940s and 1950s music was a required subject in school, and all children learned it. When in the '60s, they shared and exchanged their common musical knowledge and differing traditions - be it gospel from church, jazz from a club, or banjo tunes from Appalachia. Through their evolving musical configurations, and infused with their newly acquired styles, they inspired one another to create an original sound for a transitional moment in American culture. In *Gettin' Kinda Itchie*, Richard Campbell magnificently documents these events by telling the extraordinary story of the paths that led John, Cass, Denny, and me, to each other. With incredible research and an unwavering commitment to the facts, Richard meticulously puts together the puzzle of how The Mamas & The Papas were made, and he gets it exactly right.

MICHELLE PHILLIPS
Original Member of The Mamas & The Papas, Actress, and Songwriter.

As "the guy" I call to double-check any information I'm given about The Mamas & The Papas, Richard's vast and impressive historical knowledge was born out of a true love for the band and their timeless music. His dedication to keeping my mother's memory alive is second only to mine! Telling the prequel story of the journey that led to the creation of The Mamas & The Papas, *Gettin' Kinda Itchie* finally completes the picture. It is a must-read for any true fan.

OWEN ELLIOT-KUGELL
Daughter of Cass Elliot.

For me, *Gettin' Kinda Itchie* was an enthralling, riveting, and revelatory read, unlocking direct quotes I'd never heard and photos I'd never seen. Richard Campbell is an incredible historian, not only for the folk-rock movement, but for me and my family as well. His eye for detail and thirst for the whole story is so wonderful and satisfying. For readers, it will feel as though you were there as these brilliant, wild, and flawed artists found their destinies.

MACKENZIE PHILLIPS
Film and Television Star, Singer, and daughter of John Phillips.

Richard Campbell's incredible wealth of knowledge and dedication to The Mamas & The Papas has always been impressive, and I'm so glad he has built a home for it. Meticulously researched and highly engaging, *Gettin' Kinda Itchie* blew me away.

EMBERLY DOHERTY
Daughter of Denny Doherty.

Gettin' Kinda Itchie, Richard Campbell's odyssey into my father's early days, and those of his cohorts, was eye-opening, touching, and thorough. Featuring many photographs that I had never seen; it was wonderful to get a peek into those emergent years that led to The Mamas & The Papas.

JEFFREY PHILLIPS
Son of John Phillips.

As a self-proclaimed expert on The Mamas & The Papas I learned so much from *Gettin' Kinda Itchie*. Names from my childhood now fit. It all makes sense now.

JESSICA DOHERTY WOODS
Daughter of Denny Doherty.

Richard Campbell knows more about The Mamas & The Papas than anyone I have ever met. It's a pleasure seeing this book come to life.

JOHN DOHERTY
Son of Denny Doherty.

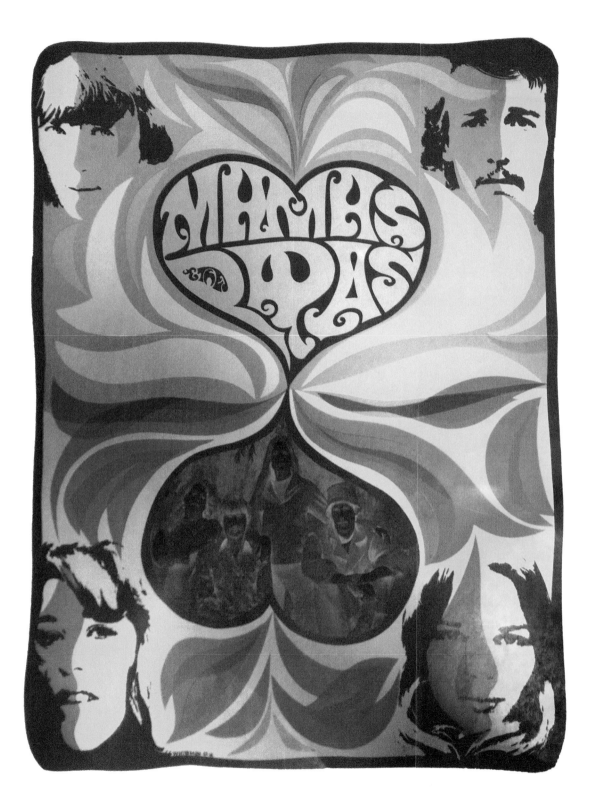

Gettin' Kinda Itchie

The Groups That Made The Mamas & The Papas

RICHARD B. CAMPBELL

For Karen
Who helped me dream this little dream

www.gettinkindaitchie.com

ISBN 979-8-9884903-0-2

Library of Congress Control Number . 2023909949

Book design by Adam Hay Studio, UK

Contents

Preface   6

Rock-a-Ballad: The Abstracts and The Smoothies   10

That Easy on the Ears Trio: The Journeymen   32

A Round, Fat, Beautiful Sound: The Colonials and The Halifax Three   78

Neither Reverent, Doctrinaire, Nor Spuriously Iconoclastic: The Big 3   110

Thundering, and Met with Stunned Silence: The Mugwumps   156

We Were the Crossroads: The New Journeymen   188

Epilogue   206

Notes   211
Appendix   221
Acknowledgments   238
Credits   239
Author   240

Preface

Come and look, see what I have found...

I remember the first time I heard the opening verse to "Come Away Melinda" by The Big 3.[1] It was 1983, I was fifteen years old, and I had just landed the 7-inch white label promotional single at a record collector's show in Richmond, Virginia. I knew, with this 1964 radio station copy, I had found a rarity. As I placed the 45 on my bedroom turntable, I heard a clarion call: the childlike voice of a young Cass Elliot, plaintively singing over sparse, plucking guitar: "Mommy, Mommy, come and look, see what I have found." The heartbreaking ballad went on to tell a story of girls and fathers who had died in war. I was captivated. In my hunt, I had also found an album featuring the song. The color photograph on its cover showed Cass between two tuxedoed men, laughing in a black dress with a white lace collar. She looked far older than her 22 years, and a bit matronly, but appearance aside, the LP showcased that incredible voice, which I knew from The Mamas & The Papas.

Around that same time, I heard The Journeymen's first album at a friend's house. Again, the voices. Such harmony and such arrangements. Studying the record cover, I wondered if the debonair fellow in the carriage in Central Park was really the same John Phillips who, just a few years later, would be pictured in a bathtub with The Mamas & The Papas. Was this the same complex and brilliant man who eschewed the traditional and, in keeping with his Cherokee heritage, made his home in a wilder frontier?

In addition to Cass and John there was Denny Doherty, with his sunny affect and quick-as-lightning wit, and mysterious Michelle, who seemed to take everything in stride and in whom still waters ran deep. These four people—the Jewish songstress from Baltimore who was huge in every way, the ruminative rhapsodist from Virginia who wove the most beautiful song stories, the charming Irish Canadian who always looked amused, and the fetching blonde bombshell from California (with a Mexican twist) who had a lot to say if you asked her—became The Mamas & The Papas. Four people on a trip together.

My forty-year fascination with these individuals has yielded friendships with them and their families, and a collection of records, photographs, sheet music, trade ads, character

dolls and film that overtook much of my house. Through hobby and study, entertainment and analysis, and eventually firsthand interviews with the surviving members and those in their orbit, my passion transformed into expertise. In the 1990s I was approached by a record label to write liner notes for a reissue CD associated with the group, and that task led to two dozen more sets of liner notes, most oriented around The Mamas & The Papas. I was contacted by television, stage productions and print media for help regarding the history of the group, assistance in reaching certain individuals as sources, or for the loan of an item from my collection.

Having read, and to a lesser extent written, much of what has been said about this seminal group that bridged the gap between the folk revival of the early '60s and the psychedelic explosion of the late '60s, I have long noticed how much less attention has been paid to the careers of Cass, John, Denny and Michelle *before* they came together as one unit. To fully appreciate their complexities and beautiful harmonies, as well as their social and interpersonal bedrock, I believe one has to consider the musically hybridized folk tableau out of which they were born. As John Phillips said in 1968, "The Mamas & The Papas were sort of a culmination of seven or eight years work of an arranging style that came together with these particular voices and particular people who were able to execute this style in the proper way."[2]

More specifically, that culmination was the result of various trios, quartets, and ensembles John, Cass, Denny and Michelle formed and reformed between 1959 and 1965. On college campuses, in coffeehouses, and at nightclubs that paid $500 a week, the four paid their musical dues in a number of groups that led to their harmonic convergence. "We'd all had so much experience in live performance through the folk music and years of playing" John continued. "It was really an inbred society—no one made a move without someone else knowing about it and everyone was on tour together continually and working the same circuit of coffee houses. You kept going and going and going."[3] Cass Elliot remembered in 1973, "Those places were at that time what they used to call basket houses. You would sing, and maybe a couple of other performers would sing also, and then they would pass the basket around and people would put in money and then you would split it up. If you made $6 that was a big night."[4]

Lifelong friendships were struck, rings were exchanged, partners were traded, and their paths constantly crossed. And as the country was fast approaching a cultural tipping point, they and other artists in their orbit galvanized, amalgamated, and sharpened the cutting edge of their musical prowess.

"And then suddenly," John explained, "a lot of them switched over to what the media termed folk rock. There was a mass influx suddenly of intelligent musicians and writers into the pop field."[5] He and his group helped lead the way.

Before they became The Mamas & The Papas, Cass Elliot, John Phillips, Michelle Phillips, and Denny Doherty toyed with the idea of calling themselves The Magic Circle. The name never took but it aptly captured their circuitous turns in and out of the 1960s folk scene.

The results were harmonies that soothed and satisfied millions amid the reverberating cacophony of the times. Social upheaval, riots, and the war in Vietnam were largely quelled with dreams of California and a song about the common reality of the first day of the week. The Mamas & The Papas stood as troubadours of a generation and a powerful American answer to the British Invasion. Between 1965 and 1968 the group garnered top ten hits like "Monday Monday," "Creeque Alley," "Dedicated To The One I Love," "I Saw Her Again" and "California Dreamin'," which would ultimately go on to sell tens of millions of records. They broke new ground as architects of the historic 1967 Monterey International Pop Festival, which kicked off the Summer of Love and the next wave of popular music. It was the end of a long path—a magic circle.

This book is about that magic and that circle. It is about the groups, music, and experiences that created The Mamas & The Papas. It is the account of The Smoothies carrying spears in costume, and of the FBI tracking The Mugwumps in Cold War Washington, D.C., and secret marriages to avoid the Draft and keep on singing. This is four musicians' journey from coffeehouses to nightclubs and gymnasiums, before leaving folk music behind and taking flight. "We started off at our peak," Cass once explained. "We had all been singing for some time. We were the accumulation of all the years of practice on an individual level and experience on an individual level… collectively. When we got together it was a composite of all the things that we had learned."[6]

Richard Campbell, 2023

Rock-A-Ballad: The Abstracts & The Smoothies

John Edmund Andrew Phillips grew up near Washington, D.C. Turning 10 years old just after the Second World War came to a close, he entered his adolescent years as the nation entered its years of post-war optimism. The son of a former Marine colonel, John's lanky six-foot-four frame opened doors via track and field and the basketball court at the U.S. Naval Academy and Virginia's Hampden-Sydney College. But young John Phillips, who was by then discovering a talent for writing and arranging songs, took neither to college nor military life.

Ukulele of John Phillips

John Phillips (#25) as part of the Bullis School Basketball Team

John Phillips' engagement picture 1954

"I had no ambition whatsoever," he once recalled. "It was one of my saving graces."[7] While academic and athletic ambitions may not have consumed him, music soon did. And music took him where ambition took others. "I got interested in music after seeing *The Jolson Story*," he told *Hit Parader* in 1967. "I got so hung up on that movie when I was a kid."[8] A fictionalized biography of 1920s singer-actor-comedian Al Jolson, the 1946 film, as one historian noted, "provides the basic narrative for the lives of jazz and popular musicians in the movies."[9] For John it was a primitive template. "I never realized that I really wanted to be a musician until I was almost already one. It sort of snuck up on me," he later admitted. "It took me a long time to figure out I wasn't meant to be an engineer, doctor, lawyer. I was meant to be a musician, a composer. I kept fighting against it subconsciously, and finally I gave in and devoted myself to music."[10] John's high school girlfriend, Barbara Nutwell, observed that devotion. Engaged to marry this traditional Catholic schoolgirl, John backed out of their wedding at the eleventh hour. "He was in love with music," she says.[11]

In hindsight, John's gifts had started to manifest at a young age. "When I was in seventh or eighth grade a friend of mine played ukulele and he taught me a few chords," he said in 1967.[12] Those chords spawned more. At a party, in Alexandria, Virginia, he sat quietly strumming a guitar in the corner when he was approached by another local musician, Phil Blondheim, who would soon enough call himself Scott McKenzie of "San Francisco (Be Sure to Wear Flowers in Your Hair)" fame, whom John asked, "Can you sing?"[13] The answer came as they began to make music together. "One of the things that attracted us to each other," Phil remembered years later, "was that we liked almost exactly the same music. We both wanted to sing. We both loved groups."[14] Phil had been in a group called The Singing Strings with high school chums. The group included Timothy Rose, a capable banjo player who would later be part of a Peter, Paul & Mary-type trio named The Big 3, which would have propitious connections with John.

"My first love has always been to sing in a group with other people," John explained, "so, I would always drive my friends crazy at parties in giving them parts to sing doo wops and all that kind of thing."[15] "John wanted to put a group together," remembered childhood friend Michael Boran, who had first met John when he was twelve. "My earliest memory of John is very vivid. It is of him and my older brother standing over me at the piano, punching me in the arm, demanding me to play 'Song of India' [a popular 1940s dance tune by Tommy Dorsey]. If I didn't, they threatened to beat me up."[16]

John's girlfriend remembers other capers:

> At my high school, St. Mary's Academy, our Glee Club performed concerts. Since it was an all-girls school we had to "import" guys from various schools and from various sources. That being the case, I asked Johnny to give of his talents. At a particular spring concert, I was to sing an aria from *La Traviata*. Johnny sang a duet with a friend of mine. The duet was "We're a Couple of Swells." Right in the middle of their performance Johnny's baggy, bum-like pants broke away from the suspenders and whoops! His pants began to fall, which necessitated the curtain having to be pulled. We have all wondered whether this was an accident or if it was planned. Anyway, the audience was in hysterics, as you can well imagine at an all-girls school.[17]

Above: Scott McKenzie
aka Phil Blondheim
Right: John Phillips and
friends in his car in 1953

"Muuver" by Arnold &
The Muvs c.1956

Trying to Find a Sound

Beyond these collaborations, John was seriously seeking something unique. He was, Boran recalled, "trying to find a sound."[18] "That's what eventually led to The Mamas & The Papas sound," John said. "It started with The Modernaires—the first time I heard those kinds of chords sung by Paula Kelly and The Modernaires. I liked the sound of men and women singing together, like in church or work or whatever. That's what we ended up with in The Mamas & The Papas—that choral blend."[19]

In the late 1950s the sound of the times was moving away from the swing music, *Your Hit Parade*, and show tune covers as the nascent sound of rock and roll was making its first waves. Doo wop groups, which combined harmonies and memorable melodies, along with telegenic teen idols, filled in some of the gaps. John and his friends tried to find their place in that field. "We were in the doorway of doing rock and roll in 1955-56," says Boran. "I was thinking of myself as a rock and roller and, believe me, there were no rock and roll bands in high school. Tim Rose and Phil Blondheim and I had all been in garage band-type playing. I fell into a situation where I could do rock and roll with other people and get paid for it to the tune of $10 a gig. No other kids were doing it or participating. They were all listening. And consequently, we had a lot of following."[20]

As he continued to hone in on a sound, John's first assemblage appears to have grown out of a street corner incarnation called The Del Ray Locals—named for his neighborhood in Alexandria. "We were not well thought of in the larger community," Boran recalled, "but we were benign and not particularly threatening."[21]

Beyond neighborhood harmonizing, John's first recorded efforts happened at Edgewood Studios in Washington, D.C. The studio was co-owned by army buddies Charles Osgood, Ed Greene, and George Wilkins. Wilkins had been part of a legitimate early '50s vocal group named The Spellbinders, while in later years Osgood became a well-known personality on the CBS TV program *Sunday Morning*, and Greene won Academy Awards for sound engineering. It was at their Edgewood Studios that teenage John recorded the song "Muuver" under the name Arnold & The Muvs.

With the lyrics "There's a man I know, oh they call him Muuva," the song mimicked the cadence and style of Ray Charles, whom John idolized at the time. In those days "muuvver" was considered a risqué word, shorthand for "motherf*!#r," which was then exclusive to the black community. Wilkins characterized it as a "joke" and said it was "recorded for laughs," saying, "John and the guys used to do it as a gag at parties. It was so stupid."[22] John soon moved towards more refined material. Wilkins was supportive and Phil Blondheim even remembered the studio owner arranging "Birth of the Blues" for the developing group.[23]

In 1957, 21-year-old John married Suzy Adams, a girl from a much more conventional world than his music life occupied, with whom he had his first two children, Jeffrey and

Suzy Stuart Adams

Mackenzie, in 1957 and 1959 respectively. When they wed, John had been working odd jobs like selling cars and cemetery plots, lifeguarding, and driving buses. But he persevered in his musical undertakings, and on their marriage certificate he listed his occupation as "Professional Singer." Jean Wyss, Boran's girlfriend at the time, remembers, "I went with Mike several times to John's apartment with the two of them, and occasionally others. Mike brought me along to babysit for John and his wife Suzy's baby boy. I think they were in the early days of getting a group together. They were working on a name for the group because when a tall girl auditioned, I suggested they call themselves The 6 Footers."[24]

A Semi-Jazz Thing: The Abstracts

After the dabbling at Edgewood Studios, John began to seriously hone his real talent of blending voices and writing music for the group. With Phil Blondheim, Michael Boran, and some other pals, he formed The Abstracts by 1959. "It was sort of a semi-jazz thing," as John described it. "It was all bobby socks with blue jeans. We just didn't want to sing that. The only thing that we could sing was jazz."[25] This quartet exhibited John's love for harmony and paid a not-so-veiled tribute to modern harmony groups of the day. "Our

The Abstracts:
Bill Cleary, Phil Blondheim
(Scott McKenzie), John
Phillips, Michael Boran

greatest influence at that time," John said, "were The Four Freshmen and The Hi-Lo's."[26] The Abstracts sang at high school proms and had matching sweaters with large letter "A"s embroidered on them. They depicted a clean-cut all-American boys' group—a prehistoric archetype of contemporary "boy bands." Boran wryly suggested with these large letter A's they call themselves "The Hester Prynnes," referring to the ignominious badge of scorn worn by the adulterous protagonist in Nathaniel Hawthorne's *The Scarlet Letter*. On weekends the group would often travel to New York where John began to learn the ropes of song-selling.

The Abstracts recorded at Edgewood, from which one extant 78 RPM record with the songs "When You Find Your Love" and "Remember" survives, although at least one other record with the songs "Cindy Lou" and "Comin' Round Tonite" was also recorded. John was writing enough at this point to deposit songs at The Library of Congress. "Comin' Round Tonite" was one of four compositions grouped as "Songs for Jeff," undoubtedly named for his infant son, with other au courant titles such as "I Fell in Love," "Golden Hair," and "Lovely Lady."

The lyrics were consistently sentimental:

> *Golden hair and soft brown eyes,*
> *Make a fella kind yearn and sigh,*
> *Sighin' for marriage type love*
> *Evening walks down lover's lane*
> *Walkin' and talkin' to a sweet refrain*[27]

At the time, The Abstracts included John's friends Phil Blondheim, Bill Cleary, and Michael Boran, with Bill Potts also possibly playing piano with the group. Boran recalls each fellow having his own place in the quartet: "I was the clown; Bill was the hunk; John was the leader; Scott [Phil Blondheim] was the voice." He also remembered their work went beyond vocalizing. "I can remember standing in front of a full-length mirror with these guys, all of us doing choreography."[28]

The Abstracts had such a clean-cut, collegiate look, it is hard to believe that John Phillips was nearly 25 with a wife and two children. For some of this time, he worked as a mailman in Northern Virginia since his music career was not carrying the full weight of his young family. But as his wife Suzy put it, "He would just disappear. There was no explanation. He heard the drums, and he heard the choo-choo train going, and he had to go."[29] There was even a storied junket to Havana in the midst of the Cuban Revolution. "He came in and said, 'Suzy I need to borrow a suitcase, because so-and-so's father died,'" she said, recalling him going into the

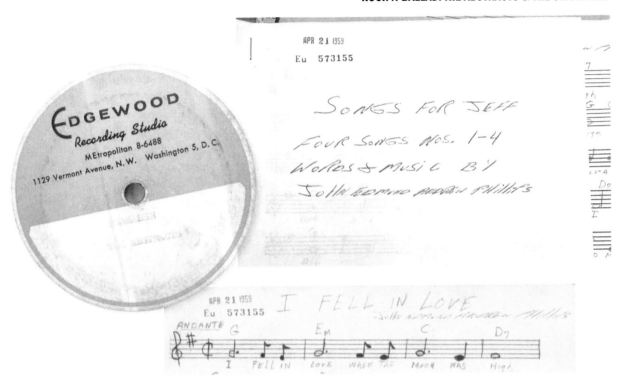

bedroom and closing the door to pack. When he emerged he told her, "I'll see you in about an hour." After three hours had passed, Suzy returned to their bedroom and realized, "That S.O.B. packed *his* clothes." Meanwhile, John was on another adventure. "We were all inspired freedom fighters," he recalled in 1986. "This was before Cuba had gone communist and they were fighting out in the hills. They were closer to Havana than we thought they were. Every morning we showed up for breakfast at a small little bodega in front and sort of a night club in the back. We started drinking rum and Coca-Cola—real Yankees. They started showing dirty movies and the next thing we knew the sun was going down and we'd missed another day of the Revolution." Of course John recognized Suzy's cognizance of his wandering ways: "She was sort of accustomed to the fact that I was a wild one and had to roam around a bit."[30]

By this time, The Abstracts had secured a manager named Mike Thornton, "a short, flamboyant back-slapper who seemed to know everybody," according to Boran. "He drove a big Caddy convertible. Whenever he pulled into a gas station, he made sure to have the oil checked; and while the hood was up, he'd turn to us and say, 'Wanna see a Cadillac motor?' We would reply in unison, 'Hell no.'"[31]

John claimed the boys secured a contract with Big Top Records, a New York pop label that produced the records of Del Shannon and Johnny & The Hurricanes, among others. It was a subsidiary of Hill & Range, which at the time controlled all of Elvis Presley's music.[32] If anything more than a contract resulted, it's been lost to the ages.

While no known recording manifested, the agent did get them a deal. By the end of 1959, The Abstracts found themselves with a legitimate engagement at the Elmwood Casino in Windsor, Ontario, near Detroit. Though it ironically had no casino, the 11-acre property with more than 100 hotel rooms and an audience capacity of nearly 1,000 was a significant spot on the club circuit, with nightly floor shows, dinner music, and comedy routines from polished performers such as Sammy Davis Jr., Jimmy Durante, Ella Fitzgerald, Liberace, and Tom Jones.

With press accounts from that December referring to them as "the vocalizing Abstracts quartet," the group appeared at the Elmwood with the comedy teams of Eagle & Mann and Antone & Curtiss."[33]

ELMWOOD—Eagle and Man, trumpet tooting troupers; Lawrence and Carroll, ball room dancers; the Abstracts Quartet; Yuletide chorus routines by the eight Elmwood Lovelies; singing emcee Chris Columbo; Jack Madden and his orchestra.

The following month they repeated the look and sound in Buffalo's Town Casino, another tony spot, again with Eagle & Mann. The relationship was symbiotic enough to yield a joint composition by John and the duo named "Ring A Ding Ding."[34] At one point their agent Thornton took them to New York to meet with a "mysterious vocal arranger who was down on his luck." Thornton paid him to create three or four charts for The Abstracts. "His name was Dave Lambert, and he later became one-third of the legendary jazz trio Lambert, Hendricks & Ross," Phil Blondheim recalled. "It was thrilling to try to sing his arrangements properly. They were standard jazz-oriented vocal arrangements, not vocalese, but they had Lambert's genius in them. I don't know that we ever did them justice but we sure tried"[35] Bill Cleary was similarly in awe, saying, "One arrangement was for 'Wagon Wheels.' I think we looked at it more than we sang."[36]

Beyond the two out-of-town gigs, The Abstracts do not appear to have ventured beyond the D.C. area until they tried their hand at the big time. George Wilkins at Edgewood Studios knew an agent in New York City named Charles V. Ryan, who had been part of a slick vocal group in the 1930s and '40s with his brother and a female singer called Babs and Her Brothers, and later The Original Smoothies.

John recalled the serendipitous connection: "After bumming around New York a while I went to the Brill Building one day. I had my guitar and all these songs...no demos, or tapes or anything. I went knocking on every music publisher's door asking, 'Can I sing you a few songs?' That's not the way you do it! Then I met a guy named Charly[sic] Ryan who was very helpful to me. He lent me some money and helped me develop the things I was working on."[37]

In the winter of 1959-60, Ryan got the boys in front of Milt Gabler at Decca Records. As the *Detroit Free Press* described it at the time, "They sold their songs and themselves too."[38]

"He just sat there and scowled while we sang. We thought we were dead," John said of their meeting with Gabler. "We sang for an hour and a half and went through practically our whole repertoire. Then he said, 'O.K. let's sign a contract.' You could have knocked us over with a feather."[39] The reaction was understandable. Gabler was a lion of the industry, having recorded hits like Bill Haley & His Comets' "Rock Around the Clock" and Brenda Lee's "Rockin' Around the Christmas Tree." "I remember how excited I was because Milt Gabler has signed and recorded Billie Holiday, Bing Crosby and Louis Armstrong," remembers Phil Blondheim. "He was a musical industry giant and a true gentleman—and Billy Crystal's uncle."[40]

Management's first order of business seems to have been to change the group's name. One newspaper claimed that The Abstracts sobriquet was "too 'far out' for Decca," so Ryan sought the path of least originality and rechristened the group after his former trio: The Smoothies.[41] "We didn't have a name and Charles Ryan, who was constantly zipping up his fly said, 'Okay, you can have my name.' We thought he was being so magnanimous," recalled Boran.[42]

Not only did the group undergo a name change but so did Phil Blondheim. With a head full of curly hair, Phil had been likened to a Scottish Terrier by comedian Jackie Curtiss a few months earlier at the Elmwood, and "Scottie" had stuck as a nickname. So he added the surname Mackenzie—after John and Suzy's daughter, Laura Mackenzie Phillips—to become Scott McKenzie.

Singin' Sweet and Smooth: The Smoothies[43]

Very much a Fifties-type vocal group, The Smoothies' sound was based on the harmonies to which John was already drawn. "I really admired The Hi-Lo's harmony and The Four Freshmen's harmony and The Modernaires, people like that," John later explained. "So we started off that way."[44] Scott sang most of their leads, with his mellow tenor equaled by his easy-on-the-eyes good looks. "He was frequently compared to Johnny Mathis," remembers

Boran, "but his was a natural talent all its own. He seemed to be almost embarrassed by how good he was. He was so very, very, very good, on so very many levels."[45]

Charlie Ryan continued to connect the group with casinos and hotels, and their engagements were typical of the entertainment scene of prior decades in which Ryan's original Smoothies had played. As John put it, "This was the old-time nightclub stuff."[46]

Theirs was a full-scale engagement with Decca, and in addition to the live appearances, The Smoothies recorded their first songs in March of 1960. The numbers were "Softly," "Joanie," "Comin' Round Tonight," and "Twenty Four Hours," with the first two comprising their debut single, released in mid-June. To put into context the strata of the record industry where they had landed, and the punch behind the boys, their recording session was within weeks of Brenda Lee's "I'm Sorry" on Decca, also with Milt Gabler at the helm. This was a major recording, with background singers and a full orchestra conducted by Jack Pleis, who had worked with Sammy Davis, Jr. The lush, ample strings and choir-like background vocals recalled the sound of Percy Faith's "A Summer Place."

These were the lost years in the early days of rock and roll. Elvis Presley was in the army and Buddy Holly, the Big Bopper, and Ritchie Valens had just died in February 1959. Filling the void was the era of the teen idol and the rise of the Brill Building songwriting engine. Between John's compositional talents, and the boys' good looks and smooth sound, The Smoothies fit right into this scene.

They even took this newfound success on the road. They were the main attraction at Mount Airy Lodge in the Poconos. Playing jazz piano there at the time was a then-unknown musician named Bob Dorough, who went on to gain fame years later from his song creations in *Schoolhouse Rock*. Scott McKenzie also recalled The Smoothies playing at the Memphis Cotton Carnival in May 1960, where they were joined by his chum from The Singing Strings days, Tim Rose. Rose recalls they wanted him mostly for his banjo-playing abilities, admitting, "Nobody thought I could sing. I didn't have that traditional style of voice."[47]

By the summer of 1960 The Smoothies were making a splash. They performed at Palisades Amusement Park on July 2 for *Teen Beat*, where disc jockey George Tucker would host and record a two-hour radio show and air it that evening on WNTA. The Smoothies appeared after teen idol Paul Anka and alongside other teenage acts The Delicates and "Seven Little Girls Sitting in the Backseat" singer Paul Evans.

The momentum built and they hit the studio again on July 15, this time recording the African-American spiritual "Michael Row the Boat Ashore," recently made into a hit by The Highwaymen, and the John Phillips' original "Ride, Ride, Ride." By the middle of 1960 the folk revival was in full swing and that sound, which had already begun to capture John's attention, can be heard in these songs. The former was the only song featuring lead vocals from Mike Boran, who remembered being intimidated by the professional choir and orchestra, with nine violins, and percussion, admitting, "We were in awe of these people who could just come in and look at the chart and sing like that." Boran was understandably nervous, and when, "after an incredible choral introduction," the director pointed to him, he missed the note. Adding to the embarrassment, Boran's subsequent "Aw sh*#!" dramatically reverberated in the imposing recording studio, "which was like an old religious temple." Just then, a booming voice made the studio-wide announcement, "'MICHAEL ROW THE BOAT ASHORE' TAKE TWO."[48]

A fortuitous connection was made in the recording of "Ride, Ride, Ride." In this original composition by John, banjo parts were played by Eric Weissberg (of "Duelling Banjos" fame) and Richard "Dick" Weissman, who would figure into John Phillips' journey in the years to come. With a "Very Fast" tempo, as the sheet music describes it, John captured the fervor of a horse chase, complete with the sound effect of a whip:

> Ride, ride, keep on movin' fast
> Sheriff's on your trail, Oh Lord.[49]

Veterans of the recording sessions have claimed that other prominent musicians who played with The Smoothies on these (and possibly other) sessions were jazz bassist Sandy Block and guitarists Tony Mottola and Don Arnone, the latter of whom had played with Frank Sinatra and Barbra Streisand.

The Smoothies also appeared on *American Bandstand* on July 25 with fellow guest Conway Twitty, who had recently achieved a number one record with the pop song, "It's Only Make Believe." This preceded Twitty's country music superstar status. "It was way back when *American Bandstand* was still black and white and actually live," recalled Scott McKenzie of the Philadelphia dance show. "The four Smoothies pulled up in the parking lot in our cold, drafty Vanagon, just as Conway pulled up in a shiny new Cadillac, driven by a swarthy tough guy in a dark suit."[50]

CLICK CORPORATION
c/o WFIL RADIO AND TELEVISION
46th and Market Streets, Philadelphia 39, Pa. - EVergreen 2-4700
-*-

STANDARD AFTRA ENGAGEMENT CONTRACT

Agreement Between

Date July 25, 1960   19____

Roland Michael Boran
XXXXXXXXXXXXXXXXX
John Edmund Phillips
William Gerald Cleary -
Phillip W. Blondheim   (hereinafter called "Performer")
DBA The Smoothies
and
CLICK CORPORATION   (hereinafter called "Producer")

Performer shall render artistic services in connection with the rehearsal and broadcast of the program(s) designated below and preparation in connection with the part or parts to be played:

TITLE OF PROGRAM: American Bandstand _____

TYPE OF PROGRAM: _____ Local ( ) _____ Network (X) _____ Sustaining ( )
                                Commercial (X)

SPONSOR (if commercial): participating
DATE(S) and TIME(S) OF PERFORMANCE * July 25, 1960
PLACE OF PERFORMANCE: WFIL-TV Philadelphia, Penna.
AFTRA CLASSIFICATION: XXXXXX group singers
PART(S) TO BE PLAYED: singers
COMPENSATION: $332.00 ($83.00 per)
REHEARSAL * none

Date   From   To   Place   Date   From   To   Place

Execution of this agreement signifies acceptance by Producer and Performer of all of the above terms and conditions and those on the reverse hereof and attached hereto, if any.

CLICK CORPORATION

Scott McKenzie
Performer

C1 5-2225
Telephone Number

By _____

224-42-4129
230-46-1290
Social Security Number
225-46-3053
227-47-5042

#158-161
8/8/60

*Subject to change in accordance with AFTRA Code.

Theirs was truly smooth stuff. The song The Smoothies sang was an original one by composer "Johnny Phillips," according to the sheet music, titled "Softly."[51] It was characterized as "chalypso," the combination cha-cha and calypso, "with a big beat."[52] John reportedly wrote it parked in a car in Washington, D.C., while the other Smoothies were nearby inside a local drugstore. [53] With Scott McKenzie's polished voice and lush string instrumentation, the group's sound fit right in with the teen idol phase that was in full force that summer. Music industry trade magazine *Cash Box* called "Softly" a "rock-a-ballad-survey" and rated it "Very Good" in its Best Bets column.[54]

Picking up the pulse, teen music magazines of the day such as *Hit Parader* and *Song Hits*, featuring teen idols and TV stars Annette Funicello and Bobby Rydell on the covers, carried small stories on the new group with photographs of the handsome boys mid-song in their matching plaid jackets. Their live appearances ramped up after recording four more tunes tilting towards the folk craze, including an original folk ballad called "Lonely Boy and Pretty Girl."

The Smoothies' recording never charted but the song showed up again in 1961 as the B-side of record of Grammy award winning English singer-songwriter Anthony Newley who wrote "Goldfinger," as well as the soundtrack to *Willy Wonka & The Chocolate Factory*.

"Lonely Boy and Pretty Girl" bears John's signature storytelling as it paints a picture of a lad who's too shy to profess his love. In addition to the male-female dynamic courtesy of backing vocalists, the song has hints of what developed in The Mamas & The Papas material, with the opening verse resembling the structure and pattern of "California Dreamin'":

> *Once there was a lonely boy,*
> *Quiet and sad,*

This is followed by the call and response chorus:

> *Lonely boy and pretty girl, (oooooo [by female voices])*
> *Could have shared a secret world. (ooooo [by female voices]))*

The main verse's group harmonies, which are more robust here than the typical doo-wop sound of other Smoothies recordings, amplify the song's texture and choral depth. The female voices, with their choral "ooo's," are all too anticipatory of The Mamas a few years later.

The Smoothies played in a Summertime Spectacular revue-type engagement for two weeks in Long Island with Connee Boswell and Jimmie Rodgers. Charles Ryan heralded their post Labor Day appearances in Atlantic City in trade publications, releasing their second, more folky single featuring "Ride, Ride, Ride" and "Lonely Boy and Pretty Girl" from their July and August recording dates. In mid-October, *Billboard* nestled a three out of four star review of this sophomore outing next to Julie Andrews' latest record, claiming,

"The Smoothies have a chance for coin with this disking" and "Side is worth spins."[55] Despite the hype, the record failed to deliver in sales, triggering a descent for The Smoothies' previously optimistic trajectory.

December brought some work and visibility for the group when they appeared with The Rocketaires, Johnny Carson, and Florence Henderson at an Oldsmobile-sponsored Christmas concert in Lansing, Michigan, attended by 4,000. Later known for her role as Carol Brady in the 1970s family sitcom *The Brady Bunch*, Henderson was a proven Broadway and television star in the 1950s, and a daily fixture on *The Today Show* as "The Today Girl." In addition to doing straight material on their own, The Smoothies performed songs like Gershwin's "Summertime" with Henderson, with whom Boran had an especially memorable exchange. "The Smoothies were breaking up, but at one point Florence came up to me and pulled me aside," he reminisced. "'I had a dream about you last night,' she shared. 'I dreamed that you pulled the group back together, and that you went on to greatness.' Ever since then, when I saw her as Mrs. Brady or on Wesson commercials, I would say, "That woman dreamt about me."[56]

THE SMOOTHIES

★★★ **Lonely Boy and Pretty Girl**—DECCA 31159—A sweet tale about a lad who was too shy to tell his girl about his feelings. The Smoothies have a chance for coins with this disking. (Northern, ASCAP) (2:53)

★★★ **Ride, Ride, Ride**—The Smoothies handle this Kingston Trio style of exciting, folk-styled ditty with excitement over a driving backing. Side is worth spins. (Northern, ASCAP) (2:09)

THE SWINGIN' SMOOTHIES

27

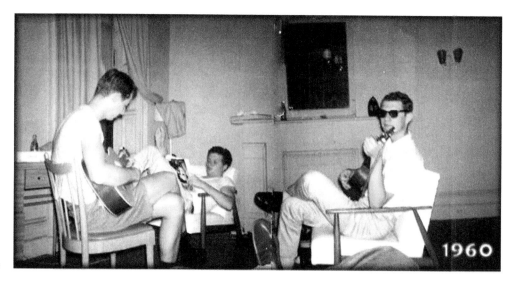

The Smoothies in New York. John Phillips, Scott McKenzie and Bill Cleary in Summer 1960

THERE'S an unusual story about the **Smoothies,** male quartet featured in the current **Elmwood Casino** show in Windsor. Songwriter **John Phillips** assembled the four to cut demonstration records of his new songs. They sold the songs, and themselves as well. Now signed to a record contract, they cut as first of their two disks the number called "S o f t l y," by J o h n Phillips. Comic **Pat Henry,** the tumbling Moroccans and singing emcee **Nick Forrest** are also in the holiday show.

Smoothies

The Smoothies had worked hard and made the gigs Charlie Ryan got them, but their lives were not as smooth as their name suggested. "We would do almost anything to survive at that time. We were living on a pound of bologna, a loaf of bread and a jar of mayonnaise each week," John recalled of their New York existence. "We had about thirty bucks a week from Charley[sic] Ryan," Scott concurred. "It was rough."[57] Both men reportedly supplemented the meager provisions with "modeling" jobs for *True Detective* and *Personal Romance* magazines as murder victims, among other things. Despite the draw of New York, Washington, D.C. remained home base for the disintegrating group. John, meanwhile, not only had two different residences, but found himself inhabiting two different worlds, spending half his time living at the Hotel Albert in Greenwich Village while Suzy and the kids remained in their Virginia apartment.

The Smoothies' swan song was a noteworthy two-week engagement back at the Elmwood Casino at the end of December 1960. "Costumes," was Scott McKenzie's one-word memory of the gigs years later. "We wore costumes," John elaborated. "We'd do like three production numbers every night. Our costumes had different themes: Canadian Mounties, Ice skaters."[58] Other times the look was more exotic or romantic. Scott explained, "We carried spears, did dance numbers and appeared with chorus girls. Sometimes we had to wear mittens and stocking caps and pretend like we were ice skating around the stage with all the chorus girls. And then we'd do our own twenty-minute act of music that was sort of like The Four Lads and The Four Freshmen."[59] Unfortunately the audiences were less than impressed, with Scott ruing, "At one convention, the men started to throw ice cubes at us and yell, 'Bring on the broads.'"[60]

THE STATE JOURNAL

GENERAL NEWS FEATURES

BEDTIME STORY THEATER

ONE HUNDRED-SIXTH YEAR — LANSING—EAST LANSING, MICHIGAN, THURSDAY, DECEMBER 8, 1960 — SECOND SECTION—PAGES 21 TO 32

Oldsmobile Will Greet Christmas Season Here

Yule Show Cast Filled With Stars

Jack Wolfram to Bring Personal Message For Holidays

A star-filled cast of entertainers will again aid Oldsmobile division of General Motors in conveying its holiday greetings to Lansing area residents this year when the annual community Christmas concert is conducted at the Civic Center Dec. 18.

As in the past, the Christmas concert will be free of charge.

The audience will hear an intriguing personal message from Oldsmobile's general manager, Jack F. Wolfram, on the subject "We Can Keep Christmas—But No One Can Keep It Alone."

Two shows—one at 3:30 p. m. and another at 8:30 p. m.—will feature many of the entertainment world's outstanding personalities, including songstress Florence Henderson, versatile comic and dancer Johnny Carson and several others.

The Rocketaires, Oldsmobile's own employe chorus of more than 100 voices under the direction of Dr. David Machtel, will weave a special Christmas choral presentation.

The Smoothies, a new singing quartet, will appear with some of their latest hit recordings, while Will Able and Graziella, well known television dance team, will also star.

Miss Henderson, Oldsmobile's

"THE SMOOTHIES"

WRECKED CRAFT—Two Cabrillo Beach, San Pedro, small boats torn loose from moorings by high winds at Cal., are battered to pieces by damage in coastal areas. (AP surf. Five boats in all were lost Wirephoto).

Space Code Is Urged

Udall Is First Arizonian in Cabinet

TUCSON, Ariz. Dec. 8 —second All Border conference bor. Two years later, Udall or A few years ago, Stewart Lee-ttam in 1940. panied an orientation school for
In 1941 he enlisted in the freshmen congressmen that wan

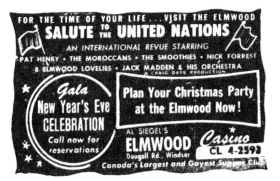

Another yarn about their final engagement nearly got The Smoothies thrown in the Detroit River. "We were supposed to be singing 'Scarlet Ribbons' every night and the owner of the club, the cigar-smoking Al Siegel was a real tough guy," remembered John. "He said something about his daughter had died and that was her favorite song. He didn't want it sung in his club anymore. We said we were artists, and we would sing whatever we wanted to sing, at any time. And he said, 'We'll see about that.' We went out and we sang it, and he was right. We didn't sing it again."[61]

Looking back at his two years in The Abstracts and The Smoothies, John reflected that their material lacked staying power. "It wasn't fish nor fowl," he recalled. "It was very insipid music that had nothing to do with anything. We didn't have an identity."[62] For his part, Scott credited that time as a woodshedding period in which they learned "working and starving."[63]

The Smoothies had reached enough acclaim to be featured on the front page of *The Lansing State Journal*,[64] but by the year's end the group became yesterday's news. John and Scott were "looking to the next thing," as Mike Boran put it, with an ear to the ground for the popularity and profitability pointing them further into the folk revival.[65] Boran was soon to join forces with Tim Rose in a folk duo named Michael & Timothy.

The boys from Virginia had a real brush with show business in 1960. Living in New York, making records in a major recording studio with legitimate session musicians, appearing on television, and performing with other prominent singers validated their capabilities. As they hit it, they experienced a style and era of entertainment that was quickly disappearing. The group was short-lived, and its recordings achieved little recognition, but the exposure The Smoothies received launched John Phillips on a course that would continue for decades. Additionally, The Smoothies contributed to the future legacy of The Mamas & The Papas in terms of agents, contracts, and business experience with a big record label. If one singular characteristic was established in the years of The Abstracts and The Smoothies, it was that John Phillips was the leader of the group—a role he would inhabit in every group thereafter.

That Easy on the Ears Trio: The Journeymen

In early 1961, The Smoothies were foundering. They were jazz types who thought of themselves more as beatniks, at the precise time when Greenwich Village had rolled over to a folk scene. "I remember everybody as trying to be very practiced at being anarchists, and yet living comfortably," recounted Scott McKenzie. "We went to the Gaslight Café and I think it was Hugh Romney, who later became Wavy Gravy, reading some poetry. I didn't know that after someone read something, the way you applauded was by snapping your fingers because it was in the basement of an apartment building and the tenants would complain if everybody clapped. So I'm sitting there and I'm trying to be really hip. I'm about twenty-years-old, squeaky clean white. And Hugh Romney finishes and me, the young cool dude there, I clapped. Everybody turned and looked at me."[66]

Notwithstanding their naivete and their proclivities for jazz, The Smoothies had picked up on the folk craze with John Phillips' song "Ride, Ride, Ride," a frontier tune that they had dressed up as a popular folk song. Recorded in 1960, the track featured Eric Weissberg on mandolin, along with a talented banjo player named Dick Weissman. Weissman was a Philadelphia native who learned banjo with a Pete Seeger book. At Goddard College, he studied the instrument and further learned with folk blues master Jerry Silverman. "Dick amazed us all," folk music godfather Oscar Brand once noted.[67] As John put it, "Dick is one of the virtuoso banjo players in the world. Pete Seeger would say that. He used to send tapes to Dick for his opinion."[68]

Weissman's talent at banjo playing was good enough to gain renown during his early years in New York. At that same time John and Scott were looking to form a folk group, since, as John put it, "I couldn't find any intellectual satisfaction to what we were doing."[69] In his eyes, The Smoothies had "evaporated" by the end of 1960. "Word sort of got around the Village that we were looking for a banjo player," he recalled, "and Dick Weissman showed up at the door."[70] The word was also swapped around at Israel Young's Folklore Center, a hub for a swelling number of folk artists. It was there that John Phillips, Scott McKenzie, and Dick Weissman created The Journeymen.

"We started rehearsing six days a week, eight to ten hours a day," Weissman remembers. Their first few rehearsals in early 1961 included Karen Dalton in the mix, presaging John's abilities to arrange male and female voices.[71] "We chose the name Journeymen," McKenzie recalled, "because we felt it represented a craftsman who is not yet a master of his trade but accomplished enough to bear the name of his profession."[72] Weissman's memory is less grand: "An agent picked the name out of a dictionary."[73]

Success came in fits and starts. After first being courted by the label, MGM Records proved to be a dead end. So The Journeymen auditioned for Rene Cardenas and Frank Werber, the Capitol Records agents who represented folk music A-listers The Kingston Trio. The audition was a success, though not in the expected way. For a first assignment, the trio found themselves collaborating on a series of commercial jingles for Canada Dry.

The Canada Dry job happened because the former Smoothies owed money to their previous manager, Charlie Ryan. When Ryan realized he had little chance of collecting that debt, he enlisted Phillips, McKenzie, and Weissman for some commercials. Phillips wrote four of the jingles. Weissman remembered the misadventure, which sounds like it could have been an episode of *Mad Men*.

We took a taxi to the ad agency on Madison Avenue. The agency, Batten, Barton, Durstine & Osborn (BBDO), was one of the major ad agencies of the time. We sat around an enormous mahogany table and [performed] the four of them. They eliminated two of them. One of their 'creatives' really liked one of the two. The others generally agreed but were non-committal. They then called in the president of the agency, who was about 100 years old. He, of course, liked version one. There was some discussion, and the creative guy held out for number two. John, being a practical guy, made some remark about number one having a "special feeling." Of course, the president got his way. As we were leaving, the defeated creative type looked at John and said, "Kid, you'll go far in this business." He got that right! I still remember the damn tune: "The voice is America, the choice is Canada Dry, America's first family of beverages."[74]

The commercial sold—providing the necessary cash to pay off old Smoothie debts—and the three musicians looked forward to the rest of 1961.

In no time The Journeymen landed a contract with Capitol Records and were booked for their first big gig at Gerde's Folk City in April 1961. "We went down to Hoot Night and insisted on wearing matching sweaters and we almost killed ourselves on stage with sweat pouring off us," remembered John, "but the guy hired us anyway for a two week gig."[75]

"Hoot Night" referred to a "hootenanny," an all-the-rage musical phenomenon of the time. A hootenanny was a bit karaoke and a bit talent show. "Actually, the hootenanny is to folk music what the jam session is to jazz," one newspaper at the time claimed.[76] Another writer theorized that the name stemmed from the phrase "hoot and holler" and was a "joining together of folk musicians…where one can bring an instrument or his or her vocal talents."[77] Other definitions described a hootenanny as "an informal party"[78] and "kind of a do-it-yourself singalong that stresses folk songs plus guitar and banjo accompaniment."[79] Bob Nelson of the Pacific Northwest Folklore Society says, "By the mid 1950's, a hoot could be found almost every weekend. These legendary events soon became a way of life for many of us as a place to listen to, and learn from, the best performers, as well as a place to hone our own performing skills."[80] As the folkie equivalent of an open-mic night, be it in a coffeehouse or a gymnasium, a hootenanny included a variety of participants. Sometimes it was all amateurs, and other times established folk groups or artists would join the fun and try out new material.

"The Gerde's thing was hard for me," says Weissman of their first big gig. "I was known as a very rootsy folkie type and there I was in a folk-pop group that most of the folkies thought was real slick."[81] John remembered, "It was with Dylan and Lightnin' Hopkins. It was Dylan's first job in New York also, and Lightnin's about four hundredth."[82]

Following their Hoot Night debut, announcements of the group's arrival frequently included references to The Kingston Trio. It was clear that if the latter faltered, Capitol was ready with their new "pop-folk group."[83] One writer even declared that The Journeymen were a "kind of insurance policy" on The Kingston Trio that would "pay off handsomely."[84] Both groups were composed of three young men, all of whom played guitar or banjo and sang popular folk tunes in the club and college settings. The Kingston Trio's original lineup played guitars and bongo drums that gave them a certain Hawaiian element. The Journeymen were more representative of East Coast and Appalachian folk tunes, adding to that vernacular with Weissman's banjo. Making the groups even more similar, The Kingston Trio incorporated a banjo when John Stewart replaced Dave Guard in the fall of 1961. John Phillips was reportedly a contender for the post too, during which time he was writing songs for both groups.

Within a month The Journeymen were in the Capitol recording studio in New York with producer Andy Wiswell. Both John and Weissman wrote pieces for what would become their self-titled debut. "The first album was the first time I played banjo and guitar on the same song," Weissman notes. "I loved doing that."[85] John, meanwhile, exhibited his knack for arranging by reworking old folk songs in new ways. One example of this is "Fennario," which derives from a Scottish folk song and is also known as "Peggy-O" or "The Maid of Fife."

The trio wove their imprimatur into the album. John did the vocal arrangements and Weissman arranged for instruments. "'Black Girl' was somewhat innovative," opined Weissman of their take on the folk standard, "because we did it as a ballad. I learned it from a Leadbelly record. The vocal harmonies are interesting, and I used different chords in different verses. I don't think anyone was doing that in folk music then."[86] The song is unusual in its quality as a Phillips-McKenzie duet as well. It was rarer for the two old friends

RICHARD WEISSMAN

SCOTT McKENZIE

JOHN PHILLIPS

to duet. John could sing but he did not think he sang very well, especially juxtaposed to Scott's brilliant singing voice. "Black Girl" is a beautiful song and shows he was wrong.

Songs like Hedy West's "500 Miles" gave the album even more folk credibility. While West had written the song, inspired by her Georgia roots, it was The Journeymen who first recorded it. Over the next two years the likes of The Kingston Trio, Peter Paul & Mary, and Bobby Bare picked up the mantle and popularized the tune further. The song brought Appalachian roots to New York and John turned in one of his better arrangements to give it just the right twist. "You gotta remember," he once said of recording their first album, "Scott and I had been singing folk music about four months at that time. Folk music to us was The Kingston Trio; it wasn't Leadbelly or anything like that. And Dick was a real musicologist, he really knew all about the Southern heritage and folk tradition."[87] Thus their take on Uncle Dave Macon's "Cumberland Deer Chase" and "Make Me a Pallet," for which Dick and John added two verses that are not in the original New Orleans composition from the 1890s. "A number of bluegrass groups have recorded it doing our verses," notes Dick, who also acknowledges his banjo solo on "Pallet" as "my favorite instrumental part of the first album."[88]

"River Come Down," with new lyrics by Phillips and Weissman, featured the talents of bass player Arnold Fishkind, "a bebopper" who had played with famed jazz musician Lee Konitz. Complementing the bass was the crescendo of John and Scott's vocals. "Chase the Rising Sun" was part of a 15-minute banjo suite written by Weissman as a senior at Goddard College, which he credits with convincing him to become a musician.

There were also original songs on *The Journeymen* LP. John reworked "Ride, Ride, Ride" for three voices, and wrote the new tune "Soft Blow the Summer Winds." Humor made its way into their repertoire in the form of two unreleased tracks penned by *Fiddler on the Roof* lyricist Sheldon Harnick: "Environment," a cynical take on nature versus nurture, and "The Ballad of the Shape of Things," "a clever song from the perspective of a homicidally-inclined, jilted lover sung somewhat like an old English balladeer."[89] The latter track, which was also often performed by The Kingston Trio, became a staple of future Journeymen concerts.

With these recordings, the three Journeymen demonstrated that they had coalesced musically, they were capable of a wide range of material, and even sophisticated humor, with John declaring, "All of the harmonies were modern, lots of contrapuntal stuff."[90] Their compositional talent was also recognized. In addition to his original songs, John often revised familiar or traditional folk tunes, thereby picking up a writing credit. One reviewer noted, "If the boys become great, they'll certainly be able to rake in the long green from both the sale of the records and the royalties from the tunes. Several of the selections are variations of different versions heard through the years."[91]

hungry i

Exbrook 7-0929

599 Jackson
at Kearny

With Capitol feeling confident in their new act, more prominent venues were in order. In addition to Gerde's, the group played the Second Fret in Philadelphia and the Herb Shriner "Pops Americana" Folk Music show in Boston. Initial press releases and news stories, as well as some of these early appearances, billed to them as "The Journeymen Three" and, in one instance, "The Modern Folk Three."

Television came next. After appearing on the Canadian program *World of Music,* one critic found rare authenticity and acumen in the group, writing,: "The only down to earth, honest-to-goodness folk singers on hand—as honest as any of the mushrooming trios are—were The Journeymen. Even with their backs to the camera, running over the horizon yards apart from each other, they sounded as if they were huddling over microphone on the O'Keefe Centre stage [Toronto's premier performing arts venue at the time]."[92] They also appeared on San Francisco television with comedian Dick Gregory.

Having headed west, they played the Ice House in Pasadena in May and June, and then landed at the hungry i nightclub in San Francisco by midsummer. Even though they were obliged to record a bread commercial in San Francisco, the big time had arrived for The Journeymen, who found themselves playing with comic heavyweights Mort Sahl and Dick Gregory. *The San Francisco Examiner* referred to them as "folk singers and warblers."[93] The hungry i was an auspicious spot in the stand-up comedy and folk world but its longest lasting impact was unnoticed at the time: it served as the meeting point for John Phillips and seventeen-year-old Michelle Gilliam.

Holly Michelle Gilliam lived in Los Angeles and attended John Marshall High School there, though until recently she had spent a sizable amount of her childhood in Mexico, following the death of her mother when she was five. Her father's home was nonrestrictive. "He was marvelous, " she told *The St. Louis Post-Dispatch* in 1977. "Our lifestyle was pretty carefree. Dad was very liberal. When it came to eating he made us at least sample everything. But we were allowed to have card parties and drink beer as long as things didn't get out of hand."[94]

In the summer of 1961, she was in San Francisco with her friend Tamar Hodel, whose father, decades since, gained infamy as the primary suspect behind the 1947 Black Dahlia murder in Los Angeles.

Holly Michelle Gilliam,
circa 1960

Tamar was a decade older than Michelle, and by 1961 had already been married and had a child. She was avant-garde and unrestrained in her gallivanting social life, making her highly compatible with Michelle, whose widower father had given her tremendous liberties with respect to the mores of the day. Added to this paternal permissiveness was the reality that Michelle, in her own right, was precocious and street savvy beyond her years.

With Tamar introducing her to fake ID's and amphetamines, Michelle was underage but moving freely in adult environments in 1961. Perhaps most of all, she was categorically beautiful. Without exception, those who knew her in her youth, remark particularly on the stunning nature of her beauty. John Phillips customarily credited her with being the first quintessential "California Girl" with long blond hair and gorgeous slim body.

At the hungry i, Michelle and her friend were mixing with the folkies. At the time folkies were the more hip and edgy type of musicians in a slightly seamy club. John was tall, handsome, and clearly the leader of his band—"the snappy patter guy," as Michelle put it.[95] Michelle was eye-catching and the allure between the two was mutual. Michelle's unabashed nature and John's attraction to her were quick off the mark. John's less than stellar track record for marital fidelity did not begin (nor end) with Michelle, and while Suzy was not caught by surprise, Michelle's open and "brazen" assurance that she would win John over did "unnerve" Mrs. Phillips.[96]

While domestic matters heated up, The Journeymen hit a lukewarm streak professionally. Their tour agenda in late 1961 had been partly cobbled together so that the group could supplement their largely yet-to-be-realized income from their unreleased recordings made earlier that year. But work was beginning to dry up. Even though The Journeymen's talent and their recording abilities were promising, Capitol Records seemed focused on the more established Kingston Trio, who were only doing better with John's compositional contributions. An anticipated rivalry between the groups did not materialize, with John Stewart of the Trio and John Phillips even collaborating on compositions.

Scott recalled, "It got so bad, Dick and I were living in a Chinese hotel in San Francisco for $9 a week."[97] The only member with a family, John was having to manage responsibilities for a wife and two young children in a marriage that had been troubled and long-distance since the days of The Smoothies.

Their record company managers had seized booking responsibilities for The Journeymen, yet the group appeared to be stalling. They landed a six-week engagement at the Joker Club in San Jose, followed by steak house venues in Spokane and Phoenix that fall. The latter was booked by Joe Glaser of Associated Booking Associates, who had mob connections and was a somewhat notorious talent agent for boxers and jazz artists such as Louis Armstrong. The trio even had to contend with a lawsuit against their managers, Frank Werber and Rene Cardenas. Eventually The Journeymen broke ranks and returned to their original booking agency, International Talent Associates, known for its inroads in the college campus scene, but this was not without legal and pecuniary consequences.

Luckily, with release dates finally set for their first recordings, there were glimmers of success for The Journeymen on the horizon. "It's a striking sound that could add a new folk team to the charts," chirped *Cash Box*, putting the group's debut single, "River Come Down"/"500 Miles," in its "Very Good" review category—the highest it offered.[98] Released in September, the 45 made some impact on local charts and in sales. Another reviewer

New Vocal Trio, 'Journeymen', In Disc Race

proclaimed "500 Miles" should "make the hit parade."[99] *Billboard* likewise deemed it a Special Merit Single with strong sales potential.[100]

The debut album, *The Journeymen*, was released in early November and also made an impression. The record cover depicted them with instruments in tow in a horse-drawn carriage in Central Park. "It seemed weird to me," Weissman recalled, "that after living in New York for five years, here I was doing the ultimate tourist thing."[101] After the album's release, The Journeymen recorded "Oh Miss Mary," a Phillips original also taken up by The Kingston Trio, and the popular spiritual "Kumbaya" in Capitol's Hollywood studios.

While big hits did not arrive in 1961, The Journeymen had come a long way in less than a year.. They had a record deal, they had concerts, and they were increasingly making the press. From their audition earlier in the year until their album's release in November, there was a big rise in their profile. It had been, as one writer of the day described it, "a rollicking trip to the top."[102] "We have a sort of feeling about folk music," John said at the time, "that the songs with the simplest chord structure and the plainest lyrics are the most beautiful ones."[103] "We try to provide a bridge between folk music and our audiences," Dick Weissman explained. "Our problem is how to make this music, which is basically simple, interesting to someone who is not simple."[104] As a promotional piece boasted, "The Journeymen perform a unique kind of chemistry on a song."[105] That chemistry is clearly heard in a song like "What'll I Do," where The Journeymen not only demonstrate their exquisite and talented harmonies, but, starting out in joined voices and then going into a clear call and response, point to the coming sound of The Mamas & The Papas. Weissman's pop banjo is not unlike what appears in 1967's "Did You Ever Want To Cry," and the presence of drums and electric guitar give the performance a much more popular feel. The recording is also indicative of John's talent with taking a well-

THE JOURNEYMEN WERE DISCOVERED A SHORT TIME AGO BY FRANK WERBER— THE MAN WHO ORIGINALLY DISCOVERED AND NOW GUIDES THE WORLD-FAMOUS KINGSTON TRIO #(S)T1629

THE DEBUT ALBUM OF AMERICA'S MOST EXCITING NEW FOLK-SINGING GROUP...
the journeymen

ON THEIR WAY!

It's been a rollicking trip to the top for the most exciting new vocal group since the Kingston Trio!

THE JOURNEYMEN

worn song and making it new. This he was doing with folk songs routinely, but in "What'll I Do" he showed that he could ably do so with a Tin Pan Alley standard by Irving Berlin, just as he and The Mamas & The Papas would do so a few years later with songs written or performed by Rodgers & Hart, The Beatles, Martha Reeves & The Vandellas, The Shirelles, and Frankie Laine.

A Guess at Big Things Ahead

The Journeymen fused their song chemistry on their second single, released in January 1962. Featuring their rendition of "Kumbaya," the familiar spiritual that came to be associated with the civil rights movement, and its flipside "Soft Blow The Summer Winds," John's collaborative composition with The Kingston Trio's John Stewart, the 7-inch earned some initial attention from the music press. "This rendition can move," *Cash Box* said of the spiritual on the A-side,[106] while others called it a "spirited version"[107] and "a guess at big things ahead."[108] Weissman admits, "It was basically an effort to duplicate the success of 'Michael Row the Boat Ashore.' We felt if The Highwaymen had a hit, we should be able to have one too."[109] Despite receiving a "Best Bet" rating from *Cash Box* and hitting the top ten in Boston and Minneapolis, the record failed to gain national momentum—even as their album continued to garner solid praise. The album's success yielded a commercially published songbook with sheet music for each song.

THE DEBUT ALBUM OF AMERICA'S MOST EXCITING NEW FOLK-SINGING GROUP...
Capitol RECORDS
HIGH FIDELITY RECORDING
the journeymen

After you've heard the Journeymen perform, you'll surely agree that the most interesting thing about this new group is its fresh, wonderful combination of swinging blend and fine musicianship. But before you've had a chance to sample the Journeymen's artistry, you might be interested in knowing something about who they are and where they come from.

introducing the journeymen

Scott McKenzie, Richard Weissman, and John Phillips are the Journeymen—journeymen in the art of singing, journeymen musicians of great skill. Young though they may be, add their natural talent to formal musical backgrounds, and it's no wonder that their music is distinctive. Thanks to each man's vocal individuality and flexibility, their singing is far more than just "another blend." Each voice holds its own while dovetailing with the others, and their tonal mixture can be modestly described as close to perfection. It provides a setting ideal for any material—English ballad to swinging spiritual—and they even sound at home with pop ballads, blues, and modern jazz. In this album their carefully-chosen, well-arranged material is folk-flavored, yet it's mingled with the group's own humor and harmonic twists, and excitingly filled out by their superb instrumentation consisting of banjo and two guitars.

The Journeymen were discovered a short time ago by Frank Werber—the man who originally discovered and now guides the world-famous Kingston Trio. He comments "These boys are so good that I think everybody should have a chance to hear them, and I don't think it will be long before everybody is hearing them. You know, folk music was a specialized field before the Kingston Trio came along, but their new, 'jazzed-up' folk style awakened a new interest almost overnight in millions of people. Now there's a tremendous public demand for really good singers like the Journeymen, who can do real justice to this kind of material. They sing in the same idiom as the Kingston Trio, yet once people have had a chance to hear them they'll realize what a fresh, new sound these boys have. I think they're going to have a marvelous future."

With this much said, it should come as no surprise that the Journeymen are already in demand as an in-person act. Beginning with a successful appearance at New York's Folk City, the threesome then joined Herb Shriner for a Boston concert, and had TV dates on the late-night "PM West," and on Toronto's CBC. So far their high-water mark was a month-long stint at San Francisco's Hungry i, long famous for launching artists into the national spotlight. Looking ahead, the group is set for a college campus tour in the near future.

Their success to this point could almost have been predicted, considering their backgrounds. John, the acknowledged group leader, showed an early aptitude for guitar playing and folk singing. Today, that aptitude has become real talent, and has been joined by a compositional flair. Scott was once lead singer with a top pop group, and has had considerable club and TV exposure. Understandably, he's the Journeymen's lead tenor and soloist. In addition to being a singer, guitarist, and banjoist, Dick is a musicologist of note, conducts seminars at New York's School of Folk Music, and regularly contributes to music periodicals.

side one

RIVER COME DOWN, originally a Jamaican melody, is heard here with new lyrics by Dick and John.

SOFT BLOW THE SUMMER WINDS is one of John's own compositions. It's a memorable contribution to our Civil War heritage, and it gives Dick a chance to embroider an intricate banjo solo on its march-tempoed but wistful refrain.

BLACK GIRL, with its melancholy tune and lyrics, makes a beautiful duet as sung here by Scott and John. The melody and first verse were unearthed in Kentucky in 1917 by the great folk scholar Cecil Sharp.

DUNYA is a traditional Israeli *hora,* sung here with lyrics by Dick and John. The trio's fine instrumental work and vocal *esprit de corps* add a lot of new excitement to this ageless melody.

FENNARIO, variously titled *Pretty Peggy O* and *Pretty Fanny O,* is an adaptation of the English-Scottish *Pretty Girl of Darby O.* This particular version is another Civil War song, reflecting the effects of the battle on the home-front, and the influence of a certain love affair on the course of the war.

RIDE, RIDE, RIDE is another of John's compositions, this time stemming from the lore of the Wild West. The dash and gallop of the rhythms realistically portray the tensely dramatic pursuit of a young outlaw by the sheriff's posse.

side two

500 MILES goes back many years in the Northern Georgia family of Hedy West, who collaborated with John on this arrangement. It is clearly reminiscent of laments sung through the years by cowboys, sailors, and railroad men.

ROCK ME LORD is the kind of head-swinging, foot-tapping song sung and clapped at old-fashioned camp meetings. It's a Negro-spiritual-derived tune, and the Journeymen give full emphasis to its original exciting beat.

MAKE ME A PALLET has been widely sung throughout the South since the days when it was popular with the pioneer New Orleans jazz bands. In the repertoire of every itinerant street singer of those days, this old blues song takes on a nostalgic-but-new sound here with original lyrics by Dick and John.

CHASE THE RISING SUN takes its melody from part of an original banjo suite by Dick, and he and John wrote the lyrics. It's a mischievous account of a flirtatious gal, and the Journeymen go all out in a flurry of peppery vocal and instrumental work that challenges any listener to sit still.

CUMBERLAND MOUNTAIN DEER CHASE is a traditional Cumberland Mountain tune which was sung by Uncle Dave Macon, an original star of "The Grand Ole Opry." In it, the hunters relax around the fire, swapping yarns while the hounds pursue their quarry. Dick's banjo runs pell-mell throughout, and manages to keep up with the dogs. Note the touch of realism in the hound's bay as the tune ends.

GILGARA MOUNTAIN, a humorous song-tale of a devil-may-care rascal and his escapades, comes straight from Ireland where it's called "Gilgarry Mountain." Containing nonsense refrains, a common feature of many folk songs, it provides a rousing finish to the album.

Produced by ANDY WISWELL

the journeymen

RIVER COME DOWN   FIVE HUNDRED MILES
BLACK GIRL   ROCK ME, LORD
SOFT BLOW THE SUMMER WINDS   MAKE ME A PALLET
DUNYA   CHASE THE RISING SUN
FENNARIO   CUMBERLAND MOUNTAIN DEER CHASE
RIDE, RIDE, RIDE   GILGARRA MOUNTAIN

Amid the swelling popularity of the folk style, and the positive reception to their album, the now-New York based trio were taking on an increasing number of campus halls. During the previous year they had played mostly club dates, including more off-color adult nightclub venues like the hungry i, as well as coffeehouses, steak houses, and community venues such as blood drives, caravans, and jamborees. The look of the trio, their sophisticated treatment of songs, and their variety of material parlayed well into the college scene of the early '60s. A survey of their live appearances reveals a clear shift to the more lucrative collegiate venues, which yielded more concerts and greater cash flow, and would remain their bread and butter for the rest of The Journeymen's existence.

The early '60s college social scene was the storied era of fraternity parties, sorority dances and formals. Typically these events were dominated by R&B dance bands playing crowd-pleasers for intoxicated undergrads. This was the time of dance crazes such as the Watusi and the Mashed Potato, and standard college musical fare such as "The Twist," "Louie, Louie," and "Shout." But rock and roll had taken a downturn after the late 1950s, with teen idols, girl groups, surf music, and some novelty songs filling the void before the British Invasion hit in 1964. That meant there was a place for a hip and sophisticated folk group on the college landscape. And so The Journeymen began to regularly play for fraternity dances, winter carnivals, and homecomings at large, conventional schools across the nation.

This 1962 move to the collegiate circuit followed in the footsteps of their elder brethren, The Kingston Trio, and by the year's end it was almost the exclusive venue for The Journeymen. Consonant with their college gigs, Capitol Records even manufactured large ceramic steins with the Journeymen motif, like those made for fraternities and sororities.

One of their first college gigs was at Hampden-Sydney College in Farmville, Virginia, a school where John had briefly attended. When The Brothers Four backed out of their contract to play at the all-male school's "Midwinters" concert sponsored by the German Club, an organization devoted to the planning of socials, formal dances and concerts, The Journeymen were quickly engaged. Their reception on campus was beyond ebullient. Playing to a crowd of 1,100 people, it "surpassed anything anticipated," according to the student newspaper, which claimed they entertained "the largest crowd ever to attend a German Club function." The paper went on to say that The Journeymen "wove a spell over their listeners so that they sat in utter silence as the ear-pleasing strains of the folk songs filled the gym. The applause was frequently tremendous and prolonged. Various comments heard during the concert were 'Terrific!' 'My God they're great!' and 'Better than the Brothers Four have ever been!' 'We certainly didn't expect them to be that good.'" Although The Drifters had been the Friday night entertainment and were also well received, The Journeymen's performance the next night was clearly the more outstanding of the weekend.[110]

"There is no definite and concise reason why folk singing has become so tremendously

popular in the last two or three years," Dick Weissman observed at the time. He pointed to the popularity of ABC's short-lived but hugely popular variety show *Hootenanny* and hypothesized "because the fourteen-year-old bracket idolizes Rock 'n' Roll and in an effort to be distinguished from this junior high group the college crowd adopted folk music perhaps because of the lack of effort involved in singing it and because of the repetition the words are very easily remembered."[111] Indeed, *Hootenanny*, which broadcast remotely from various college campuses across the nation, deserves much credit for mainstreaming folk music into millions of American living rooms between 1963 and 1964.

"The hootenanny has progressed from the coffee houses of the beatnik set to the college campuses of the nation and wherever young people congregate," as one reporter described it.[112] The folk revival had been going on since the late 1950s, but it seemed to find its home in the universities of the early '60s, where cerebral conversation and urbane or suggestive humor was appreciated. Within the world of folk, there was a fairly accepted divide: there were true folk singers, who were faithful to the origins of roots music, and then there were the more popular folk performers, such as The Journeymen, who were capitalizing on the genre and making it more palatable for general audiences.

That The Journeymen were able to so successfully nudge into this scene points to their particular nature. Crisscrossing the United States, particularly in the East, the trio typified the folk craze of time. On the other hand, they were set apart by their superior arrangements and the combination of vocal and instrumental excellence. Dick Weissman was a legitimate musicologist who had studied music, lectured in seminars, and understood the roots crowd, allowing him to introduce a song with sufficient history and authentic credibility. John Phillips and Scott McKenzie, meanwhile, drew upon their history with The Smoothies and were masters of humorous patter in these collegiate settings. After all, they had performed on *American Bandstand* just a couple of years earlier. Moreover, the highly intelligent and smooth way the group handled folk music, serving up jazzier numbers and standards such as "One Quick Martini" and "What'll I Do," permitted them to perform with wide ranging material that was not all hardcore folk music. Thus they could accompany a dance replete with coats, ties, and formal gowns. Moreover, it was hip to have a folk group in 1962. Social consciousness was on the rise and college students distinguished themselves from high school teeny-boppers with the more intellectual and acoustic sounding folk tunes.

In February 1962, The Journeymen proved their versatility by recording several more polished and commercial sounding tunes in Hollywood, such as "I Never Will Marry," "Hush Now Sally," and "Rock Island Line." Weissman remembers the sessions with Voyle Gilmore, producer for Frank Sinatra, Judy Garland, and The Kingston Trio, who had worked with the group the preceding fall when they recorded "Kumbaya" and another spiritual folk song, "Oh Miss Mary." Weissman remembers Gilmore as "classic L.A.: suntanned and relaxed.

St. Pat's Festival Concert Will Feature 'Journeymen'

MUNCIE STAR, FRIDAY, MARCH 30, 1962

THE JOURNEYMEN

..provided the other half of Spring Frolics entertainment Friday night with a pot-ourri of well-known folk tunes, banjo solos, clowning, and humor. (Photo by Carolyn Johnston)

Twin Cities' Only
FOLK MUSIC ROOM
presents
The JOURNEYMEN
plus
GENE FARMER
(comedy & folk)
Nitely thru Jan. 14
PADDED CELL
COLFAX & LAKE STS.

DON'T
TURN AROUND
(John Stewart-John Phillips)

Friendship
Music Corp.
BMI—2:40

4737
(45-37261)

Produced By:
Voyle Gilmore

Capitol
RECORDS

THE JOURNEYMEN

The studios in Hollywood were more laid back. Since it was mostly just us, though, it didn't have such an effect on us." Bass duties were taken up by Dixieland jazz great Morty Corb. "He had a 200-year-old bass," continues Weissman. "One day he took out his notebook and wrote something down. I asked what he was doing. He said he always wrote it down when he made a mistake. I asked him how often that happened and he said, 'About every six months.' He wasn't kidding."[113]

Hollywood may not have influenced the tracks, but the vintage John Phillips arrangements did. "Don't Turn Around" was a Phillips and McKenzie duet that reached the top ten in various cities after its April release. For it, Weissman "enjoyed playing pop banjo, which basically no one was doing then, and no one is doing now."[114]

Recorded in June 1962 at The Padded Cell in Minneapolis, which was emblematic of the venues they were playing, their sophomore album, *Coming Attraction – Live!*, was an audio snapshot of their itinerant forays into collegiate arenas and nearby basket houses. "The manager of The Padded Cell was Freddy Latinville," remembers Weissman. "He was great. He was about six-foot-three and was built like a linebacker. If people talked, he'd stand over them. That was usually enough, but if it wasn't, he kicked them out and refunded their money."[115]

The Journeymen's performances at The Padded Cell, recorded over multiple nights, capture not only their musical abilities, but also their charismatic anecdotes and humor. In their live performance of "Metamorphosis," another composition by Broadway legend Sheldon Harnick, one can hear some of their stage chemistry when John introduces the song: a "humorous oddity rhapsodizing the transformation of a pitiable caterpillar into the 'king of winged in-sects,'" making full use of the homonym "in sex."[116] Harnick, who wrote the tune as a nonsense poem "set to music in the style of a Schubert art song"[117] was "delighted that The Journeymen chose to use my work." As he heard it, "The vocal sound they made—clean, bright, spacious, 'alive'—was wonderfully satisfying."[118] Of his song "Environment-Heredity," Harnick notes, "They made it sound like an authentic folk song, although it certainly was not written as one."[119] In Harnick's "The Ballad of the Shape of Things," which the trio tackled in their first recording session, the innuendo and double-entendre of their delivery showcased John, Scott, and Dick's cleverness and comedic timing.

Folk music was also never far separated from politics. All three Journeymen were prone to satirical political jabs and puns. Commentary and topical humor came along with the singing. Referencing an international political sex scandal of the day, John's joke, "Christine Keeler was voted cabinet maker of the year," put one college crowd in an "uproar" of laughter.[120] At another outdoor college show, John was greeted with a racial slur from an audience member when introducing a song written by African American singer-songwriter Josh White. His quick-draw retort, "You're very crude, sir," prompted a standing ovation from the rest of the crowd.[121]

The group's rapport with an audience is clear on the crowd-pleasing "Gypsy Rover," which the group always did as a singalong. At William & Mary, where the group performed inside a gymnasium, John wryly advised those who didn't know the words to "take a few free throws."[122]

In one student newspaper, a creative writer captured Scott, Dick, and John respectively like this:

> Old King Cole was a merry old soul,
> A merry old soul was he,
> He called for his pipe,
> And he called for his bowl,
> And he called for the journeymen three,
> The first was short, he could croon and sing
> The second could play excellently,
> The third a comedian Said most anything
> His language was pretty free.[123]

CAPITOL FULL DIMENSIONAL STEREO

COMING ATTRACTION—LIVE!

Capitol RECORDS HIGH FIDELITY

A FABULOUS ON-STAGE PERFORMANCE BY
AMERICA'S SENSATIONAL YOUNG FOLK SINGERS . . .

THE JOURNEYMEN

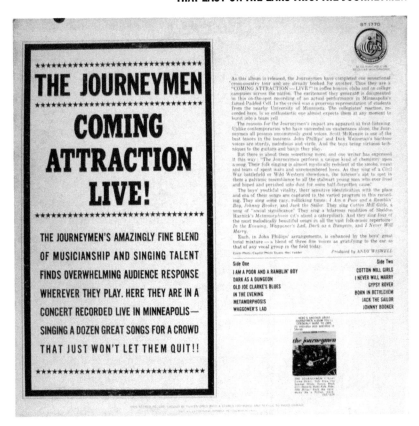

Traditional fare was served up in the live album with innovation. Dick Weissman's friend Hedy West offered the group "Cotton Mill Girls," a song that she learned "from my family, my father and his siblings, who with my grandmother inevitably sang and played and drank my grandma's blackberry wine, whenever they got together." Explaining the song's development, West continued, "They had learned the snippet of the song from a close relative who worked as a spinner in the Atco Cotton Mills near Atlanta. I wrote new verses adding what I remembered from the stories that I'd heard from my family's removal from mountain farm life to the life of mill hands."[124] John subsequently added a verse himself.

Of the numbers from the Padded Cell recordings, "In the Evening " best demonstrated The Journeymen's versatility with a jazz number. "We were drawn to jazz because we were sort of beatniks," John remarked. "So, we wanted to sing modern harmonies like Lambert, Hendricks, and Ross," hearkening to unfulfilled jazz aspirations of several years prior.[125] Dick adds that no one else was doing this kind of material. A long unreleased number from

the show, "How Mountain Girls Can Love," is a tune he remembers John learning from a bluegrass record by The Stanley Brothers.[126]

As the live album proved, The Journeymen's mutual gifts of voice and instrument distinguished them. "Many groups had one or the other," remembers Jerry Haskew of The Cumberland Trio, "but few had all of it. I remember booking them on their first big time college concert at the University of Tennessee for the fall of 1962." Haskew recalls the boys being down to earth, with John calling Haskew's fraternity house and asking him to find the group an economical hotel while they were in Knoxville. When they arrived in town, they changed clothes at the fraternity house. As head of campus entertainment for the university, Haskew sat with the university president during the concert, which was to a packed 3,000-person house. He remembers that when the group performed "Cotton Mill Girls" the president exclaimed: "Damn they're good." Haskew continues, "After that, John, Scott, and I, along with a few other folkie friends, stayed up all night jamming." He credits this experience with inspiring him to form The Cumberland Trio. "The Journeymen flipped the switch for me."[127]

A flyer from Florida State University echoed the growing acclaim of their unique status: "The Journeymen have found the solution to being popular folksingers. Just what they have found cannot be named and can only be assessed by hearing them sing."[128]

Coming Attraction – Live! came out in September 1962. One curious distinction was that the title was printed in different colors on some mono and stereo covers. The cover showed The Journeymen sitting relaxed on their instrument cases and equipment trunks, clad in cardigan sweaters and open collars. Their more informal university fashion was conspicuous compared to their prior album cover's buttoned-up, coat-and-tie apparel. *Billboard* deemed it a "Special Merit Album" and politely observed that The Journeymen "come through with pleasant performances…neatly and with occasional excitement."[129] The reception at *Cash Box* was a bit less tepid, stating "With youthful vitality the gang offers top drawer renditions."[130] *The Louisville Courier Journal* said, "Three young folk singers still after that big record hit, are caught during a personal appearance in Minneapolis."[131]

It seemed something was catching on. Around that time, WNEW in New York was playing the B-side of their inaugural 1961 single, "River Come Down." A year after The Journeymen had brilliantly recrafted the Jamaican song in their own style, the song's popularity motivated the group's booking agency to re-sign them. They also signed a lucrative $25,000 deal to write and record commercial jingles for Schlitz Beer. The group ended the year playing for homecoming festivities at American University in Washington, D.C., where they were characterized as "singing a dozen great songs for a crowd that just won't let them quit." They "left the crowd spellbound" a student said, and "got the only standing ovation I have ever seen accorded any group that has performed here."[132]

CENTER WOMEN PLAN BENEFIT—The Center Women's League of the Jewish Community Center will sponsor a benefit program by The Journeymen Sunday, March 18, at Lewiston High School Auditorium. Proceeds will be used to help equip a nursery school at the center and to replenish supplies.

Mrs. Sumner Cohen (left) is chairman of arrangements, and Mrs. Stanley Bernard (right) is publicity chairman for the event.

A number of additional recordings from 1962 were absent from their album. In fact, the trio released more singles during that year than any in their almost four year existence. "Don't Turn Around" backed with "Hush Now Sally" featured John's joint writing efforts with John Stewart and Dick Weissman respectively. It made a little noise commercially in the late spring, was picked up as a "selected single"[133] in some outlets, and dubbed a "pleasing portion that many teens will feel for," by *Cash Box*.[134] Paired with the Irving Berlin standard "What'll I Do," their take on the Merle Travis song "Loadin' Coal" was recorded as a single that summer and was one of Dick Weissman's rare vocal solos. It caught the attention of *Billboard* in the fall as a "Breaking Hit" and was seen as having "Strong Sales Potential." The review called it, "a folksy effort sung with enthusiasm" and predicted it "could attract attention." [135] These more mainstream offerings complemented the folk fare and served to keep the group's name in trade publications, newspaper reviews, radio stations, and record stores in between the album releases.

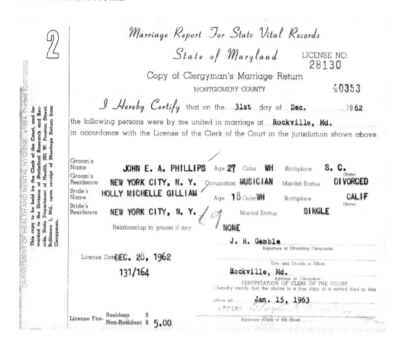

In their sojourns, the group's members were also maturing and undergoing personal changes. They missed about six weeks when Scott underwent a throat operation, which understandably worried his partners about the effect it might have on his voice. Their fears dissolved when McKenzie started to sing at a Canadian University appearance and, to Weissman's ear, "sounded ten years younger."[136] Meanwhile, John had begun to intensify his romance with the young Michelle Gilliam, which coincided with the final days of his marriage to Suzy. Since the two had met the previous year, Michelle was at his side during engagements from Springfield, Massachusetts, to Juárez, Mexico. John reportedly was also increasingly experimenting with marijuana and amphetamines.

By the end of 1962, The Journeymen were traveling the nation as an extremely popular act on campuses. Besides John's reliable contributions, Dick was writing more music for the trio. Topping it off was an event of even greater significance: John, now divorced, married Michelle Gilliam on New Year's Eve at the First Baptist Church of Rockville, Maryland, after which she described herself as "without a doubt, the happiest person in the world."[137] Scott and Dick gave her a "thirty year old Martin guitar" as a wedding present, which she found "absolutely beautiful."[138] The newlyweds celebrated their nuptials at The Shadows, an up-and-coming club in Washington, D.C. The effect of John and Michelle's union would mean new directions for The Journeymen and beyond.

FRESH SOUND FOR FIESTA — The Journeymen, vigorous new singing trio with a fresh and swinging blend of sound, takes over the star spotlight Monday at La Fiesta Theater Restaurant in Juarez. Discovered by Frank Werber, the man who organized and still guides the world-famous Kingston Trio, the Journeymen will be following in the footsteps of the popular Kingstons, who hold audience attendance records for their two La Fiesta engagements. The Journeymen are, from left, John Phillips, Scott McKenzie and Richard Weissman.

Citybilly Folk Singers

The year 1963 started with promise and ended with angst. At the year's start, *Father Knows Best* was still on television, Kennedy's New Frontier agenda entered its second year, and folk music was riding a high crest of mainstream popularity. Twelve months later, The Beatles had hits no father knew best, the President had been assassinated, and folk music was becoming a thing of the past.

Folk Groups Come...and Go
THE JOURNEYMEN ARE HERE...TO STAY!

OPENING TUESDAY
HOYT AXTON
AND
THE **JOURNEYMEN**
Doug Weston's   9083 SANTA MONICA BLVD.
                     Near Doheny
Troubadour   CR 6-6168

The Journeymen were enjoying a rejuvenated success in early 1963. As John Phillips characterized them, "We were the Four Freshmen of folk music."[139] A pop-folk group in the purest sense, they recorded their most progressive and creative album—appropriately titled *New Directions in Folk Music*—that spring. Renowned folk music authority Alan Lomax had written an article about the city dwelling folk singers whom he called "folkniks" or "citybilly" singers. A more apt description for The Journeymen could not be found.[140]

The trio was polishing their performing skills while generating a great deal of writing during their third year. With two albums and several singles under their belts, they had racked up no less than 250 live appearances over the previous twelve months. John had also written five songs recorded by The Kingston Trio. Virginians John and Scott, and Philadelphian Dick were a bona fide East Coast folk group, born out of the era's defining Greenwich Village scene. Denny Doherty described them as "very Ivy League: clean cut, Brooks Brothers suits, Princeton haircut."[141] For John, the time and place were catalysts and inspirations, explaining, "When you are from Virginia out of a high school, college, fraternity thing, and then you are thrust into the middle of the Village, it is sort of a culture shock to suddenly find people who are interested in the same things you were interested in. You can't make it in your hometown. And you can't make it by singing stuff that's been made famous by other people. You've got to have an idea of where you're going. You've got to get an individual sound."[142] Scott agreed, saying, "Especially in those years because John was one of the first singer-songwriters. There wasn't any such thing. Not on a big scale."[143] John, however, shared the credit: "Whenever we need some songs we just tell Dick to sing for a couple of hours and we pick the ones we like. He could sit down and sing folk songs for twenty-four hours and never repeat himself."[144]

John, Scott, and Dick were ready to test uncharted waters with their third album. While Dick was the product of the folk purists and "slowly educated us toward the folk tradition," as John described it, Scott and John were still "pop musicians at heart, and jazz musicians."[145] This combination allowed The Journeymen to continue to cover a variety of material at the nexus of traditional and progressive folk.

Jazz, ragtime, and blues influences manifest themselves on these 1963 recordings. Considering themselves the last of the beatniks, their first recording of the year, "Rag Mama," was indicative of these leanings. Produced by Kermit Walter, "a real character"

who arrived in New York driving his feed truck, "Rag Mama" was recorded in February and featured banjo work by Artie Ryerson, a veteran of records by Bill Haley, Eartha Kitt, and Tony Bennett.[146] It was released in March with a picture sleeve of Michelle—the new Mrs. John Phillips—clad in a 1920s gun moll getup. The record was called a "contagious showing" and one reviewer predicted it "could be making a lot of airplay," comparing its sound to the number one hit "Walk Right In" sung by The Rooftop Singers.[147]

The Journeymen recorded *New Directions in Folk Music* between March and April of 1963. "Country Blues," "Ben and Me," and "Someday Baby" offered a fresh take on the folk idiom with bluesy features and jazzy flourishes. Departures are heard in Muddy Waters' "Someday Baby," which features a drum, and "Country Blues," with its use of a lower tuned banjo in the tradition of Dock Boggs. Scott McKenzie remembered that during one of The Journeymen's long engagements at the hungry i, the group "used to like to go to different nightclubs and heard Jesse Fuller do 'San Francisco Bay Blues.'"[148] As Weissman puts it, "everybody was doing it," and so The Journeymen recorded their own two versions.[149]

So while they innovated, the group did not abandon traditional material. Instead they improved upon prevailing versions. "All the Pretty Little Horses," "Virgin Mary," and Ian & Sylvia's "Four Strong Winds" were all presented in a new light. Not unlike Picasso with visual art, John would take songs such as these and strip them down or deconstruct them and then assemble and arrange them in a fresh way, maintaining the lyrics and melody but varying the sound with a new tempo or harmonies. These adapted to the flow of the album alongside new material by Dick and John.

Dick's increased writing endeavors also yielded "Someone to Talk My Troubles To," composed after meeting the woman who would become his wife, which was subsequently recorded by at least twelve other artists. He describes "One Quick Martini" as "a real departure—The Journeymen's 'Scotch and Soda,'" referring to one of The Kingston Trio's trademark tunes.[150] One of the most inventive jazz renditions on the album is "Ja-Da," complete with John and Scott mimicking trombones and other Dixieland sounds in a kazoo-like, but realistic fashion. Another effect the group used was in response to the emerging

22 The Macon Telegraph and News Sunday Morning Oct. 20, 1963

The Journeymen Discover A New Musical Innovation

The Journeymen And An Admirer

[l-r] Scott McKenzie, John Phillips, Suzy Sumner, Richard Weissman

CAPITOL IS MAKING this special goal-post display piece, one of five, available to dealers in line with its fourth annual college promotion. Campaign is designed to push new and catalog product of artists popular on the nation's campuses.

"stereophonic" technology in recording. Scott recalled The Journeymen's extensive use of "ping-ponging" tracks "to obtain multiple vocal overlays on the tapes of the time, which typically had only two separate tracks."[151] That layering of harmonies was a harbinger of things to come when The Mamas & The Papas hit the studio in a few short years.

Besides recording, the group was ever on the move and in demand. They played a series of college dates, many of which were return engagements from the previous years. In the spring, one student newspaper remarked, "They had the image (rumpled Ivy League), they had the guitars (and one banjo) and they had the gall."[152] At their October 1963 appearance at Mercer University in Macon, Georgia, the group experienced a humorous mishap. In the "scramble" to get to Mercer after a late plane landing, Scott's trousers were lost. Before the show started, an announcement was made with a request that a student donate "one pair of black, 32 waist, 29 length pair of pants." At first the announcement was taken as a joke but the students soon "came to realize that no pants meant no concert." A willing benefactor saved the day.[153]

FORUM

One Performance Only

SUNDAY Eve. OCT. 13

at 8.30 p.m.

Featuring famous recording and TV stars

★ *In Person*

ODETTA
The JOURNEYMEN
IAN & SYLVIA
The TARRIERS

HOOTENANNY

Tickets $1.50, $2.00, $2.50, $3.00 tax incl.
NOW ON SALE AT FORUM BOX-OFFICE

That summer they also played new club venues in places like the Alan B. Shepherd Auditorium in Virginia Beach and the Troubadour in Los Angeles. Capitol tried again with "Kumbaya" and "Ja-Da" as a single release at the end of the summer, earning the 45 a "Pop Spotlight" in *Billboard*.[154] Another reviewer claimed it would be "a good bet for deejays" and termed its Canadian issue a "Class Release" several weeks later.[155] About this time, the group started singing Armstrong Tile commercials live on *The Danny Kaye Show*. Dick Weissman remembers, "I was amazed at how long it took to do an on-camera commercial since I'd played on dozens of them off camera."[156] Michelle Phillips, who was there for the rehearsals, remembers every line to this day and considers John's jingle "*really good*."[157] The following year, the commercial was voted the best videotape production by 150 television executives.[158]

ESDAY, OCTOBER 29, 1963

SIU HOOTENANNY

John Phillips, Dick Weissman and Scott McKenzie, professionally known as "The Journeymen", appeared Saturday evening at the Southern Illinois University Hootenanny held in the Edwardsville Junior High School auditorium.

New Directions in Folk Music came out a few weeks later and reviews of it were robustly, categorically positive. One critic wrote, "The trio sings the traditional folk song, but they do it with magnificent spark,"[159] while others pointed to the creativity of the group, the commercial appeal of the record, and the variety of its song choice, with another saying, "That easy-on-the-ears trio, the Journeymen, decide folk music can be just about anything American folks sing."[160] The pop-folk nature of the recording placed it nicely alongside records by The Beach Boys and Wayne Newton, with which it was frequently advertised. For this record's cover the trio was photographed on a movie lot in Hollywood, back in their coats and ties, and looking incredibly handsome. The label acknowledged that the thrust was to the university crowd and copious ads for The Journeymen's album hit college newspapers nationwide with the italicized admonition, "*Look for - ask for - The Journeymen on your campus.*"

Hootenanny U.S.A.

In many ways, the folk revival was at its apex that fall, and so were The Journeymen. In October, *Cash Box* made mention of the group's ten-day, seven-city tour, where they would be the guests of honor in each place, and the center of attention at a cocktail party hosted by Capitol Records.[161] The following month they covered tremendous ground with several other groups in a *Hootenanny USA* tour throughout the Southeast and Midwest. The tour included the comedy group The Geezinslaw Brothers, solo singers Glenn Yarbrough and Jo Mapes, and a Canadian trio with two albums to their credit named The Halifax Three. That group's tenor—one Denny Doherty—began a friendship with John and Michelle, who sometimes joined The Journeymen on tour. John was instantly smitten with Denny's voice, which he likened to Mel Torme, a.k.a. The Velvet Fog, later saying, "I have only heard three or four people in the world that can sing like Denny, that Irish tenor beautiful quality. My Dad was one of the others. I grew up listening to him—so mellow and beautiful."[162] Unlike Torme, Denny truly was Irish-Canadian, and in addition to his lyrical, natural voice, he was strikingly handsome.

This cavalcade type tour was popular at the time and exposed the group to large audiences in arenas and coliseums, sometimes in conjunction with local universities. The *Hootenanny* television show continued to ape the folk trend and The Journeymen appeared on it twice during the year. The tour was fast paced and constantly moving and slated to hit more than two dozen cities in about a month's time. One student newspaper described backstage: "You go to a backroom where a small riot is taking place. Everyone is singing or shouting. Coat hangers fly through the air. You are asked to hold a pair of trousers for a minute."[163]

The Journeymen received top billing among the groups and were clearly at the top of their game. "John Phillips," one reporter gushed, "is characterized by the critics as having a style and musical outlook not unlike the poetry and mood of a young pioneer American who has found himself in the mid-twentieth century life but who prefers the music and style of the past."[164] Scott was similarly lauded as "one of the best tenors on the entertainment scene."[165]

Perhaps the most publicized of these appearances took place in mid-November when the tour was scheduled to play in Jackson, Mississippi, where the audience was to be segregated. John explained at the time, "It was more than segregation in the Auditorium. They wouldn't even let negroes in the place. The city wanted to make a test case out of it. They had police around the building ready to arrest the first negro that came within 200 feet of the door. We didn't feel that we could play before people like that."[166]

Appearance Canceled by Song Group

FOLK SINGERS WON'T PLAY AT MCNEESE

Give Show at TSC College

Instead, the groups rerouted to nearby Tougaloo College, a predominantly black school. Michelle Phillips recalls getting off the buses and being astonished to see men standing with guns as they disembarked. The episode made the news wires and quickly circulated nationwide. As a result, their next tour stop in Louisiana was canceled out of fear of similar unrest. Pat Lacroix of The Halifax Three further recalls, "When the bus pulled into the venue at Baton Rouge we were met by the KKK, who greeted us with baseball bats and bicycle chains pounding on the bus. The bus did a quick exit and we headed north to our next concert."[167]

One of the next engagements was on November 21 at Kansas State University, where a story in the college newspaper captures their life on the road: "The Journeymen are dressing together near the door. One says they will leave for Des Moines as soon as they can get out to the bus. 'We've got 33 one night stands in a row. If the stops are within 400 miles we take the bus. Otherwise we fly.' He tucks the tail of an unbelievably wrinkled shirt into a pair of Levis."[168]

For their Des Moines concert Michelle flew in to join The Journeymen and visit an aunt and uncle. As she got off the plane, she noticed that everyone in the airport was crowded around the televisions inside, which was a new thing at the time.[169] President Kennedy had been shot.

The tour more or less ended and wended its way back to New York, where they had a couple of appearances the day before and after Thanksgiving. The final performance was to a half-filled Carnegie Hall, which earned a mention by *Cash Box*[170] and a small story in *The New York Times*.[171]

The Journeymen regained their balance in mid-December. They put on a twenty-song program at the State University of New York in Delhi before an audience "primarily of high school and college students…a hootenanny type affair."[172] At the end of the year, the group was listed in a *Billboard* article titled "Who's Who in the World of Music."[173]

Following this, the group more or less went dormant until the winter college gigs started up again in early 1964. The itinerary was very similar to the previous year. Many college concerts were on the schedule, including "The Big Hoot" at Ohio State where The Journeymen played to more than 11,000 people with The New Christy Minstrels and Josh White. "We've been quite busy," declared John. "We play mostly for college audiences and occasionally for a few night spots."[174] They ventured throughout the South and Midwest again, and traveled west to Oklahoma and Texas. At Louisiana State they were called "the intellectual" folk group who were "risque" as they pushed the limits of their ribald lines. One such quip by John: "This is a song about a mountain boy, who loved a mountain girl — often."[175]

One paper seemed to presciently pick up on the boys' eventual separate directions: "After three years and three albums together the future of The Journeymen is somewhat undecided. As Dick is thinking of leaving the group and continuing his song writing while

THEIR PERMANENT NEW DIRECTION IS UP!

T-1951

he studies music in New York, John and Scott may add another member to the set, stick together, or merely split up."[176] After years of relentless pushing, group dynamics with the trio were disintegrating, with John and Scott not speaking to each other, and Dick serving as intermediary. Sometimes they even traveled separately. "That's true," acknowledges Michelle. "It was about me being on the road with them. They had an agreement: 'No Chicks On the Road' and John was taking me along every time they were on the road even before he was divorced. Scott and Suzy were very good friends and it put Scott in a very awkward position. Eventually they had a big blowout and that was it."[177]

Dick and Scott were both weary and ready to quit. Signaling his ability to go it alone, Dick had already cut a solo album in March with a somewhat descriptive title, *The Things That Trouble My Mind*.

For several of these spring dates The Journeymen performed with Ian & Sylvia, and twice appeared on the Canadian TV show *Let's Sing Out*. The group's last documented concert was at Clarkson College in Potsdam, New York, on May 17.

By the summer of 1964 something seismic was happening in popular music and it all had to do with the reverberating sound from across the Atlantic. The Beatles had squarely

75

hit the United States earlier that year with "I Want to Hold Your Hand," and the British Invasion was fast consuming airwaves and record sales stateside. The folk revival waned as tectonic rumblings were giving way to new sounds. In addition to this, John attributed to *Hootenanny* both the mainstreaming of popular folk and the extinguishing of it with packaged tours, observing years later, "The Beatles came along and started doing intelligent music and harmonies that were acceptable to folk musicians who were used to using minor chords and diminished chords in their own music and proved that it would be palatable to the public."[178]

At the time, however, John "didn't really like" the new sound.[179] He was part of a successful group in a milieu that was still generally popular, albeit diminishing. The fissures in his trio were inescapable, but taking a cue from other newer, innovative ensembles, he started to think of regrouping and returning to an old love—the combination of male and female voices—with his wife Michelle. To add a distaff element to The Journeymen, was a huge step towards what would ultimately become a response to the British volley of 1964.

Wednesday, April 22, 1964

WARM-UP TIME. The Journeymen, popular folk singing group, warm up in the dressing room of the Cameron fieldhouse before performing in Aggieland.

THE Journeymen FREE! with Drury ID ★ ★ ★ in the FIELDHOUSE ★ ★ ★ Thursday APRIL 2, '64

GENERAL ADMISSION $1.50

A Round, Fat, Beautiful Sound: The Colonials and The Halifax Three

The much-heralded British Invasion of the Sixties revolutionized popular music. But while the main invasion came from across the Atlantic, a lesser-known flanking movement invaded folk music from Canada, sounding a battle cry for the confluence of The Mamas & The Papas, as well as groups such as The Lovin' Spoonful, Steppenwolf, and Blood, Sweat & Tears.

The Four Winds, with Pat LaCroix (Far Left) and Gordon Lightfoot (Second from Right) 1958

Among the ranks of this Canadian Invasion was future Papa Denny Doherty. With Patrick LaCroix and Richard Byrne, Denny forayed into the New York folk scene in 1962 as part of the Greenwich Village folk revival and eventually became known as The Halifax Three.

Each man in this trio possessed a different musical pedigree. LaCroix was a jazz singer from British Columbia who had his own TV show before joining the group. While attending Westlake College of Music in Los Angeles, he sang with Gordon Lightfoot in a vocal group called The Four Winds. Byrne had sung since boyhood, with experience mostly in classical and folk. One 1962 newspaper article described his "fairly lengthy career" spanning the continent "with a harmonica, guitar and bongo drums."[180] Denny Doherty, meanwhile, had most recently been singing rock and roll.

Denny Doherty on a Dare

Denny was a true Haligonian whose dockyard worker father had been in the marching band of the Princess Louise Fusiliers, a regiment of the Canadian Armed Forces. Irish-Canadian Denny had grown up in Wellington Court in Halifax, a modest and unprivileged community of hundreds housed in former army barracks. It would be the equivalent of today's public housing. The youngest of six, Denny was jaunty, devilishly handsome, and extraordinarily gifted of voice. The elder Doherty was not keen on his son pursuing a musical career, insisting, "Get something you can put in your ass pocket."[181] But Denny had other plans, saying, "My father had been at me to get a trade, but the life I chose was to become a gypsy as it were."[182]

On a dare, Denny started singing publicly in 1955 at the Halifax Forum, a skating rink-turned-dancehall near Wellington Court. He "came straight from high school glee clubs," according to one reporter.[183] "I was singing in the car," he reminisced. "And the boys told me to shut up. 'If you want to sing, get up on the stage and sing with the band at the Forum. There's a dance up there tonight. Go and sing there.'" The song Denny dared to sing was Pat Boone's "Love Letters in the Sand." The stunt went better than he could have imagined:

> Six hundred people on a wooden floor over an ice rink stopped dancing and turned around. I was petrified. That's it, I thought, they're going to charge the stage and kill me. They came closer. They came to the stage. The girls were going 'Ahh.' The boys were getting really mad at me."[184]

The bandleader, who knew Denny's father through military reserve service, liked young Doherty's singing so much he invited him back to play with his band, The Peter Powers Orchestra.

Later, while working in a Halifax pawnshop, Denny was "banging away" on the various guitars and musical instruments pawned by sailors and seamen on merchant marine ships in the Halifax Harbour.[185] The familiarity and access to the equipment fostered his growing interest. Richard Sheehan, a classmate at St. Patrick's High School who had seen Denny singing at the Forum, describes their connection: "I had a job at Sears Department Store and this guy I worked with, Eddie Thibodeau, knew a drummer, Michael O'Connell, and we used to get together and play songs. I told them, 'You know, I've got this friend at school who can really sing. We need to invite him over.'"[186] Denny accepted the invitation, with Sheehan

Denny Doherty (Far Left) at the Barrington Pawn Exchange

distinctly recalling, "I think it was probably by the end of the first verse that we realized that we had to get about two dozen numbers down really good and get out and start doing some gigs."[187] Calling themselves The Hepsters, the local rock and roll group played in venues like Knights of Columbus halls, social clubs, and weddings as far as Indian Harbor and St. Margaret's Bay in Nova Scotia—about an hour's drive away. Describing their repertoire as the "songs of the day,"[188] Sheehan says, "I remember 'Sloop John B.' as The Kingston Trio was starting up then, and the Everly Brothers were popular. We did Jimmie Rodgers songs like 'Kisses Sweeter Than Wine' and 'Honeycomb' and of course, Elvis. It was sort of the Top 50 of the day."[189] Denny recalled covers of material by Santo & Johnny, The Platters' "Harbor Lights," Chuck Berry's "Johnny B. Goode" and Mark Dinning's "Teen Angel."[190] The band was four pieces, with Sheehan playing guitar and a tenor sax, and Denny in front on vocals. He also occasionally "tortured a trombone," as he put it.[191]

"Denny would bend at the waist and belt out a song. On stage he had that kind of swagger," recalls Sheehan. "He always liked the hand mic. I remember trying to get him to play guitar and he didn't at the time. He didn't want to. He was more comfortable with the hand mic and he was very good at it. Denny was a charismatic guy." In the roughly two years The Hepsters were together between 1956 and 1958, Sheehan avows, "We drew crowds wherever we went."[192]

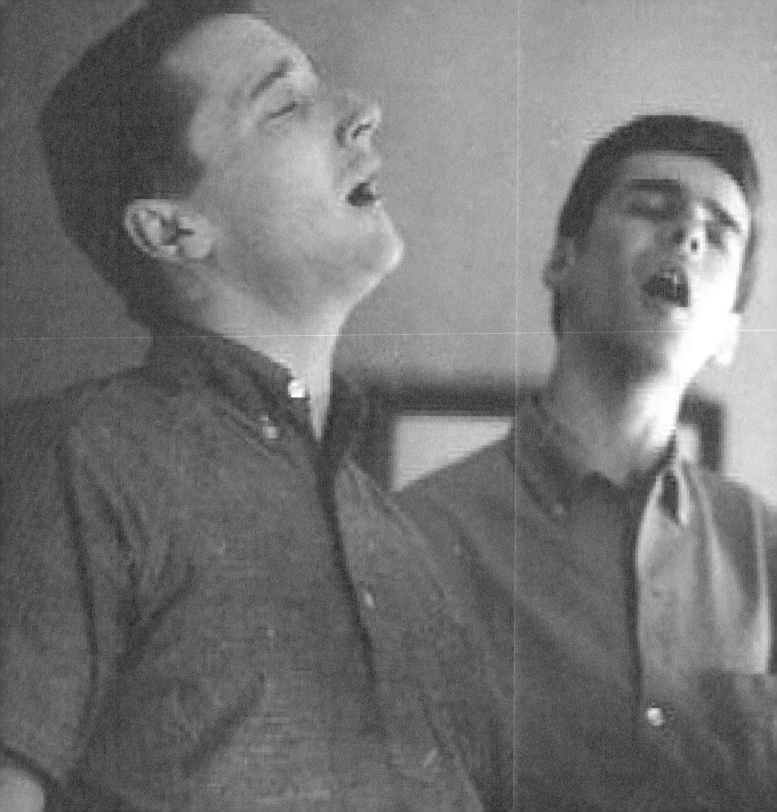

THE COLONIALS

on

"TRAVELLIN' ON HOME"

WEDNESDAYS AT 8:30

starring

Denny Doherty   Pat La Croix   Dick Bryne

with

hostess Pat Leith

MADE IN CANADA
RODEO
INTERNATIONAL

ASCAP
Time: 2:43

RO. 280

THEY CALL THE WIND MARIA
(Lerner - Loewe)
THE COLONIALS
(45)

In 1960, at a New Year's Eve Party in Halifax, Denny sang for the first time with Pat LaCroix and Richard Byrne. The point of origin was a jazz club near Denny's job at the Barrington Exchange Pawn Shop. A month later, under the name The Colonials, the three entered into a contract with Canadian label Rodeo Records. The contract bespeaks its era with its mention of 78 RPM records and 45s, in addition to "Long Play Records." Byrne was the only signatory, a fitting harbinger of his dominant role in the trio.[193]

The next month they had a single and made the rounds in Nova Scotia. They played fraternity parties at nearby Dalhousie University and even on international freighter ships docked in the Halifax Harbour. At first they were simply working for libations. "Our earliest repertoire was basically covers of The Kingston Trio and some songs that we knew from our families," recalls LaCroix.[194] The trio gained prominence on their local television show, *Travellin' On Home*, of which they made sixteen weekly episodes and Byrne wrote the theme song.

"Right from the get-go we were in it for the dough," admits Pat LaCroix. "My first love was the music of the Great American Songbook in a jazz style, and Denny was a rock and roller. However, folk music was the hot item, and we were hellbent to cash in on it."[195]

They recorded one long forgotten album with the hackneyed title *Hootenanny*, that accompanied their single on Rodeo Records: "All My Trials" paired with "They Call the Wind Maria" from the musical *Paint Your Wagon*. The former was dubbed a "colorful track in a calypso vein" by one review and featured a conga player named Billy Ince. The single made a showing in *Cash Box*, which awarded it a "Good" rating, noting the show tune was also deemed to have "good teen market appeal."[196]

This accolade was taken to heart in Nova Scotia. When a local newspaper critic panned the group after a performance, the president of Rodeo Records issued several letters in Halifax. With their *Cash Box* rating in mind, he defended the trio and touted the esteem of the group in the United States. "It may be of interest to your newspaper and readers," he wrote, "that the views of the critic involved are not shared by the professional critics of the American market. It seems strangely consistent that the local critics have no faith in local talent standing up to American competition."[197] That the label was going to the mat for their newfound group seems to indicate some conviction on Rodeo's part that there was a promising talent in The Colonials.

Their reputation seemed to have survived, and soon found them singing in a commercial for grocery store chain IGA, for which Byrne penned the lyrics to a "sea shanty type melody," as LaCroix remembers.[198] "After that in Halifax we had done it all," Denny recalled. "We had the TV show, we did the coffeehouses, played the fraternity houses, that was it—it was time to move on."[199]

Long Rough Road To the Top, But There's Always a Crowd

Move on they did. "As soon as our TV series finished," LaCroix remembers, "we got in a red '57 MG with guitars, suitcases, and an overinflated sense of self-worth, and headed for Montreal. Richard had managed to weld the roof of a Studebaker Low Boy on top of it, turning it into a very bizarre looking sport station wagon. Denny and I took turns curled up in the back."[200]

On their way to Quebec the MG broke down in Eastport, Maine, and, as Denny put it, "we had to sell a guitar to get the car fixed," after which they sang a set at the Red Roof Inn for a meal and a room. "That was our first professional gig in the US," laughed Denny, "singing for our supper."[201]

Once back on the road they soon reached Montreal, a city Byrne had previously worked with his wife in a sort of exotic nightclub act. "He had some kind of strange little South American animal—a kinkajou—on her shoulder," Denny described. "He dressed à la Lash LaRue with a big bullwhip. She had a little skimpy outfit on and he whacked cigarettes out of her mouth."[202]

"There were 300 nightclubs, so if you could get some kind of act together and get up on stage, you could get work up there," Denny further recalled of Montreal in 1961. "Byrne knew we had a viable commodity in The Colonials. We sounded good, we sang good, we looked good, and it was perfect timing for this new folk thing. All the clubs in Montreal really wanted to feature folk music."[203] At the time, LaCroix told one newspaper, "Canadians just don't seem to go for Canadian folk songs. They want the American numbers they've grown accustomed to hearing."[204]

Life in Montreal soon took on an itinerant route when, as Denny remembered it, "this guy gave us an apartment and $50 a week to do a gig in his back room." The guy was Robert Silverman, who owned the Seven Steps Bookshop. "He had a rather 'pinkish' bookstore," Denny recalled. "There was some communist material. They were into banning the bomb and all that. In the back they had a little coffeehouse and we performed there."[205] Silverman was a Trotskyite but he attracted some of the Greenwich Village folkies at the time for his back room coffeehouse named the Embers, which featured performances from the likes of Bob Dylan and Leonard Cohen.

"We were working the Embers," Denny continued, "then we'd finish a gig and we'd run down St. Catherine's Street to the Venus de Milo Room. We'd finish the gig there. We'd run back up to the Embers, do a gig there. Run back down to the Venus de Milo Room. That went on all night for weeks."[206]

As they were quickly maturing in this large cosmopolitan city, their horizons broadened beyond coffeehouses. "A repertory of numbers that can only be described as extensive," advertised Lou Black's Living Room, the tony, high end dinner club where The Colonials spent an extended stay in the first weeks of 1962.[207]

The Colonials, Dennis Doherty, Pat Lacroix and Dick Bryne

Long, Rough Road To The Top, But There's Always A Crowd

The trio made a strong showing at Lou Black's, but when Black experienced problems with organized crime, the three decided to change venues. The Mafia was entrenched in nightclub life in Montreal and had tried to strongarm Lou Black, who had been the maître d at a mob affiliated club called the Living Room in New York. He was not swayed, but as a result of his intransigence The Colonials learned that he was thrown down the stairs of his own club. Denny said later that ultimately one half of Black's body was found in the St. Lawrence River and the other half in town.[208]

After playing in smaller Eastern townships, as well as Quebec and the Laurentians, The Colonials made their way to Toronto in the spring of 1962. The company was terrific, with the group rubbing elbows with The Raftsmen and Ian & Sylvia, but profitable gigs were hard to come by. "At the time, Toronto had a plethora of coffeehouses and bars that featured folk music," remembers LaCroix. "Unfortunately, most of the coffeehouses were just open mic free performances—places like the Bohemian Embassy, the Village Corner, and the Purple Onion."[209]

Eventually, the group secured an agent, Harold Kudlets, and even though their efforts at getting on television shows were unfulfilled, not all the jobs continued to be gratis. "We played a joint called The 5th Peg, opening for Bill Cosby," says LaCroix. "Our group made $350 for the week and Cosby made about the same."[210] A reviewer noted, "They present a pleasant appearance, their voices blend well, their material is less esoteric than is sometimes the case with folk groups and perhaps best of all, their chatter between numbers is light and slyly humorous."[211] Denny concurred, "We weren't trying to educate, we were trying to entertain."[212]

It was such praise that got them to a New York audition on May 1, 1962 with Epic, the folk music imprint for Columbia Records. Going to the States was the ambition. As Denny put it at the time: "What else can we do? It's the big market especially for folk music."[213]

"We were working Niagara Falls," remembers LaCroix, "and we drove down to Buffalo and auditioned at a big supper club for an old impresario named Harry Altman who had people like Eddy Fisher and Sammy Davis, Jr."[214] The supper club was none other than the Town Casino, the same venue where John Phillips and The Smoothies had played two years previously. With Altman on their side, The Colonials had entrée in New York.

Name Change and Novelty Hit

Driving all night to Manhattan, the Canadian threesome found themselves, mere hours later, auditioning for Columbia's Epic Records and International Talent Associates—the same booking agency that handled The Journeymen and The Kingston Trio. The day ended with a contract with both the agency and the record label, an individual room for each Colonial at the Plaza Hotel, and a name change.

"The Americans changed our name," Denny explained. "At the New York audition this guy said, 'The Colonials? I don't think so. Where are you from?' We said, 'Well, we're from Nova Scotia.' And he said, we'll call you The Dorrymen…or The Oarlocks… Say, what town are you from?' We told him and he said, 'You're The Halifax Three.'"[215]

In a scene surfeited with numerically nomenclatured folk groups, The Halifax Three fit right in. And yet, being Canadian, they could bring their own folk songs and phrasings to their records and performances, in addition to their renditions of American fare, adding a quasi-foreign panache that was particular to them. Other Canadians such as Gordon Lightfoot, Ian & Sylvia, Joni Mitchell, Leonard Cohen, and Buffy St. Marie capitalized on this too.

Once signed, the three took up residence at the Albert Hotel. Pat LaCroix's wife Patti waited tables on Bleecker Street and the group played for baskets in coffeehouses around Greenwich Village. Baskets were passed because, if an establishment did not have a liquor license, hired entertainment was prohibited. To get around this, baskets were passed around like church offering plates to remunerate performers. "This is how we paid our hotel bill for the next few months until the new gigs started to emerge," LaCroix says.[216] Others working for baskets on the Greenwich Village coffeehouse circuit included Tiny Tim, David Crosby, and Bob Dylan.

At this stage, having material to record was a priority, and, in addition to Richard Byrne's original compositions and arrangements of old folk songs, the trio was referred to Art Mogull,

a song promoter for Warner Bros. Publishing. He gave The Halifax Three a tape, Pat LaCroix recalls, "saying that he thought the song on it would be a good choice for our album. We took it back to the hotel and listened to Bob Dylan playing an out of tune guitar and singing badly, 'Blowing in the Wind.'" "Well that will never sell," was Byrne's response.[217]

With new opportunities and pressures in front of them, the group worked to polish their unique sound. Remembering Byrne as the Svengali of the group, producer Bob Morgan said that he hoped to make them the next big thing since his success with The Brothers Four. Traveling to the Colonial Hotel in Sarnia, Ontario, Morgan told them they had "a round, fat, beautiful sound," remembering, "Denny and I managed to find some bottles of beer and went out and sat on the shore of Lake Huron, and threw pebbles there, and got to know each other."[218] Within the month, they were in the studio, recording the songs "Something Old – Something New," "Far Side of the Hill," and "Fare-Thee-Well."

A fortnight later, they were back recording their first single, a railroad tune called "Bull Train," paired with "Come On By," their own spin on "Kumbaya." When the single came out in December, *Billboard* gave it "Four Stars," dubbing it a "Special Merit Single" and declaring "it comes across with much authenticity."[219]

In the new year of 1963, The Halifax Three shared a manager and a stage with famed comic Shelley Berman, who recalled how well received they were: "I had to follow them. I

Eric Hord with The Halifax Three

had trouble coming on stage because the audience always wanted more."[220] High praise from a wildly successful comedian who was enjoying a television special and critically-acclaimed albums. Comedy seemed to pair well with the droll threesome, who also shared the bill with comedian Adam Keefe at the Village Gate.

Their self-titled first album, *The Halifax Three*, yielded by their sessions the previous summer, followed in early 1963. Momentum was building. The album's cover showed the trio mid-song, centered around Pat LaCroix playing a washtub bass. "The washtub bass was built by us in New York out of a hardwood rake handle, a round galvanized washtub, and the fingerboard of a bass fiddle with a gut G string and a cello tuning peg," LaCroix remembers. "I played it on the up-tempo numbers and, due to the fact that it had a tuning board, it was one of the few washtub basses played in tune, since I was able to finger the notes and not just push the handle back and forth to get the pitch."[221]

The group was different. "The Halifax Three," bragged the back of their first album, "were not striped shirt weekend party boys."[222] One Canadian critic observed, "The Halifax Three have a lot on their side. They are not fresh out of college, neither do they rely on re-arrangements of current hits. Rather they are hard-working, well-travelled, youngish men who know what a chancy thing success can be."[223] "We were doing folk songs like 'Oh Mary, Don't You Weep' more as performers, not as folkies trying to promote roots music," remarked Denny. "If we found a song we liked, we'd sing it. It happened to be that folk music was the vehicle that we got gigs with."[224] LaCroix agrees, saying, "Later on we started listening to old time folk artists like [Woody] Guthrie and some blues people, but at the beginning we really didn't know very much about the folk genre."[225]

The sound of The Halifax Three was, in a word, smooth. Denny's range spanned three octaves and Byrne's arrangements and adaptations were velvety. They were harmonious, polished, and unabashedly commercial. "We were not musicologists," acknowledged Denny.[226] The previous summer, this commercial capability cost them a snub at the Mariposa Folk Festival. Contrasting themselves with folk purists who either embraced or ignored their flaws as a badge of authenticity, LaCroix adds, "We wanted to sound good."[227] Songs such as "I Passed By a Stream" and "Far Side of the Hill" were highly produced and perfected in the studio and were representative. Yet the group was innovative as well. Along with LaCroix's washtub bass, Byrne achieved a bongo-like sound by thumping his guitar on songs like "All My Trials." One paper characterized their sound as "the folksy Nova Scotian trio's brand of swing."[228]

Unplanned but nearly simultaneous with their album's release, a unique opportunity arose for their second single, which came out in February 1963. It was a novelty song called "The Man Who Wouldn't Sing Along With Mitch," lampooning television song-meister Mitch Miller. "It was an attempt to do something that might get them some attention,"

Produced by Robert Morgan

The Halifax Three

BULL TRAIN
I PASSED BY A STREAM
SOMETHING OLD—SOMETHING NEW
HUSH LITTLE BABY
ALL MY TRIALS
COME ON BY

•

COME DOWN THE MOUNTAIN KATIE DALY
FAR SIDE OF THE HILL
WHEN I FIRST CAME TO THIS LAND
FARE-THEE-WELL
HEADIN' ON HOME AGAIN
OH MARY DON'T YOU WEEP

Denny Doherty · Pat La Croix · Richard Byrne

Above the many young voices in the folk music world, three exciting and supremely talented young men are making themselves clearly heard. The Halifax Three were discovered "down east" in Canada just a short time ago and were immediately brought to New York for an audition with Epic Records' Executive Producer, Bob Morgan. The rest of their discovery story is condensed into two words by Bob: "I flipped!" And so has everyone else who has heard them.

The Halifax Three are in the "new wave" of popular folk artists. Their sound is one of truth, of a natural reality, an essence of knowing and living that breathes from deep within. These are not three collegiate, striped-shirted, weekend party boys. These are young men who have learned life the hard way and are strong and vital because of it. But most important, they have a gift, the ability to communicate, not just to entertain but to engage the listener emotionally.

Individually, they have wandered the length and breadth of North America and Europe, learning first hand about the hardships and exaltations out of which folk music arises. They have acquired a deep capacity to live a song. Accomplished musicians before they began their travels, the group brings a meticulous yet deceptively effortless technique to the music they play, a sure sensitivity to the lyrics of the songs they sing.

The songs they have selected for this album are varied. Some of them, from a purist point of view, are not folk songs at all. Come Down the Mountain Katie Daly, for example was first heard last year—as the "number one" record on the Irish Hit Parade. Others, such as Oh Mary Don't You Weep and Come On By are a definite part of folk heritage. Yet in all these selections, from their rousing rendition of When I First Came to This Land, to the narrative unfolding of I

Passed by a Stream (written by Richard Byrne), the Halifax Three demonstrate a fascinating versatility.

Richard Byrne, who writes many of his own songs and arranges all of the music for the Halifax Three, comes to folk music with a first-hand knowledge of his material. At fourteen, motivated by a sincere desire to know people, to know their roots, he began to roam from his native Nova Scotia. To date, this curiosity about the land and its people has taken him all over the North American continent, given him an enormous backlog of material for his song and, before the formation of the Halifax Three, had taken him through such assorted jobs as artist, radio announcer, health studio manager and wild animal trainer.

The solo voice on most of the songs in this album belongs to Dennis Doherty, the youngest and most Irish member of the Halifax Three. In addition to being an accomplished trombonist, he has sung on CBC-TV for many years and, before he joined the Halifax Three, as vocalist in a rock and roll group. As Denny clearly demonstrates on this record, his voice, with its three-octave range, lends itself to any type of song.

Pat La Croix shares the solo leads with Denny and plays his own variation of a washtub bass at live performances. Except for two years as a professional golfer, Pat has stayed with music all his life, first singing with his brother's jazz group, then studying piano, voice and arranging in Hollywood. Then he traveled to Europe where he wended his way as an itinerant singer through Germany, Scotland, England and Holland. Returning to Canada, he divided his time between his own TV show in Halifax and various club dates in Montreal. It wasn't long before he met up with Dick and Denny—and the Halifax Three was formed.

A

THE SELECTIONS—PUBLISHED BY M. WITMARK AND SONS (ASCAP) EXCEPT WHERE NOTED—ARE FOLLOWED BY THEIR TIMINGS

SIDE I		SIDE II	
BULL TRAIN BMI Canada, Ltd. (BMI)	2:15	COME DOWN THE MOUNTAIN KATIE DALY - Leeds Music Corp. (ASCAP)	3:21
I PASSED BY A STREAM	2:42	FAR SIDE OF THE HILL - Lee-Wall & Sons (ASCAP)	2:40
SOMETHING OLD SOMETHING NEW	2:03	WHEN I FIRST CAME TO THIS LAND - Ludlow Music, Inc. (BMI)	2:35
HUSH LITTLE BABY	3:03	FARE THEE WELL	1:59
ALL MY TRIALS	3:19	HEADIN' ON HOME AGAIN	2:46
COME ON BY	2:34	OH MARY DON'T YOU WEEP	
	16:12		16:30

(COVER PHOTO) HENRY PARKER

© EPIC RECORDS 1963 / ALL RIGHTS RESERVED ● "EPIC," "CBS" MARCAS REG. T.M. PRINTED IN USA

recalled producer Bob Morgan.[229] Mitch Miller was a famous musical conductor and record executive with a hit weekly television show in the early 1960s called *Sing Along with Mitch*. The program was more or less a community sing-along program with a male chorus and song lyrics depicted at the bottom of the television screen.

The song's genesis began on a January 1963 episode of *The Merv Griffin Show* where Miller was a guest. As a joke, Miller's personal manager commissioned the song for Griffin to sing as a surprise gag at Miller and his show. The public response to this good-natured jab was so positive that *The Merv Griffin Show* actually received requests for a recording of the song. Epic Records was contacted and The Halifax Three were enlisted to record it a week later—the very day their album was released.[230]

Mischievous Merv Inspires Mitch Hit

A little ditty titled, "The Man Who Wouldn't Sing Along With Mitch," commissioned by Merv Griffin as a joke the day Mitch Miller appeared as his guest, is turning into a hit.

After they'd had their laugh, Merv and Mitch were ready to forget the whole thing until mail started coming in asking where to buy the record, so the ditty was quickly developed for recording purposes, and waxed by The Halifax Three for Epic.

 POP SPOTLIGHT

THE HALIFAX THREE

THE MAN WHO WOULDN'T SING ALONG WITH MITCH
(Brookhaven, BMI) (2:09)   Epic 9572

A real cute novelty here, in the folk idiom. The lyric tells the tale of the stubborn man who just wouldn't sing along with the bearded one. The number's a foot-stomper. Flip is "Come Down the Mountain, Katie Daly" (Leeds, ASCAP) (2:51).

"The Man Who Wouldn't Sing Along with Mitch" spoofed the bandleader and profiled its non-conformist subject. With the space race in full sprint, it incorporated a cute reference to then-very-culturally relevant "Cape Canaveral," as well as the Cold War bureaucracy in Washington's secret service.

He got a job in Washington and worked up to the top
Then the secret service heard someone snitched (someone snitched)
So then the boss got real upset
And dropped him from the cabinet
'On my team we all sing along with Mitch'

He fled to Cape Canaveral to really get away
He jumped inside a rocket, pulled the switch
On landing he discovered soon
He wasn't welcomed on the moon
'Up here we all sing along with Mitch'

We'll have to hang him from the rafters
Burn him as the witch
The man who wouldn't sing along with Mitch[231]

The song ended with an impressive imitation of a few bars of one of Miller's most famous sing-along records, "The Yellow Rose of Texas."

In 1959, The Kingston Trio had great success with their satirical story-song, "M.T.A." about a man stuck on the Boston subway. The Halifax Three hoped to play off that kind of success with their novelty song which charted in New York and received widespread national press. Gossip columnist Walter Winchell, with one of his typical morse code-like entries, called it "A Daffy Ditty."[232] *Billboard*'s "Spotlight Picks" characterized The Halifax Three as "newsmakers" and their new song as a "musical potshot at you-know-who."[233] *Cash Box* reported that Epic pressed 400,000 advance copies of the record "in anticipation of the expected dealer panic in its release."[234] This story further theorized that a New York City newspaper strike at the time was forcing publicity and advertising professionals to seek innovative ways to promote new records and that "Mitch" was a winning example of alternative public relations.

The Halifax Three — EPIC

THE MAN WHO WOULDN'T SING ALONG WITH MITCH

COME DOWN THE MOUNTAIN KATIE DALY

5-9572

"EPIC," "CBS" MARCAS REG. T.M. PRINTED IN U.S.A

Indeed, "IMMEDIATE RELEASE – 7 Day Special" is memorialized on the recording documents. A picture sleeve with a caricature of the titular "Man" throwing a can of beer at the TV was rendered under a photograph of the trio, and sheet music was published as well. Denny claimed, "It was a way of giving Mitch Miller a nod, since he was the president of Columbia. I remember he came to the sessions and gave it his blessing."[235] Hopes were high with the novelty tune that one reviewer called "a real foot stomper,"[236] and about which another wrote, "The trio really blasts this nonconformist, and they hope in turn that the record will blast them into the conformity of fame and fortune."[237]

One curiosity that drove viewership of Mitch Miller's TV show was the unannounced, uncredited cameo-type appearances of stars in the chorus who happened to be in New York. The guests camouflaged by dressing like the male chorus and on different occasions would be interspersed in the chorus during the show's closing sing-along. Camera closeups would reveal the likes of Johnny Carson and Jerry Lewis making such appearances, which is how. The Halifax Three appeared on the show that spring.

Harnessing the synergy of the album and the single, a *Billboard* ad for the group boasted "THEY'RE UNUSUAL, THEY'RE HOT, THEY SELL."[238] The single earned "Billboard Pick" status and the album received a 4-Star review.[239]

In concerts, the three had become four with the addition of banjo player Eric Hord, who also backed up Ian & Sylvia. Hord grew up in San Diego and was largely self-taught as a musician. He had some success with a folk group named The Neighbors in 1962 with

Accompanist Eric Hord

a similar kind of novelty song to The Halifax Three's "The Man Who Wouldn't Sing Along with Mitch." The record was titled "The Ballad of John Glenn (The Biggest Ride Since Paul Revere)," a reference to Glenn's historic voyage into space that year. After this success, Hord proceeded to accompany Ian & Sylvia. He was a "musical genius," according to his former girlfriend Daveen Koppel Saimo, and this is borne out not only in his accompanist roles but in his lecture-performance at the 1963 Mariposa Folk Festival and in his later efforts on albums with Barry McGuire as well as Denny Doherty's first solo album, *Watcha Gonna Do*.[240]

As early as February 1963 the group was sometimes billed as "The Halifax Three Plus One." "The impetus for adding an extra instrument was really just to fatten the sound," explains LaCroix. "When Eric was with us, we had the added voice of the banjo, which was great on the bluegrass and cooking country-type tunes."[241] That wasn't all. As one newspaper put it, Hord "served as the placid butt for their humor in their night club act."[242] Hord would surface again to play live with Denny in The New Journeymen a few years later, and eventually with The Mamas & The Papas, particularly in their concerts. Hord was affectionately called "The Doctor" by The Mamas & The Papas because at times he literally "held the bag" of their recreational drugs.

In March, The Halifax Three were in Fort Lauderdale playing the Café House of Pegasus during Spring Break. The House of Pegasus was a hot location, known as "Fort Lauderdale's

Center for Folk Music," that comedian George Carlin called "a pot and coffee place."[243] Carlin, Phil Ochs, and the nascent Spanky & Our Gang all performed there around the same time as The Halifax Three.

The augmentation of the trio's sound in concert continued. During their time in Florida, Jonathan Talbot, who had been a flamenco guitarist known as Juan Moreno (and sometimes John Panken), accompanied the group as an "extra instrumentalist," adding "texture" to their sound. Even though Talbot's invitation to play with the group came from Richard Byrne, who gave him a cold call just before the month-long engagement began, the accompanist found the de facto bandleader the most challenging to get along with. "He was heavily into being in charge and like a rooster preening on stage," Talbot recalls. "Denny was a much more lyrical personality and into imaginative flights of fancy. I remember Pat as gentle and laid back in comparison to the other two." In a letter from the time, Talbot wrote, "I have succeeded in establishing good relationships with both Pat and Denny, but it is becoming increasingly difficult with Dick. His obsession with getting ahead causes him to continually fight with both me and the others and I must spend time apologizing to people who aren't in the group." Talbot also recalls Denny's "personality was what connected with the audience," despite Byrne's efforts to receive that adulation.[244]

Accompanist
Jonathan Talbot

In Fort Lauderdale, a local couple befriended the trio and offered up their yacht as a floating residence. Fellow Canadian folkie Buffy St. Marie was also performing in the vicinity and joined them for some of their voyaging. LaCroix remembers "the days cruising Florida's Gulf Stream and the nights having a hell of a good time entertaining the college kids."[245] For his part, Talbot observed at the time that, for him, the beach was "too crowded with college inebriates in search of beer."[246]

When not afloat or on stage, The Halifax Three were doing a very different gig by day. "We were the Triple S Triplets giving away Triple S Trading Stamps to 400 old people in shopping centers," laughed Denny. "We'd ask them questions like, 'What day is St. Patrick's Day?'"[247] LaCroix most remembers being driven around in a 1932 Maxwell during these lucrative days of wearing straw hats and seersucker jackets.

While The Halifax Three glided along in Fort Lauderdale, unbeknownst to them, Tim Rose, and his bandmates Jim Hendricks and Cass Elliot, were at the same beaches, figuring out how to reformulate an act they had called The Triumvirate. And several weeks later, John Phillips and The Journeymen were playing in nearby Miami. Thus, like the intersecting circular patterns of a spirograph on a map, the orbits of the future Mamas and Papas were ever-tightening.

Soon the Canadian trio finished in Florida. Denny and Pat were baffled, if not spooked, by what they considered Talbot's vampiric aversion to being outdoors. "He had some thing about never seeing the sun or letting the sun touch his skin," said Denny.[248] But Talbot's correspondence at the time boasted of a suntan and accompanying the trio to some daytime events. In reality, he had a dental abscess in a molar that had to be pulled and did not go well. The painkillers were not strong enough to squelch the pain, with the guitarist writing, "I managed to go on every night but because I couldn't sleep well, I hung out after the show at the Cafe Pegasus."[249] Talbot's talents were evident enough that he stayed on at the Pegasus after The Halifax Three's run. It was their departure that had the real spookiness factor for Talbot who reports that Dick Byrne bought a hearse to make the trek back to New York.[250]

The dark specter of that hearse was more than countered by the brightness of the group's prospects. All this attention from "Mitch" resulted in a vigorous concert schedule on the American and Canadian folk circuit that merged with several television appearances. One memorable opportunity occurred when "The Man Who Wouldn't Sing Along With Mitch" was a pick of the week on New York radio station WNIS. The reception of the record was strong enough to land the group offers for Canadian television shows in Toronto that earlier would not even grant them an audition. One of these was *The Juliette Show*, a prominent variety program north of the border. As fate would have it, the group was subsequently offered a chance to perform their new hit that same night on *The Ed Sullivan Show*, an incomparable break for performers at the time. They begged the Canadian team at *The*

Juliette Show for a rain check but fell short in their valiant efforts to make *Sullivan*.[251]

A different kind of near miss happened around the same time. "Sometime while we were doing these CBC shows, Denny made a fast trip to Halifax to check in with the family," recalls Pat. "While he was there, he got arrested for nonpayment of debt." As it turned out, Denny's old boss at the pawn shop was after some money owed. "A panic phone call from Denny ensued. Somehow, we had to raise $200 in a hurry or we would have blown *Parade*, a national CBC variety show." A desperate call was made to the show's producer, who, all too "familiar with the lack of funds that most artists suffered," covered the debt to make Denny a free man.[252]

Denny recalled another foolhardy experience when "we did a gig for a week in Grossinger's in the Borscht Belt," an area in the Catskill Mountains of New York with nightclubs predominantly patronized by Jewish clientele. Grossingers was a swanky hotel and resort that "had it all," according to their advertising, and indeed it commanded big names for entertainment. Denny remembered nearly liquefying their luxurious quarters there, saying, "We decided it was time for a steam bath one night. We all had laryngitis so we turned the showers on and then went and did the show." Having neglected to turn off the water, when they returned "the hotel room was melting."[253]

MONAURAL/LN 24060

the exciting new folk sound of
The Halifax Three
The San Francisco Bay Blues
and the rest of our best

© EPIC RECORDS/A PRODUCT OF CBS

"A trio of swinging Canadians with a light touch" is how The Halifax Three were described in the spring of 1963, when they were following up their popular parody single with the recording of another album.[254] Cut mostly in April and released in July, *San Francisco Bay Blues* was marked by a more sophisticated approach. In songs such as "Rocks and Gravel" and "He Call Me Boy," the three ventured to the edges of folk music, incorporating soulful touches of blues. On the former track the three sing complicated contrapuntal harmonies, as Denny's bluesy, somewhat syncopated and echoey lead points to the plaintive singing heard in Mamas & Papas songs like "Monday Monday." "One of my favorite tunes was 'Little Sparrow,'" LaCroix says of the album's harmonious third track. "I think it really shows off the sound we had as a group."[255] In a review *The Toronto Daily Star* called the album "an enormous improvement," declaring, "They're now succeeding at things they earlier stubbed their voices on."[256]

New Connections and New Directions

That summer they did gigs at the Shadows in Washington and Virginia Beach, and the Night Owl in the Village, while they continued to live at the Albert Hotel in New York. Among their peers in the Village was a remarkable woman named Cass Elliot who sang with a trio called The Big 3. The Bitter End was her group's main base of operations in the summer of 1963, but just next door was a bar The Halifax Three frequented called the Dugout. It was there that Denny first became friends with Cass. He affectionately recalls them challenging one another to "drink each other under the table," which led to a long evening of imbibing that literally ended with them sitting on the floor under the Dugout's table.[257]

At this point manager Bob Morgan recalls Denny and Pat being somewhat frustrated with Byrne, who was still "definitely leading the charge."[258] In late summer, another fortuitous association came about with the addition of a new fourth member, fellow Canadian Zalman Yanovsky whose political cartoonist father had immigrated from Russia. Paul Winter of The Paul Winter Jazz Sextet recalls Zal Yanovsky playing with The Halifax Three in Virginia Beach when they performed at The Shadows, July 31, 1963.[259] Others have pegged the addition of Zal later in August after the Mariposa Folk Festival. "He played lead blues, kind of a single string picking, when I met him," Denny recalled. "He had been into rhythm and blues, and folk music: an unorthodox style of playing, to say the least. There was not any book anywhere that he followed. Our gig paid him a couple of hundred bucks a week, and we toured a lot, so through that he met other musicians and started hanging around New York."[260]

For Fun . . . .
For Food . . . .
For Inexpensive . . .

OR 4-5060

THE DUGOUT

Zal Yanovsky with
The Halifax Three

Coming Soon! The American

HOOTENANNY FESTIVAL

Friday, September 20

W. K. KELLOGG AUDITORIUM

Starting at 8:30 P.M.

A full 2 hours of fun
Featuring Nationally
Known TV Stars

★ THE HALIFAX THREE
★ ELAN STUART
★ THE TAILSMAN FOUR
★ BILL BIEDLER
★ RON HALLER

plus . . . Sing Along Song
Sheets Supplied

TICKETS $1.50 No Reserved Seats

Available at Grinnell's or Lil's Record Shoppe

Sponsored by
BIRCHWOOD METHODIST MEN'S CLUB

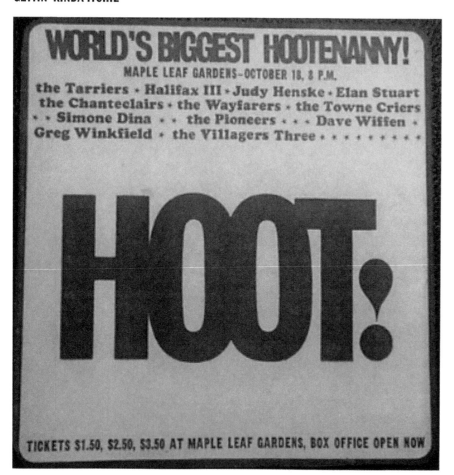

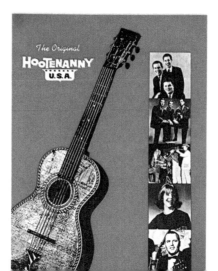

In October, The Halifax Three performed for the televised United Givers Fund Rally in Washington with Judy Collins and Rod McKuen, featuring keynote speaker, Attorney General Robert Kennedy.[261] They bounced back and forth between New York and Toronto, and performed increasingly often with other folk artists. Later that month they were part of the "World's Biggest Hootenanny" in Toronto's Maple Leaf Gardens, where they appeared with The Tarriers, Elan Stuart, The Spokesmen, and Judy Henske, to name some of the more famous players. This was a raucous event that saw The Halifax Three accompany a character named Birney the Beachcomber and his Limbo Show by "starting in with a heavy beat" and getting the crowd to "clap rhythmically" as the Beachcomber, "blond, bearded, and barefoot," sang satirical political songs.[262]

Alongside The Journeymen, Jo Mapes, The Geezinslaw Brothers, and Glenn Yarbrough, The Halifax Three joined the *Hootenanny USA* tour of November 1963. At the time of its announcement, dates to schedule it were "falling in so fast" that, according to its producer, its original duration of four weeks was contemplated to be extended to six or seven.[263] Touring primarily by bus, the Canadians brought some flair to this particular company. Several newspapers featured them when heralding the show, since they were the only non-domestic act. Pat LaCroix recalls his own distinction: "My lot in life was I had to take the washtub bass on the bus everywhere. I got more aggravation from more bus drivers."[264]

With *Hootenanny USA*, the group played coliseums and convention halls to enormous crowds, particularly in university towns. Pinpointing it as the time John Phillips's interest was piqued in him, Denny recalled one night in Memphis when he sang and the girls in the audience "started to scream," after which John began to invite Denny to smoke marijuana surreptitiously on breaks along the trip.[265] It was the burgeoning friendship between Denny and both John and Michelle Phillips that was perhaps the most lasting and important development of this experience.

Remembering his own version of the tour's ill-fated stop in Jackson, Mississippi, Pat LaCroix recalls, "John got a call from some civil rights people who told him that the venue in Jackson was segregated. We took a vote and decided to cancel the concert." Unlike the other acts, however, The Halifax Three and The Geezinslaws did not proceed to do the alternate concert at the predominantly black Tougaloo Institute, instead taking the night off. LaCroix remembers talking with locals in bars, as well as the hostility they encountered in neighboring Louisiana.[266]

According to press accounts in late 1963, the trio's size had increased, writing, "The Halifax Three actually are The Halifax Five. Three who sing in varied style while one masterfully plucks and strums a guitar and a fourth on bass and the fifth on a second guitar. Whether it is folk or rock and roll they are enthusiastically brassy."[267] One of these five continued to be Zal Yanovsky, and it is likely his rock-leaning influence that provoked another less favorable review: "They had to give a display of the worst trend of the Hootenanny craze. 'It's the latest thing.' They said, 'It's a combination of folk music and rock 'n' roll.' They christened the half-breed "Folk 'n' Roll." The nickname may not have stuck, but it shows The Halifax Three were pushing the edges of their repertoire.[268]

Yanovsky constantly had a transistor radio to his ear during the long bus rides of the *Hootenanny USA* tour. About a week after the incident in Jackson, on a drawn-out trek between concerts, he suddenly piped up, "Hey, the president's been shot." Given his zany and sometimes unorthodox sense of humor, LaCroix recalls telling him to "knock it off" and that it wasn't funny, saying, "Of course it wasn't a joke…"[269] Meandering their way back to New York, the *Hootenanny* tour closed to a half-filled house at Carnegie Hall. Many have said that the president's assassination knocked the wind out of the sails of the folk revival, and this tour's experience bore that out. "Everything just stopped. Everything," was Denny's lasting impression. "It shattered everything. The tenor of everything changed."[270]

Back in September 1963, in a black church in New York City, the group had recorded its last song, "All the Good Times." A somewhat fitting valediction, the B-side to their third and final single virtually prophesied the group's future: "All the good times have passed and gone, All the good times are over."[271]

At the end of the year, *Hair-Do* magazine did a hootenanny themed photo spread featuring a young girl and various coiffures, with The Halifax Three in the background. It was reported that the trio performed their "newest song, 'Come Away Melinda' during the photo session."[272] Written by Fred Hellermen of The Weavers, this poignant anti-war tune had been recorded a few months prior by Harry Belafonte, and would be recorded in 1964 by The Big 3. No copy of The Halifax Three's rendition is known to have survived.

After the *Hootenanny USA* tour, The Limeliters' former manager Burt Zell promised the group bigger things in California. He proposed they head in not only a new geographic direction, but also a new artistic direction. After a final engagement at the Royal York Hotel in Toronto's Imperial Room, the group headed west to make good on this offer. The promised new chapter never started. Stalling out at the Colonial Hotel in Los Angeles, The Halifax Three realized the act had run its course, with no recording or performing dates scheduled. LaCroix and Byrne returned to Canada, while Denny and Zal retreated east to regroup in New York. Whether they knew it or not, The Halifax Three's Canadian incursion into the folk scene pollinated the seeds of folk rock, which germinated and reached fruition in the next year.

CARNEGIE HALL / 72nd Season

Saturday Evening, November 30, 1963, at 8:30 o'clock

FELIX GERSTMAN

presents

A Holiday Folk Festival

continued on next page

continued from preceding page

A HOLIDAY FOLK FESTIVAL

stars

The Journeymen

The Halifax Three

The Geezinslaw Brothers

Jo Mapes

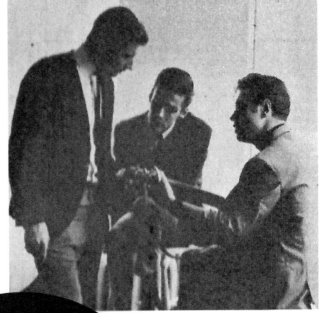

Neither Reverent, Doctrinaire, Nor Spuriously Iconoclastic: The Big 3

It has been said of the folk revival era that if you had a guitar and a couple of fellows at Washington Square in Greenwich Village, you could be a folk group. That remark was confirmed by conventional groups in the mold of The Kingston Trio, The Journeymen, and The Halifax Three. But if a girl was added to the mix, the sound filled out, creating a different effect. The vocal range and harmonies were greater, a broader type of material could be performed, and in performance the combination of the sexes added a verve that was absent in the more homogeneous all male groups.

Mixed gender groups were more unusual, but in popular music, The Fleetwoods or Nino Tempo & April Stevens demonstrated that male-female harmonies had a richness all their own. In the folk field, this was most notably achieved by Peter, Paul & Mary. That group was created by legendary manager Albert Grossman, who auditioned various singers to create a trio with male and female voices in 1961. The group was a leader in popularizing the folk revival of the early 1960s, carrying the torch of social consciousness previously hoisted by The Weavers.[273]

The Big 3, Cass Elliot's first successful folk group, adapted this male-female modification and combined it with a pioneering repertoire to stand out in the panorama of folk groups. Moreover, it was in The Big 3 that Cass developed that powerful, unconventional female component she ultimately brought to The Mamas & The Papas sound.

"She knew how to make an entrance"

Cass Elliot was born Ellen Naomi Cohen in 1941 in Baltimore. From an early age she was precocious, and as her sister puts it, "knew how to make an entrance."[274] By the time she was in high school she had made an impression in community theater, playing the part of the French Maid in *The Boy Friend* when she filled in for the last few weeks of a successful 1959 run at the Hilltop Theatre in Maryland.[275] On the heels of this acclaim, *The Baltimore Sun* mentioned her role in a follow-up production called *Prior To Broadway*. Not much is known about this show except that it boasted a score with lyrics by *Fiddler on the Roof*'s Sheldon Harnick—just a few years before The Journeymen were performing some of his songs—and that according to reviews, Ellen Cohen was "good."[276] While the parts may have been small, the impact was big, and, as she put it years later, "Somehow the thought of going on to be a doctor just didn't make sense."[277]

After the theater forays of 1959, Ellen began calling herself "Cass Elliot." True to form, there is much mystique and murkiness around the name, about which she was asked with some frequency. One account is that Cass named herself after Cass Daley, the comedienne and musical star of the '40s and '50s, or Peggy Cass, another comedic actress known for her role in the 1958 film *Auntie Mame*. Cass dismissed the latter story on more than one occasion: "That must be very annoying for Peggy Cass!"[278] Other theories about the Elliot part of her name were that she took it from the poet T.S. Eliot or that it was some alteration of Ellen. Additionally, the reversal of her true initials E.C. to C.E. has been observed and speculated as part of the name change.

More likely, the name finds its roots in her family's love of music, particularly opera. "We sang opera around the house because my father was an opera fanatic," Cass told *Hit Parader* in 1967. He used to make up words in any language just to fit with the music."[279] In *Les Troyens*, a French opera about the Trojan War by Hector Berlioz, the character of Cassandra was portrayed as an ancient red-headed prophetess of doom, who declared to those around her what peril might befall them, with, tragically, no one taking heed. Ellen's father, Philip Cohen, operated mobile lunch buses, the forerunners of today's food trucks, and while working with his daughter, he would tell her she was just like Cassandra. As she put it, "My father always called me the Mad Cassandra. That was when I was young and had a lot of energy and was always running around." Cass took the name Elliot from one of "her favorite actresses-teachers, named Jessie Elliot," who "was killed in an accident," saying, "She always encouraged me. So, I took her name."[280]

About the time Cass decided to pursue acting and change her name, she landed a writing job, recalling, "I wrote obituaries for *The Jewish Times* of Baltimore by looking through *The New York Times* for Jewish names and rewriting them."[281] She soon left this post and ventured into the cabaret scene of 1961 New York, where she reportedly worked at the Showplace.

TONIGHT
NEW **SUMMER STOCK**
Hilltop Theatre
Owings Mills, Md.
"Liveliest," smash musical
"The Boy Friend"
Fourth Hit Week!
Tues. Aug. 25-30th.

Special Mat. Today—2:30 P.M.
Evening—8:40 P.M.

Tickets: Box Office   TE. 3-0400
S. & N. KATZ   SA. 7-2900

'Boy Friend' Held Over

FOR the first time in Maryland's summer theater history, a production will be held over for a fourth week. "The Boy Friend," the Sandy Wilson musical at the New Hilltop Theater at Owings Mills, will be held over through August 30. There will be a special matinee today at 2.30 P.M.

Mitzi Hoag and Joe Warfield will continue in their original parts. John Hampton has taken over the male lead opposite Judy Tillman. Ellen Cohen is new in the part of the French maid.

The "Tunnel of Love" will open September 1 and run through September 6. In the cast will be Sandra Swann and Richard Neilson.

She remembered the time like this: "I lived in a $36 a month apartment that had a john in the hall and was constantly being burglarized. But I had a great time. I worked for $40 a week under the table as a hat-check girl in a nightclub."[282] While there, she rubbed elbows with other ambitious young theater types like Ruth Buzzi and Joan Rivers, who recalled, "She was the 'I'll Show You' girl."[283] She also appeared on a quiz game show hosted by Johnny Carson called *Who Do You Trust?*, later telling him, "I was so broke. I was walking down 7th Avenue and these pages were handing out cards to appear on the show at the Little Theater. So I played on the show and it was my first television appearance."[284] The premise of the show involved male-female couples chosen for their particular backgrounds. Carson would interview the contestants and the man, once told the category, would choose to either answer or "trust" the woman to answer with correct answers. In Cass's case, as she lamented years later to Carson, "You didn't give me any money."[285]

Cass grew up in a home filled with music. "My parents used to sing, not professionally though. The first piece of music I really remember was 'Nutcracker Suite.' The second piece was 'Peter and the Wolf,' which I still love with a passion. During the war there was a record 'Myrtle the Turtle.' It was about a defense plant turtle who went to work for the war effort. I liked that song."[286]

"She was hoping to be a Broadway kind of person. And really it was to earn money along the way that she got into folk singing," Cass's sister, Leah Kunkel, recalls.[287] After vying with Barbra Streisand for a role in the musical comedy *I Can Get It For You Wholesale*, Cass toured in a company of *The Music Man* in the middle of 1962.[288] The company was an outgrowth of the National Touring Company of *The Music Man* in which the majority of that cast continued on as the Summer New England Touring Company. From the handful of performances documented, Cass earned mentions in local newspapers for her comedic timing, and the show's choreographer Myrna Galle-Van Buren remembers her "outstanding" voice in the performances.[289]

Cass Elliot, Far Right, in The Music Man

THE CAST

Traveling Salesmen .... BRUCE CARRITHERS, ROLAND IRELAND,
JOE KIRKLAND, JERRY QUINN, EDDIE RYAN, THOMAS SELLERS

Charlie Cowell	GRANT WALDEN
Conductor	RON ALEXANDER
Harold Hill	ROBERT COSDEN
Mayor Shinn	ARTHUR TELL
Ewart Dunlop	ROLAND IRELAND
Oliver Hix	JOE KIRKLAND
Jacey Squires	EDDY RYAN
Olin Britt	BRUCE CARRITHERS
Marcellus Washburn	ART WALLACE
Tommy Djilas	BILL STANTON
Marion Paroo	LEIGH GREEN
Mrs. Paroo	ADNIA RICE
Amaryllis	JOY SHEPPARD

(Ewart Dunlop, Oliver Hix, Jacey Squires, Olin Britt } Model - T 4)

Winthrop Paroo	SCOTT BLOOM
Eulalie Mackecknie Shinn	LIDIE MURTI
Zaneeta Shinn	SANDRA RICHARDSON
Alma Hix	JESSIE FOSTER
Maud Dunlop	CHARLOTTE MESMER
Ethel Toffelmier	MARIAN BLOOM
Mrs. Squires	CASS ELLIOT
Conductor and Marshal Locke	RON ALEXANDER

River City Townspeople and Kids
Dianne Ackerman, Myrna Gallé, Andrea Katz, Loi Leabo, Sean Leabo,
Bonnie Leigh, Arlene Pianin, Mark Rose, Shawn Stuart, Dan Taylor
Costumes Supervised by Leonard Dunn.
Scenery Constructed by George Baur Theatrical Equipment Co.

'Music Man' Starts Second Week At Playhouse Monday

"THE Music Man," Meredith Willson's musical hit, enters its second week at Pocono Playhouse in Mountainhome, on Monday night, July 16, with Robert Cosden and Leigh Green in the starring roles.

During the past week overflow audiences found keen enjoyment in the delightfully nostalgic musical that moves with the speed of a rocket and the conviviality of a county fair.

It tells the humorous story of a traveling salesman charlatan who cannot read nor play a note but who sells the townspeople of River City a brass band and gorgeous uniforms. His motives are dishonest but even with the law hot on his heels, he transforms a dull town into a singing and dancing community.

Cosden, in the role of the con "Music Man" gives a triumphant performance and proves that he is nimble in dancing, ingratiating as a mountebank and utterly inventive in his singing.

Leigh Green, his co-star is captivating as the prim librarian who learns that life isn't just to be found in books.

Salutes also must go to the "Model T 4," a barbershop quartet and to young seven-year-old Scott Bloom who stops the proceedings with a solo number called "Gary, Indiana."

Others captivating the audiences with their performances include Adnia Rice, Art Wallace, Lidi Murti, Joy Sheppard, Bill Stanton, Sandra Richardson, Jessie Foster, Cass Elliot and a host

Top: TIm Rose
Center: MIchael & Timothy (with former Smoothie Mike Boran),
Bottom: John Brown

By late 1962 Cass was back home in Washington, D.C., where she sang on occasion at the Unicorn Café.[290] Later accounts describe her as taking classes at American University and doing a jazz radio show on campus. During this time, she met Tim Rose, whom she characterized as a "smooth talking banjo player."[291] Rose told her, "You sing good. Did you ever think about singing for a living?" Her response: "My whole family sang but I had never thought about anybody making a living at it."[292]

This modest answer is not quite true. Cass was not only precocious as a child but driven to perform. "When I was about 4 years old," she shared, "there used to be a kiddie show that came from Baltimore called *Saturday at the Hippodrome* in a movie house. They used to go down into the audience and pick people to do things. I sang 'Don't Fence Me In.'"[293] Cass recreated this experience in a comedy skit on her 1973 television special. Former Smoothie Michael Boran remembered seeing her at a George Washington High School talent show, where she lip-synched the Fred Astaire showtune "How Could You Believe Me When I Said I Love You When You Know I've Been a Liar All My Life."[294] After that, at Forest Park High School, she told *Motion Picture*, "I was with a singing group called The Soultette. It slowly occurred to me that I'd love show business."[295] Then there was *The Boy Friend* and her experience at the Hilltop Theatre. She had also, by this point, gone to New York to try her hand in performance, and after that, finished *The Music Man* tour several weeks earlier. Making a living in entertainment was exactly what Cass wanted to do.

Cass wanted to succeed in musical theater and singing in a folk group was not part of that plan. At that point, "Her heart wasn't into folk music," Michelle Phillips puts it later. "She wanted to be doing *Oklahoma*. She wanted to be doing *Annie Get Your Gun*. She would love to have done *On A Clear Day [You Can See Forever]*. That's what she gravitated to."[296]

For his part, Tim Rose had not always been singing for a living. At the end of September 1962, he had just finished performing with ex-Smoothie Mike Boran on a Mediterranean cruise, as part of a duo called "Michael & Timothy." Before that, he attended college in Kansas and served in the Air Force. Like Cass—and John Phillips for that matter—he had grown up in Northern Virginia outside Washington, D.C. In high school, he had played with future Smoothie Scott McKenzie in a group called The Singing Strings, before playing banjo with The Smoothies at the Cotton Carnival in 1960. A gifted musician, he played both guitar and bluegrass banjo from the age of 17. According to Rose, at the end of his stint with Mike Boran, they were playing in Greenwich Village when Albert Grossman, famed manager of both Bob Dylan and Peter, Paul & Mary, commented, "the banjo player has some talent."[297]

Tim had a gruff voice but he was kind and an intelligent conversationalist. Before his death in 2002, the years had given him perspective on the happenings four decades before. "As long as there's interest in The Mamas & The Papas," he declared, "there will be interest in The Big 3."[298]

The Triumvirate, Tim Rose,
Cass Elliot, John Brown

Wait Until You Hear Her Sing

Tim's memory of meeting Cass in the fall of 1962 was somewhat like hers. "I was invited to a party in Georgetown and this friend of mine said, 'I want you to meet this girl. She's a great singer.' Cass had a job selling cosmetics in a drugstore near American University." His initial callous response was not atypical, admitting, "I saw her sitting on a couch and I said, 'I don't care how well she sings, forget it.'" His attitude quickly changed, however: "We got to chatting anyway that night and I drove her home. We went to my basement, and I played her some songs. She had never heard of Jimmy Reed or Flatt & Scruggs. I asked her if she could sing something and we did little two-part harmonies and I said, 'Look, I have this friend in Chicago. why don't we go and form a group?'"[299]

Cass was game, later saying, "I took some money and bought a Volkswagen, and we went to Chicago and we formed a group."[300] Tim adds, "We got an apartment, met Johnny Brown, put together a trio, and called ourselves The Triumvirate."[301]

John Brown was already an established folk singer in 1962. Earlier that year he had met Tim while playing a coffeehouse gig in Omaha, Nebraska, when Tim was still in Michael & Timothy. Rose "played good guitar and flashy banjo," Brown recalled. "He called me in the fall of '62 from D.C., saying he had broken up with his partner and would like to try a duo act with me."

"It was November," Brown continued, "when a knock came on my front door of my Old Town flat. There was Tim with this huge Jewish girl suggesting we form a trio. The two guys and a girl concept was well established, but Cass was no Mary Travers. I took Tim aside and said, 'You've got to be kidding.' He asked me to just give it a listen and then make up my mind."[302]

As it so happened, Brown had booked a gig to perform at The Fred Niles film studio Christmas party. "I said, 'O.K., we'll rehearse as a trio, play the gig, and depending on the 100-plus audience response, decide if it looks workable,'" Brown recalled. "We rehearsed for two weeks, improvising harmonies and solos, getting seven songs down, and had one weak encore. Tim and I both had green flannel blazers and black slacks, so we bought matching rep ties. Cass had one nice black dress, and with her hair piled up she looked large, but interesting. On stage it looked like an act."[303]

The three gelled quickly. "When my 12-string and Tim's banjo needed tuning," Brown reminisced, "Cass would step up to the mic and spritz off the top of her head. She was very funny, and when we were in tune the music would resume. We did our seven songs and got vigorous applause. We did our one weak encore and got more applause. It was that good from day one." The Triumvirate's first gig was such a success that someone in the audience inquired, "How long have you been together?'" Cass quipped, "Oh about 45 minutes."[304] As she recalled several years later, Cass's memories of their wintry woodshedding were not particularly auspicious: "We spent a horrible, miserable, starving winter. Putting it together. Singing. Learning songs. Twenty-five below zero. It was one of the roughest winters they ever had in Chicago.[305] It was very, very cold and I did not have a coat."[306] Years later, John Brown went to see Cass in concert as a solo artist. After one of her songs he called from the audience "Bass!" (In 1962, "Boss" was superlative slang for something being good. The Triumvirate amended it to "Bass" as part of their personal vernacular). Cass recognized the voice and the decade-old reference, replying "Ah. The voice of Christmas past."[307]

In January 1963 The Triumvirate played at Old Town North and the Fickle Pickle in Chicago. Rose recalled landing gigs by making good on prior contacts from when he was playing with Mike Boran the year before. In the Windy City, folk artist and civil rights activist Josh White introduced them to his manager, who in turn got them an engagement at White's regular cellar club in Cleveland called La Cave.

"Then we left Chicago and went to Cleveland," remembered Cass. "All of us in the Volkswagen: an ancient Volkswagen. I mean really ancient. With guitars and banjos. It was really something." The cramped car was not the only hindrance. "We were very broke, and we had so little money I did all the cooking and I used a lot of tomato sauce. They used to call me 'The Tomato Sauce Queen.' If I had a can of tomato sauce and a cup

This is us! The one on the left is Jimmy and Johnny. Brown is the tall one. This picture was taken at a Hootenanny at the Fickle Pickle about 10 Days ago.

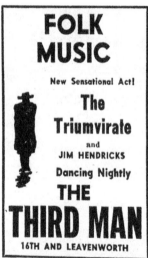

of rice I could feed about twenty people. A little bit of cheese," she laughed, "that was a treat. Those were hard times. It was always a hassle to get food and transportation to our next stop."[308]

According to Brown, the owner at La Cave got The Triumvirate a two-song appearance on a 90-minute daytime TV show out of Cleveland called *The One O'Clock Club*, which aired during the same time slot as *The Mike Douglas Show*. "We did our two songs, and after the show the producer offered us a six-month contract to appear on the show five days a week at union scale, $250 each, which was $100 a week more than I was earning in Chicago for five nights at Mother Blues," Brown recalled. "I was ready to move my family to Cleveland. What an opportunity: a demand for new material, and wardrobe, and decent money, and night and weekend gigs, and film of ourselves on TV, and then head to New York."[309]

Brown's hopes were quickly dashed, however, as Tim Rose did not want to be "stuck in Cleveland." Brown also detected that Cass had a "crush on Tim,"[310] while Rose says it was Brown who was trying to cozy up to Cass.[311] "We didn't take the offer," Brown rued. "I call it 'My brush with fame.'"[312]

The Triumvirate was just about finished when Brown got the ultimate brush off. In February 1963 the group went to Omaha for a gig where a singer named James Hendricks opened for them at a coffeehouse fittingly named the Third Man.[313] Hendricks was born and bred in Nebraska and had recently graduated from Hastings College where he was part of a folk group called The Faymon Trio.[314] When The Triumvirate arrived, he was teaching music in school, directing choir in church, and singing in coffeehouses on the weekends. "Customers sat on cushions or low-slung chairs, listened to folk music and sipped esoteric concoctions such as spiced espresso, cappuccino, and café macha," a patron later said of The Third Man, recalling how Cass was "very quick with the funny ad-libs and was always bantering back and forth with the crowd."[315]

Jim Hendricks recalls, "Every night they were there, whenever I would sing, Cass would sit right in the front row and just give me the eyeballs like you wouldn't believe. And I was saying, 'What is the deal with this girl?' I immediately locked in with her."[316]

The deal was that Cass and Tim asked Jim if he would consider replacing Brown in The Triumvirate. Rose remembers, "Cass said, 'That's him.' And I said, 'Who? What do you mean?' And Cass said, 'That's the guy we should get. Look at the way the girls look at him.'" Rose adds, "He was this real Presbyterian kind of guy. I said 'Jim, how would you like to give all this up, take your car, and come with this nice Jewish girl and me and form a folk group?'"[317] Cass likewise recalled, "The minute we heard him we said, 'Drop that teaching contract. Come with us. We'll make you a star.' Jimmy was so great. He has this high, clear, well-trained tenor, and I must admit I was totally infatuated with him. I had never seen such a good-looking clean-cut kid."[318]

Jim Hendricks in
The Faymon Trio

The three snuck out at night and rehearsed in Jim's red convertible Tempest. "We used to go out and get in the car and harmonize," Hendricks recounts. "It was just a magical thing and we all said, 'This is it.' I could feel it. Both of them were very warm but Cass really captured everything. She did it for me. She was so dynamic. I could hear her voice and I thought, 'This girl can flat do it.' She was so warm and caring."[319] Hendricks was persuaded. When he quit his job, his boss later said: "He told me he wanted to try this just to see what might happen. He said he might regret not giving it at least a try. Who knows, something really may come of it after all?"[320]

When they lowered the boom with Brown, Rose recalls the fury. According to Tim, John put his fist through Tim's Martin guitar and destroyed it. The manager of another coffeehouse in Omaha, The Crooked Ear, lent Rose the money for another guitar. Tim claimed he next took the new threesome to Florida, while Jim remembers Tim and Cass getting a rental and driving back to Cass's mother's house in Virginia, where he later met them. Jim had just bought the new Pontiac Tempest and drove to Virginia once he closed out at home. It was then, Jim claims, that they made their Florida plans, with him financing the trip.

Hendricks and his new partners ditched the name The Triumvirate, which Tim thought "sounded too academic."[321] In Florida they rehearsed sitting on the sandy beaches of Fort Lauderdale: three improbable individuals honing their vocal harmonies during college Spring Break.

They returned to Washington and soon arranged an audition in front of Roy Silver, who managed current club headliner Bill Cosby, and Bob Cavallo, who owned The Shadows. As Rose put it, "The Shadows was 'the room' in Washington," as far as folk clubs went.[322] The group showed up an hour late for their audition and Silver recalls the light coming on the stage and seeing Tim, Jim, and Cass "in sneakers and cut off shorts."[323] He took one look at her and was amazed at her size. Even Cavallo asked Tim, "Why are you on stage with the fat girl?" to which Rose replied, "Forget what she looks like. Wait 'til you hear her sing." He did and told Rose to give him a call the next day.[324]

It was Roy Silver, however, who really saw the group's promise, claiming, "The first second I heard them sing I knew they were great."[325] Rose echoed that Silver called the next day and proclaimed, "The Big 3!" Rose queried, "What's that?" and Silver replied, "That's who you are, and how soon can you be in New York?"[326]

The Big 3 journeyed to New York immediately. "It was fresh and wonderful, we were all young kids feeling the wind in our hair. We were making music and listening and doing a *lot of walking*. We were free!" Cass reminisced, continuing, "There was an innocence you just don't find that way again."[327] Jim remembers their arrival: "It was like a fantasy because when we hit New York we had already been talked up. Roy had done such an incredible job of publicity."[328] In late March the *Omaha World-Herald* reported they were "negotiating a recording contract."[329] The advance work was the result of Silver's far-reaching connections, established in part by his representation of Bob Dylan, Bill Cosby, and Joan Rivers. The Big 3 began playing in Greenwich Village on May 9, 1963, at the Gaslight Cafe. And the group delivered.[330] As one critic put it, "The trio displayed savoir faire and control while producing some fine folk art."[331]

Bound to be Big

By May 25, The Big 3's picture was in *Billboard*, where they were described as having "a new sound that's hard to describe but bound to be big."[332] The article previewed their forthcoming recordings on the brand new label FM Records. FM Records was the brainchild partnership of jazz producer Monte Kay and Fred Weintraub, owner of the Bitter End, a "folk talent emporium and coffeehouse" in Greenwich Village.[333] Some speculated "FM" was for the newly emerging FM radio, or perhaps for the "F" in Fred and the "M" in Monte.

For more than 60 years the Bitter End has been the launchpad for performers ranging from Lenny Bruce to Lady Gaga. Boasting itself as New York's "Oldest Rock and Roll Club" and "America's Night Club," its famed brick wall has been the backdrop for album covers and filmed performances. One of its managers described its ambience: "As you walked in the club, the stage was on the right hand side, about ten inches off the ground...There were church pews to the left where the audience sat. The pews were the kind with wooden backs

and the backs had ledges on them where you could rest your hymnbooks. The ledges became the tables for the sodas and ice-cream drinks that were all that could be served since there was no liquor license. It would also hold the ashtrays and the clay flowerpots that were used as ice buckets. It all had a beat-generation feel to it, and the people loved it."[334] The Bitter End got its name for being the last thing on Bleecker Street "before you got to desolation" in an area then described as "pretty close to a slum."[335]

In 1963 the club was just two years old and a hotbed of folk talent. Hootenanny nights were a weekly happening with open mic opportunities for the Village folkies. It was in this epicenter that Silver achieved a major engagement for The Big 3, allowing them to entrench themselves in the folk scene for much of that summer. Weintraub had selected them as one of his "picks" for up-and-coming folk talent, and thus he placed them in front of the club's iconic brick wall. The relationship between the Bitter End and FM Records only fueled The Big 3's rise. The label was founded for the purpose of issuing a "Bitter End Series of albums" orienting on folk and jazz artists and performances at the club.[336]

The Big Three making the big sound.

Journalist Ellis Nassour described The Big 3's Bitter End debut in June:

I can remember their opening night well. As Cass was getting into her dress, the zipper broke. It seemed as if everything was going wrong on Cass' big night. 'I need a drink,' she exclaimed. There she was…standing in the middle of the room in her slip….'Where's that drink?' Someone said 'About the best you'll do here is a glass of apple cider!' (The Bitter End does not serve liquor). Cass looked up and said loudly 'Apple cider!' Then, quickly changing the tone of her voice, she asked, 'Hey, does anybody know anything about zippers?' And all at once all hands went to work getting Cass into her opening night gown–after a few minutes she sighed "I should have sewn a couple of sheets together!' The dressing room must have been no larger than 2 x 4 but there were at least ten people in there. Somehow everything worked itself out, though and The Big Three went on. They captivated the audience crowded into that small cafe and completely satisfied the music critics.[337]

With his clout, Silver set about securing more visibility for The Big 3. Hendricks says, "We were already on the way. Every night was a super night. I can't remember anything but total highs."[338] On July 2 they appeared on *Arthur Godfrey's Talent Scouts*, a live program that had been broadcast since the 1940s, first as a radio and then TV show, and was well known for introducing new acts to the general public. It was a sort of *American Idol* of its time, with Patsy Cline, Tony Bennett, Pat Boone, Rosemary Clooney, and Steve Lawrence all being former contestants. (Famously, Buddy Holly and Elvis Presley were turned down for the show). The Big 3 were on the debut of a Summer Series version of the show with Merv Griffin hosting and Liza Minnelli and others appearing on the same night.[339] Rose declares, "We looked good on television, the two of us against Cass, it was an interesting visual thing."[340] A reviewer amplified this visual, writing, "The two dapper fellows on either side of Miss Elliot provided more than just an ethnic appearance: their accompaniments swung into a folk rhythm without theatrics."[341] Silver recognized this too and secured them a series of upcoming appearances on *The Tonight Show* with his friend, and the show's new host, Johnny Carson. Ultimately, The Big 3 would appear on it nine times. Yet as good as they looked on TV, one reviewer pointed out their "television appearances haven't done them justice" compared to seeing them live.[342]

Silver quickly bolstered the already strong threesome with additional features. Robert Bowers became their musical director, arranger, and bass player. A trained jazz musician, Bowers had just successfully finished writing and producing an off-Broadway revue called *Digging for Apples*, in addition to becoming the house bassist at the Bitter End. He remembers laying eyes on The Big 3 for the first time: "I see this monstrously big woman and these two

guys. One of them looks like a punk and the other is the sweetest, best looking, handsome kid you've seen in your life." Appearance aside, their sound was even more remarkable. Upon hearing them he says, "I was absolutely knocked out," recalling The Big 3 as talented but unschooled musicians.[343] Bowers raised the bar, with Hendricks remembering how they "rehearsed and rehearsed for hours" at the Bitter End with their new director.[344] Of their fairly regular *Tonight Show* appearances, Bowers proudly recalls, "During Johnny Carson's first year, I wrote an arrangement for the entire orchestra and the group doing "The Far Side of the Hill" with flutes and woodwinds.[345]

As with the lore surrounding her real name, even Cass's pseudonym took on variations at the time. Bowers and his writing associate Jim Butler, who also worked with Cass, both claimed different diminutives. Butler was the House Doorman at The Bitter End in 1963 and went on to have a 40 year career as a Show Handler for ABC-TV. He recalls that in 1963 and 1964 "Cassie" was how he knew her.[346] This is borne out by some autographs from the period. Bowers, meanwhile, boldly claims he was the first to call her "Mama," maintaining he found Cass to be like 1920s singer Sophie Tucker, known as a "The Last of the Red Hot Mamas," and so when Cass came to rehearse he started greeting her with,

"Hey, Mama."[347] Interestingly, Cass incorporated Sophie Tucker's signature song "Some of These Days" in her concerts during the last two years of her life.

Bowers also distinctly recollects their constant struggle performing with broken strings. Hendricks confirms the memory: "Tim was notorious for breaking strings. He dug in so hard. Cass would always fill in."[348] One reviewer noted that Cass "ad libbed gracefully when one of the guitar strings broke. She kept the near-capacity audience chuckling and satisfied as she introduced the next tune."[349] Bowers reflects, "That's why Cass became such a brilliant spokesperson. She had to talk to keep the audience alive at the Bitter End while they were getting the guitar strings fixed or replaced. She was brilliant at it—she was so very funny."[350] In one such instance, introducing their song "Ringo," Cass representatively digressed with a hilarious and fictitious yarn:

> This song is dedicated to all the movies that Mickey Rooney ever made. I'm sure you're familiar with the one where Guy Kibbee plays a Kentucky Colonel who raises race horses for a living. Mickey Rooney is his grandson and the mortgage has been called in on the ranch and they had to sell all the horses except this one old kind of swayback, broken down horse. And Mickey Rooney cuts school one day and enters this horse in a race at a county fair. The horse wins and Mickey Rooney gets a lot of money and he pays off the mortgage and everybody's happy and for being such a good boy Mickey Rooney gets Judy Garland and a 1934 Packer convertible with leather seats and Patsy Kelly waves goodbye.[351]

Despite his habit of snapping strings, Bowers found Tim to be a superb banjo player, saying, "Tim played very aggressively. And very clean and clear. He was a very good live-performance musician."[352] Bitter End manager Paul Colby gave Rose even more credit: "Tim Rose was the real creative force behind The Big Three."[353] Tim was clever with some of The Big 3's repertoire. As John Phillips was doing, he rearranged, adapted or added a verse to old folk songs like "Silkie," "Glory, Glory" and "Wild Women," sometimes with Cass and Jim's help, thereby achieving a new copyright that might lead to additional royalties.

Their residency at the Bitter End was accompanied by appearances on television and gigs in places such as Palisades Park in New Jersey and the Shadows in Washington, D.C. The trio had come far, fast. In early September, a full-page ad in *Cash Box* bragged of their upcoming album, and appearances on *The Tonight Show, Hootenanny,* and *The Danny Kaye Show.*[354] The trio had recorded their first album that summer. Issued in October, their first single, "Winkin' Blinkin' & Nod," with B-side "The Banjo Song," received a promising 4 Stars from *Billboard.*[355] At the time, the head of Vee-Jay Records, which distributed the single, described them as a "Weavers-type group with a fine down to earth sound."[356]

THE BIG 3

A relatively new group, the Big 3 has brought a new sound to the folk scene. First, there's Cass Elliott, who's been singing professionally since 1959. She was a drama major at American University, sings lead on ballads. Second is Tim, left, who plays guitar and banjo. He was a psychology major in Washburn University. Last, but not least, is Jim, a former music teacher who sings melody and harmony, plays the guitar. Write FM Records, 200 W. 57, N.Y., N.Y.

Both Silver and Bowers insist that the group recorded their debut album—simply titled *The Big 3*—in one session. Sound engineering duties were handled by William Schwartau, who had worked with Ray Charles, Peter Paul & Mary, and Duke Ellington. Eminent soundman Phil Ramone called Schwartau an "unsung hero" in the ranks of sound recording, likening his abilities to "the same way a painter uses light and color" and claiming that Schwartau's "ability to hear 'through the microphone' was impeccable; and when Bill set up a session, what you heard in the studio matched what you heard in the control room."[357]

Bob Bowers witnessed this genius when he played bass for the album. Schwartau had concerns since he had never recorded a bass before. "He had me stand on a low riser built to act as a resonator for the bass which for this bass was redundant. Bill tried several different microphones but was dissatisfied with them all. Finally, he came up with a perfect solution. He wrapped an omnidirectional mic in a thin sheet of foam rubber and wedged it in the opening of the bridge of the bass. It didn't dull the resonance of the bass but picked up the vibrating strings and the attack, plus enough for the sound emanating from inside the body of the bass through the *f* holes."[358] The group's recording of "Rider" reveals this brilliance as one can hear the bass in a physical, palpable way.

Merging exceptional vocal abilities with their more progressive arrangements, The Big 3's self-titled debut demonstrated what they did at The Bitter End: they stood out distinctly in the folk scene. Spirituals, bluegrass, ballads, even bluesy jazz numbers and folk standards

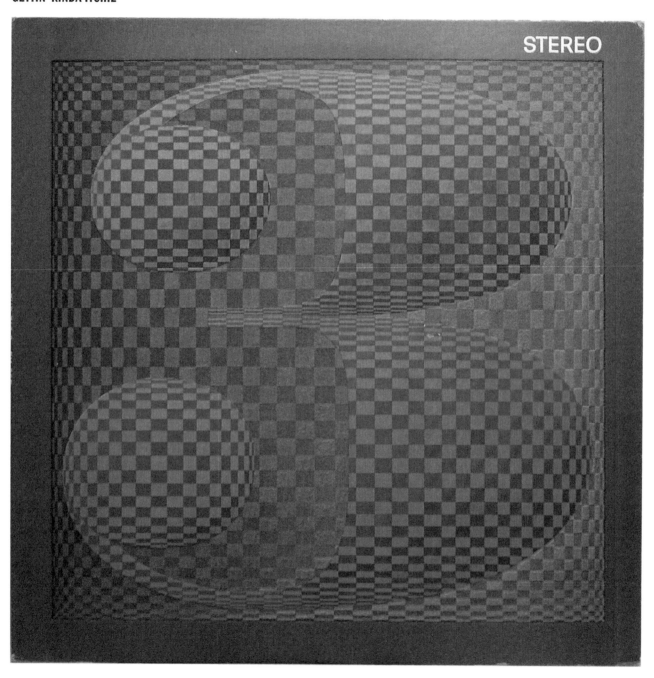

STEREO

comprised their wide-ranging repertoire. "Folk music had to change or risk losing its young audience," declared Paul Colby of the Bitter End about the musical scene in 1963. "The logical thing was to take a folk song and rock it." That, he insisted, is what The Big 3 "did exceptionally well."[359] A radio host characterized "The Banjo Song" as "their own very dynamic rendition of a Stephen Foster classic," referring to Tim's brilliant reworking of "Oh Susanna."[360] "Dynamic" was probably a civilized way for the host to refer to the rock and roll quality of the song. With its driving rhythm, this was really an early folk rock tune, and it spawned quite a legacy. A year later it was recorded with Cass and some others in Greenwich Village, again with electric guitar and drums. Then, it has long been argued, it surfaced again when The Shocking Blue used it as the foundation for their 1969 hit "Venus," which went to number one on the *Billboard* Hot 100 and bears an uncanny resemblance to the song. In fact, Robbie van Leeuwen, the leader of The Shocking Blue, has acknowledged "The Banjo Song's" influence. In turn, Bananarama revived "Venus" with their own hit cover in 1986, which Korean star PSY then sampled in his 2001 song "Bird."

"Rider" was a banner tune that Hendricks remembers as "an 'up' kind of thing. We opened or closed with it and it was very powerful. Everybody would flip out."[361] He introduced a performance of "Winken Blinken Nod" as "our own arrangement of a children's classic poem."[362] Their array of material actually further propelled their strength, as that range was complemented with their vocal talent. Bowers observes, "They just had the proper timbres that blended—and the ability to *listen* to each other."[363] "Come Along" and "Ho Honey Oh" hearkened to Rose's love for bluegrass and the Virginia roadhouses where he cut his banjo-teeth.

Bowers recalls "Cass wore a schmatta" at the 10 a.m. recording session for the album, "which was early for The Big 3, what with them being night owls."[364] Music Makers Studio in Midtown Manhattan was a large facility compared to the Bitter End. Recording was new for the trio, but not for two members of the session band: famed drummer Panama Francis—who had played on hits for Bobby Darin, The Four Seasons, The Platters, and Neil Sedaka—and electric guitarist Carl Lynch, who was well known in the New York recording scene, playing with Pearl Bailey, George Benson, Phil Spector, and the Isley Brothers. When these musicians worked with new or lesser known acts like The Big 3 it was "off the books" as a sort of moonlighting gig.

Cass, Jim, Tim, and Bob were accustomed to close quarters on the stage at the Bitter End, "which at best could accommodate ten people, if they squeezed together," recollects Bowers. At Music Makers, the musicians had to be spaced to avoid "leakage" from each other into their respective mics. Bowers recalls everyone was distanced, with his "gigantic 7/8 bass" borrowed from the symphony, fifteen feet away from the group, saying, "The spatial relationship was weird."[365]

Bowers says The Big 3 were nervous as they began, and so was he. "Rider" was the first song the group recorded. "The tune begins with just bass and drums, then the voices come in and ultimately the guitars join the melee, which is what it quickly turned into." The trio was not familiar with a drum keeping time and "the guys had a tendency to rush," he recalls, "especially when approaching the last chorus of the song." Panama Francis kept saying, "Relax." Soon a voice came on the intercom and called for break, inviting Bowers and Cass into the control booth. Upon entering the booth, as Bowers remembers it, "Roy brought out a big piece of hash. Cass fashioned a pipe and stem from the foil that at that time lined the inside of my Benson & Hedges cigarette pack. We all had a few tokes. We all relaxed."[366]

Bowers then recounts a transformation: "'Take ten,' Schwartau announced. He was not referring to a break, we'd just had one. On the next take we nailed it. Jim and Tim must have gotten a contact high, and were now as relaxed as the rest of us." Bowers further relates, "Tim asked Schwartau, 'Isn't that a lot of takes?' Bill said, 'Not at all. I also record Peter, Paul & Mary. They never do less than sixty takes. Even then, we have to do a lot of intercutting

Roy Silver

from previous takes to get one right.'" Bowers and Silver recall the entire album being recorded in about an hour and a half, with most tracks done in no more than three takes.

While Roy Silver was the group's producer, that credit, at least on the album, was also attributed to Alan Douglas and Pete Kameron. Douglas was a former jazz producer who went on to produce Jimi Hendrix. Kameron was one of the co-founders of FM Records who had managed The Weavers, later producing films and establishing the *L.A. Weekly* newspaper. Kameron was responsible for the album being distributed by Vee-Jay, a deal for which he made money and the group did not. "It was some kind of chicanery involving Pete Kameron who set up the distribution deal," Bowers says. The reality was that there was no distribution. "There was a big falling out between Kameron, Roy, Fred Weintraub, and Monte Kay [the progenitors of FM Records] in Monte Kay's office," he remembers. "Roy and Fred eventually split up over it. Alan Douglas threatened to kill Pete."[367] The ultimate result was no financial realization for the musicians. As Tim Rose put it, "We were all naïve. Everybody made money but us."[368]

The look of the album was bold. Its cover boasted a huge fuschia-colored "3" styled in "optical art," an abstract art form that can give the impression of movement when viewed. Tim Rose claimed it was one of the first examples of Op Art, while Bob Bowers called it the first psychedelic album cover. The design was created by renowned graphic artist Benjamin Frazier Cunningham, who had been a supervisor of the famous WPA murals at San Francisco's Coit Tower during the 1930s, and later taught at Cooper Union in New York.

With the album completed, their first single released, and three appearances booked on *The Tonight Show* within a month, the group hit the road. They started making inroads on campuses with rapid succession appearances at Fordham, Cornell, Northwestern, and Boston University. At Northwestern, The Big 3 played with Paul Winter's Jazz Sextet. Winter, now a jazz legend, had played with the group a couple of months previously at the Shadows in Virginia Beach, as well as with The Halifax Three a few weeks earlier. When Winter walked alone across the Northwestern gym floor before the concert that night, he heard a voice yell from high in distant bleachers, "HEY PAUL!" Instantly he recognized the voice of Cass, whom he hadn't seen in months. "She was full of fun," he reminisces. "It was the kind of yell that only someone who can razz you yells."[369]

That Fall The Big 3 embarked on *A Folk Festival* tour with the host of ABC's *Hootenanny*, Jack Linkletter, along with Les Baxter's Balladeers, Raun McKinnon, and Joe & Eddie. Sometimes local folk acts would join the caravan too. The *Folk Festival*'s territory was primarily the Midwest, and the tour covered at least "sixteen one-night stands." Described as "the headliners" and a "swinging, singing group," The Big 3 was scaling heights quickly.[370] They were frequently singled out in reviews and with almost as much frequency Cass's size was specifically mentioned: "You'll know the reason for the name [The Big 3] when you see their

soprano, a female Jackie Gleason with a very funny between numbers patter, and incidentally, a very good voice."[371] Others remarked, "the rather rotund Miss Elliott,"[372] "a girl with a huge voice and physique to match,"[373] "featuring large Cass Elliot,"[374] and "a chubby girl singer flanked by two thin males."[375] This kind of commentary on Cass's appearance was almost routine, but it was almost always accompanied by marvel at her vocal gifts.

One newspaper during the *Folk Festival* tour reported they had recently received the "Hall Neustadter Award for the Best New Act of 1963."[376] Given that there is no other record, historical or contemporaneous, of such an accolade, one wonders if this was some clever management and puffery on Silver's part.

Another kind of puffing was going on too. Raun McKinnon recalls some of the revelry of the *Folk Festival* tour after hours: "Cass became very good friends on that tour with David Crosby, Mike Clough, and Bob Ingram, who were in Les Baxter's Balladeers. They used to hang out with her in her hotel room and smoke dope."[377] Bob Ingram remembered the two groups not only shared pot, but Ingram shared a bed with Cass too, simply as a fellow broke musician.[378] David Crosby has recalled that the tour was in Baltimore at the time of President Kennedy's assassination. While certainly absorbing some of the aftershocks felt in the folk revival and the culture at large, The Big 3's rise was still very much underway with a major television appearance on *The Danny Kaye Show* just a week after the president's death.

How the group ended up on Kaye's show, which was then in its first season, was again due to Roy Silver's genius. Danny Kaye had been persuaded to visit Greenwich Village to hear the best talent available at the time. Silver became involved in the happening and planned to showcase four acts at the Bitter End: The Big 3, actor-comedian Danny Meehan who had played with Barbra Streisand in *Funny Girl*, comedic duo Allen & Grier, and Bill Cosby. "It was the most exciting night that any of us had ever participated in," claimed Silver. "They came to the Bitter End in limousines and all the guys were in suits…and we were from the Village." As the acts began to go on, Silver remembers after The Big 3's performance: "Danny Kaye leaped out of his chair and said, 'They're great. That's it. They're going on.'" Then the second act, Danny Meehan, went on and Kaye did the same thing. Allen & Grier followed with a similar response from Kaye. But with that, Silver recalled Kaye declared, "That's enough, I don't want to see anymore," and summarily left the club. So, declining to see Bill Cosby, Danny Kaye was on his way. A very big argument with the comedian ensued and was seared in Silver's memory.[379]

Yet for all their fast-moving success, a dyad was beginning to develop within the triad. Hendricks attributes some early fragmentation to one particular event in November of 1963: he was drafted. "I took my draft notice to Roy and Cass. We were always real close, but Cass and I had gotten very close. We ran around together a lot—she used to go out and buy me clothes. I still wear a black cashmere topcoat that she bought for me in the fall of 1963."[380]

Cass Elliot 2nd from left in The Big 3; David Crosby 5th from right in Les Baxter's Balladeers

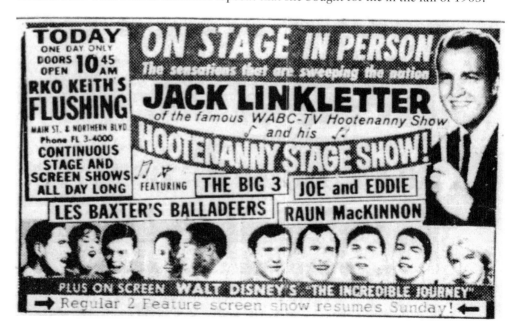

The draft notice was a huge potential check on The Big 3's new success. The solution seemed simple for Cass, according to Jim. "We were wondering what in the world we were going to do. As we got to looking into the situation we found out because I had been a schoolteacher I had been exempt, and so when I left teaching then I became eligible. The only other thing that would exempt me besides teaching was to be married. So, Cass said, 'Hey let's go get married.' We went down to Alexandria and a judge that she knew married us."[381]

Mr. and Mrs. Hendricks's December 1963 marriage was secret, platonic, and pragmatic. Consequently, as Jim declares, "We didn't tell anybody."[382] The marriage certificate shows a Fairfax, Virginia, location near Cass' mother Bess in Alexandria, and there is some indication they actually tied the knot at Roy's place, in the area where the group had met Silver and where they frequently played the Shadows and the Cellar Door. The link to Roy's residence may be because Jim gave Roy's 57th Avenue office address in New York, as his own on the Marriage Certificate. Wherever they tied the knot, Roy was there.

"Tim didn't know," Hendricks explains, "and that's what started the whole thing," referring to early division within the group. At that point Cass and I became really, really close, and Tim was always kind of on the outside. Not the enemy, but kind of that way. It was a funny situation."[383]

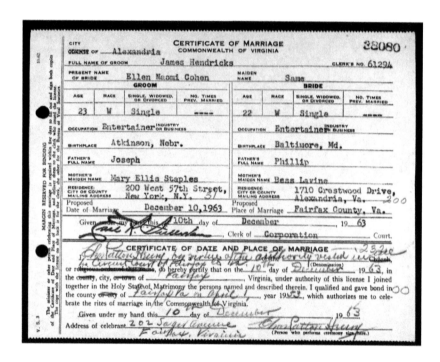

Still, for the most part, the group was going great guns. Staying close to home, they also remained busy at the end of 1963, playing a folk festival in Richmond, homecoming at American University, and another gig nearby at the Shadows. Marilyn Moren was also on the bill with The Big 3 in Richmond. The group's success and prospects was apparent to her as she met Cass for the festival:

> I went through the door and stood alone for an uncomfortable length of time. Suddenly a very short female in a spacious cotton dress ran over to me with a huggable talk and took me behind the stage to introduce me to "the boys." They were working on some guitar runs and stopped just long enough to be introduced. Then the super friendly lady said, "and I am Cass." She asked me to work out some harmonies with them but of course I had turned into stone from all of my excitement. Cass bubbled. I have no idea where she got it all from. She begged me to join up with them and head to California and Florida on the way. I told her I could not financially make a trip like that. I was in school at Richmond Professional Institute, [now Virginia Commonwealth University]. Cass didn't give up on having me go with them to sing and make records and we all would make money. My heart ached for doing that but I just couldn't. I had never played for a crowd that large. I couldn't see anyone past the first three rows and the applause was frightening to me. The audience was well pleased with my performance and generous with applause. I couldn't stop thinking of Cass. She was amazing.[384]

In mid-December The Big 3 appeared, in color, on *The Tonight Show,* where they sang the French Christmas carol, "O Holy Night" arranged by Tim. Bowers recalls rehearsing for the song and calling Cass down in her initial treatment, "It's a Christmas carol, Cass. Stop singing it like you're in a whorehouse"[385]

Commercials, Canadians, and a Coda

The new year brought forth another endeavor: commercial jingles. Once again Silver's connections helped secure these deals for the group, who recorded commercials for McLean's Toothpaste, Thom McAn shoes, and Ballantine Beer, among others. Tim Rose also claimed that The Big 3 did ads for Brylcreem and either Schaefer or Schlitz beer, although this has never been confirmed. In the 1970s and 1980s, Rose reportedly recorded jingles for Wrangler and Big Red chewing gum, while Cass recorded radio and television commercials for Hardee's restaurants in 1973 and 1974. Ironically, Cass once joked, "You can be a good singer from here, to Hell and back and if you haven't got material you will be singing commercial jingles for the rest of your life."[386] She may have been right, but as advertisements go, the Ballantine and Hardee's jingles were well-written, well-received, and well-remembered.

In fact, The Big 3's Ballantine commercials got more airplay than anything else The Big 3 ever did. "You get a smile every time" was played regularly in New York. In an interoffice circular, Ballantine referred to the commercial as a "smashing success" and the group apparently thought the same, using the ditty as a warm-up for their *Tonight Show* appearances and even incorporating it into their concerts.[387] The three flew to New York for one day in January 1964 and recorded a handful of minute-long spots after running through more than sixty versions of the new year's rendering. They amplified the sound by adding two guitars, a bass fiddle, a bass saxophone, and a recorder or flute. Phil Ramone engineered the session and Tony Mottola, one of the guitar players, arranged the commercial's music.[388] Mottola was playing in *The Tonight Show* orchestra and worked with Ray Charles, Johnny Mathis, Frank Sinatra, and Perry Como as a jazz guitarist. He had also played on recordings with John Phillips and The Smoothies a few years prior.

At the same time The Big 3 were doing ads for Ballantine, John Phillips and The Journeymen were recording Schlitz Beer ads, while The Halifax Three had done a grocery store jingle a year earlier. Brewing companies were clearly tapping into the folk craze for the beer drinking public, especially with the college crowd and sports events audiences. In fact, Ballantine was the "Official Beer of the New York Yankees."

The strategy was the same for Thom McAn Shoes, whose advertisers were unabashedly playing the folk hand with The Big 3 commercials. The lyrics sounded like the start of a hootenanny night at any local coffeehouse:

If you wanna walk for freedom
Tell you what you gotta do
You gotta put your foot
In a particular shoe

Hoot-nanny-nanny-nanny-hoot-nanny-hoo
Hoot-nanny-nanny-nanny-hoot-nanny-shoe

Show your spirit
Show your spunk
This is what you gotta do
You gotta put your foot
In a particular shoe
Be a man

Or be a woman
Tell you what you gotta do
You gotta put your foot
In a particular shoe

Hoot-nanny-nanny-nanny-hoot-nanny-shoe
Only from the man
Thom McAn[642]

BALLANTINE RECORDS A COMMERCIAL

"The Big Three" does their 60-second version of the new 1964 Ballantine radio jingle

The Big Three finished their last encore at The Shadows club in Washington, D.C. at 12:20 Thursday morning, January 2nd. By 9:00 a.m. that same morning they were on a plane for New York, where they went directly to a recording studio and worked until 1:30. They went from there back to the airport, flew to Washington, and sang their first number at The Shadows at 8:30 that same night.

Why did The Big Three go to New York? To make a 60-second radio commercial for Ballantine Beer. Although they actually worked for only two hours and a half, six long months went into the preparation for this single recording session.

A radio commercial begins with the words. To give Ballantine Beer's 1964 commercials more sales impact, to make them more competitive, it was decided last fall to revise the lyrics of the 1963 commercials. They were made simpler, brighter, happier, more direct. This began six months before The Big Three made their version, and ended after 64 different versions of lyrics and music had been tried. When the final version was accepted and approved by Ballantine, the first three commercials were made (these are now on the air). The Big Three was used for the fourth because their 1963 commercial has been such a smashing success. A great many more will be made, with different recording artists, for the 1964 radio pool.

It took 17 people to make The Big Three commercial (some have taken as many as 50). To The Big Three's single banjo were added two guitars, a bass fiddle, a bass saxophone, and a recorder (flute). One of the guitarists was Tony Mottola, who plays for Mitch Miller and Perry Como, and who arranged the music for the commercial. About 15 actual tapes were made before one was acceptable to the musical and creative directors of Ballantine's advertising agency, William Esty Company.

Not only must a radio commercial sound right, it must run exactly 45 seconds (to which are added 15 seconds of announcer talk). This is not as easy as it may sound, and requires precise timing on the part of the artists

Cass Elliot, female member of "The Big Three," once toured in "The Music Man."

recording the jingle. It's not easy because after you've been listening to the same commercial for two and a half hours, it's hard to tell when you've got it right — exactly as you want it. It takes a good ear.

So successful is this particular "Smile" commercial that The Big Three now include it in their act wherever they appear (they call it their biggest hit record). And if you visit TV's "Johnny Carson Show" as a member of the audience, you'll hear it played during the "warm up" period before the show goes on the air. It's one of the country's real hits!

You get a smile every time,

(Smile every time),

With the heads-up taste of a Ballantine.

You get a smile every time,

(Smile every time),

With the heads-up taste, of a Ballantine.

You'll liven up your livin',

With lively Ballantine

Good taste! Good time!

So get a smile every time,

A smile every time,

Enjoy the heads-up taste,

Of a Ballantine Beer.

On the other side of the glass, *The Big 3*, run through one of sixty-four versions of the Balantine commercial. Recorded in Gotham between appearances at the Washington club on successive nights, the spot is so high in folk-tune bluffs' esteem that the group uses it as part of its act. *The Big 3's* manager is in the lower right photo.

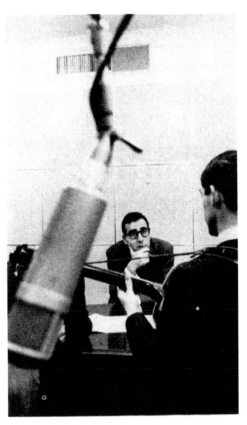

Top: *The Big 3*, Cass Elliot, Jim Hendricks, Tim Rose consult with vocal arranger Bobby Bowers and music arranger Tony Mottola in New York.uses it as part of its act. *The Big 3's* manager is in the lower left photo. Above: Arranger Tony Mottola, at left music stand, augmented the banjo and guitar instrumentation used by *The Big 3*.

The Big 3's powerful harmony drove these jingles. The spots demonstrate how good these singers were and how their vocal prowess enabled them to transcend the folk context into a more mainstream platform.

At some point that winter, Cass and Jim ventured north of the border. In New York, the previous year, they had met and made friends with Canadians Denny Doherty and Zal Yanovsky of The Halifax Three, who were touring heavily in late 1963. "We got to know them and started hanging out with them whenever they were around," Hendricks recalls. "Denny would come to the Hotel Albert. Cass and I had a room there. He would drop in there and we would sing together."[389]

"Cass and I went up to see them in the early winter months of '64," remembers Jim. "We went up to Toronto to have fun and hang out in the folk clubs." At this time, The Halifax Three was on its last leg, as the folk craze waned. During the trip, Hendricks' recollection is that the four friends talked about forming a group among themselves. "When we were in Toronto we sang together. We were doing that a lot because that's what everybody did at that time, especially in folk clubs or coffeehouses on hootenanny nights. It wasn't a big deal. If people liked to sing together it was one of those things that happened."[390]

That same winter, The Beatles arrived. Zal was at Cass's place in New York the night the Fab Four appeared on *Ed Sullivan*, and it is there he met Cass's friend John Sebastian, who formed The Lovin' Spoonful with Zal the following year. Bob Bowers recalls being stuck in a Midtown Manhattan traffic jam with the group, traveling to Gotham Studios where The Big 3's second album was being recorded. As they waited, Cass explained to her cohorts, "This is because The Beatles are here."[391] That may have been the week after The Beatles were on TV because police were required to block off streets on February 12 when The Beatles performed back-to-back concerts at Carnegie Hall, not far from Gotham Studios.

In March 1964, Vee Jay Records announced a new subsidiary label called Tollie Records, which released The Beatles' "Twist and Shout" as its debut single, before re-releasing The Big 3's first single a few weeks later. *Music Vendor* magazine deemed The Big 3 record a Highlight of the Week.[392] Up until this time, Beatles records in the United States had been carried, and not very profitably, only by Vee Jay. In an attempt to capture a more hip market, Tollie's vice president, Jay Lasker, planned "to concentrate heavily on the current type of pop."[393] To that end, a trade ad at the time heralded, "Tollie-Schmollie....They're in the Groove and That's What Counts."[394] That the Tollie label put The Big 3 in the same mix as The Beatles, points to the promise of the progressive folk trio. A year or so later, Jay Lasker would help start Dunhill Records, the label that ultimately signed The Mamas & The Papas, before before he eventually ran Motown Records.

At the end of March the group performed for the final time on *The Tonight Show*. "We did not talk to Carson until the very last time we were on," reminisces Tim. "We sat on 'the couch' and Cass froze. So I ended up doing the conversation. He did not want to talk to me, he wanted to talk to Cass."[395] Shel Wildes, an NBC page, recalls the group's *Tonight Show* appearances: "I held their autographed records for prizes with 'Stump the Band,'" a recurring contest on the show. Wildes also recalls that after one show during The Big 3 years, Cass collapsed and needed paramedics due to intense health problems.[396] (Uncannily, she later collapsed in rehearsals for an April 1974 appearance on *The Tonight Show*, just three months before her death).

The Big 3 was recommended by *Billboard* in April 1964 as a "Pop Standard Programming Special," grouped with records by Burl Ives, Mel Torme, and Woody Herman.[397] They were potentially marketable as a broad-spectrum vocal group, as much as a specialized folk trio. But though their sound tended toward the mainstream, the subject matter of their newest record, "Come Away Melinda," was Grade A political. It is a harrowing apocalyptic anti-war poem, sung by Cass in a child-like voice, asking her one surviving parent, "Why can't it be the way it was before the war began?"[398] Harry Belafonte had first recorded the song several months earlier with a faster tempo and using a children's chorus to ask the questions. The Big 3's slowed down version and Cass' compelling performance made it all the more eerie. Rose took this further a few years later when he recorded it as a solo artist with war-like sound effects.

That song was among those on their second album, which audaciously vaunted the group with a full color picture of The Big 3 as its cover. The name of the record was curiously paradoxical: *Live at the Recording Studio*. The group continued to innovate and offered blues, spirituals, and Western type tunes such as "Down in the Valley." In recollecting "I May Be Right," written by Dick Weissman of The Journeymen, on which Carl Lynch played electric guitar, Jim Hendricks says, "We stole it from Dick Weissman who lived upstairs from me. That was a Peter Paul & Mary type song."[399] Rose agreed at the time, saying, "We work in the style of the Kingstons and Peter, Paul & Mary. Tasteful spiel and evening clothes," preening further, "Our music is traditional and authentic enough, but we don't do the down-home bit. After all, we're college people. That would just be putting the audience on."[400] John Sebastian held the same opinion: "The Big 3 were in the mold of Peter, Paul & Mary."[401] But Bob Bowers further clarifies the comparison: "Unlike Peter Paul & Mary, where you could hear three individual voices, these people had a sound. And this sound would pin you to the wall just like Stan Kenton's Big Band, or those sheets of sound from Coltrane and people like that. It was just extraordinary."[402] Hendricks claims that "the arrangements were what did it,"[403] with Rose adding, "I've often said we were the only folk group that sang in tune."[404] Apart from the musical comparisons, Cass and Mary Travers became friends in those Village days. Cass still had her mother's credit card and spending sprees together at Bloomingdale's were just some of their adventures as newly successful femmes of folk.[405] In 1969, Cass invited Mary to appear in her first prime time television special in which they sang together with another old friend, Joni Mitchell.

Bowers recalls recording "Wild Women" for the second album: "That is Tim on electric guitar. At the end of the song, you hear it kind of falls apart. We don't end together. There are supposed to be three voices behind her, but one of them is mine-from across the room, not Tim's. And Panama Francis, who was drumming, hadn't the slightest idea. We were only rehearsing. Roy loved it so much he refused to do another take because the feeling is so right. It is possibly the best cut on the album."[406] "Wild Women" originated with African American blues singer Ida Cox in the 1920s. Gusti Hervey claimed to have taught Cass the song in Chicago, possibly during The Triumvirate's time there in late 1962. She and Ginny Clemons were active in that folk scene and had sung with Cass impromptu in an assemblage with the politically incorrect name "The Ofays of Faith."[407] (An "Ofay" was an African American derogatory slang term for a white person, akin to "Honkie.")

Along with "Young Girls Lament" from the first album, "Wild Women" proved Cass could sing the blues with conviction:

> *Well, you never get nothin' by being an angel, child*
> *Girls better change your way of livin', and get real wild*
> *I wanna tell you somethin', you know I wouldn't tell you no lie*
> *Wild women are the only kind that ever get by*
> *'Cause wild women don't worry,*
> *Wild women don't get the blues*[408]

John Sebastian

Her lead vocals in these tunes would point to the bluesier solo numbers she did with The Mamas & The Papas, such as "I Call Your Name" and "Dream a Little Dream of Me."

While the album was being finished, Bowers recalls nineteen-year-old John Sebastian coming to the studio with an apron full of harmonicas. He wanted to play on The Big 3's record. Cass stepped outside the control room and "diplomatically explained that wouldn't be possible because it wasn't the sort of thing we were doing."[409] What the group was doing on this second album was more original. In addition to "Wild Women," their hip, up-tempo redux of the 1870s standard "Grandfather's Clock" put the song squarely into the groovy folk rock vein that pointed ahead. Not unlike the way The Mamas & The Papas would soon strip down and reconstruct Rodgers and Hart songs such as "Glad to Be Unhappy," the three really let go in a number that sounds like rock and roll.

On the heels of their second album, The Big 3 pressed on with a sixteen-day, seven-state tour of the Midwest. In the *Midwest Hootenanny Festival* (also called the *Midwest Hootenanny Jamboree* in other accounts), they played with Gale Garnett, Jimmy Rodgers,

PRINTED IN U.S.A.

FM 311

SFM 311

FM 311

M 659

The BIG 3
Live at the Recording Studio

By KAY REYNOLDS

CAST:

Cass Elliot: Around 23, warm, very hip, sharp-witted and enthusiastic about everyone but herself. Vocally capable of reaching emotional heights surpassed by no one.

Tim Rose: Twenty-four years old, at odds with the world, very frank, and possessing an unerring accuracy with his not-too-tactful manner. An exciting performer.

Jim Hendricks: America's 24 year old answer to Cary Grant, former high school music teacher and owner of more than 100 female hearts. He is steady and at the same time full of surprises and revelations.

Roy Silver: Manager of The Big 3. Maintains an air of stolid reserve, chain smokes, and will play Big 3 records for anyone who wanders into his office, including postmen and delivery boys.

The Musical Director, Bob Bowers: Debonair, sophisticated, short-tempered, will not admit any love for anything . . . also plays bass on this album.

Recording Engineer — Frank Kulaga: Tall, young, cooperative and a near-genius at the control board.

Our scene opens at the recording studio. The time is 10:00 p.m. The room is about 30' x 40', with music stands, chairs and assorted instruments like clavichords, etc., pushed into the corners.

The Big 3 are standing around a set-up of microphones which looks like an abstract stick-figure painting. At one end is the control room, with Roy and Frank seated and watching through the glass window.

Bob is tuning his bass, The Big 3 are finishing the first of at least 14 cups of coffee, tea, etc. during the night, and Roy is smoking the first of a long line of cigarettes. This is the second session for the album. The first consisted of putting on tape all the songs which were being considered for inclusion in the album. At least eight songs have now been definitely decided upon, and at this point during this one three-hour recording session, they hope to finish at least three and possibly four songs.

SCENE 1

Frank: Everybody ready in there?

Tim: Which one shall we do first?

Roy: Let's try Grandfather's Clock so we can get it out of the way.

Bob: (Aside to Jim) Let me hear your A.

(Jim starts tuning, Tim joins in and the next ten minutes are spent in tuning and retuning and tuning. Cass roams around the studio making remarks about her throat, the air conditioning, the coffee, the out-of-tuneness of the others, and the state of the world in general. They finally appear to be ready.)

Roy: Okay, let's try and get one all the way through . . . and then we'll quit.

(Smiles appear on all their faces.)

Frank: Grandfather's Clock, take 1.

(It is quiet. Tim whispers the tempo . . . "one, two, three, four . . ." and they start playing. They stop, and a summit conference takes place at this point

about the tempo.)

Frank: Grandfather's Clock, take 2.

It is quiet again. Tim sets a slightly different tempo, and they start.

Frank: Sorry, hold it . . . my fault. Okay, take 3.

(This time they get halfway through the song.)

SCENE 2

(It is 45 minutes later, and we fade in on the last chords of Grandfather's Clock.)

Roy: Okay . . . that sounds like a good take. Let's go to another one for a while. What have you done on Silkie?

Tim: Well, why don't you listen to it and see what you think.

Cass: Yeah, listen to it, and never mind telling us what you think.

Tim: We've changed a few words here and there. I think it's a little clearer now.

Jim: I don't think it's any clearer . . . but I dig the song anyway.

Roy: Can I hear it?

Frank: Silkie . . . take 1.

Tim: Hey, Frank, don't make this a take, we're just running through it.

Roy: No, I want to take on everything, just in case something good comes out of it.

Frank: Silkie, take 1.

(They sing the song through. When they finish there is a short silence.)

Roy: It's beautiful. I don't think anyone will understand what you're singing about. We'll have to put an explanation on the back of the album.

Cass: It's clear to me. It's a song about a silkie.

Roy: (To Frank) You were listening . . . do you know what it means?

Frank: Was it about the Civil War?

(There is another silence.)

Jim: Well . . . what the hell . . . we can explain it in the liner notes.

Cass: Somehow that seems like cheating.

Tim: Well, we can't change the words any more than we have. It's either "cheating" on the liner notes or not doing the song.

Cass: Let's do it and not explain it, and get a reputation for obscurity.

Bob: Let's have it for obscurity!

Roy: Let's have it for getting it on tape and worrying about the explanation later.

Cass: Yeah, let's have it for getting on with it.

Jim: Yeah.

Tim: Yeah. Let's have it for tuning.

(There is another brief pause while they tune . . . for about the 30th time.)

Frank: Silkie, take 2.

SCENE 3

(It is 30 minutes later. A short break is in progress. Cass is now in the sound booth talking to Roy.)

Cass: Roy, I can't help it . . . I'm very hoarse. I can do maybe one more song, but that's stretching it.

Roy: Why are you hoarse?

Cass: (In that confidential voice she does so well.) Listen, we've been rehearsing six to eight hours a day, and I haven't had enough sleep for about a week . . . I'm surprised it's held up this long.

Roy: Uh huh. (With resignation) Hey, what can I tell you. Let's try one more . . . we've got to finish this album, and it's got to be a good one.

Cass: What can I tell you? One more song today and I might make it . . . two more and I'll blow my voice for sure.

Tim: Hey, can we get on with it?

Roy: Yeah . . . what's next?

(Cass lingers for a minute, then wanders back out to the others.)

Roy: How about Wild Women?

Cass: How about not Wild Women . . . Roy, I'll never make it.

Jim: How about Glory Glory?

Cass: Oh . . . all right.

Tim: No, let's do I May Be Right.

Roy: Yes. I May Be Right.

Frank: Are you ready?

(Short pause for more tuning.)

Frank: I May Be Right . . . take 1

(Fade from the scene as the usual stopping and starting get under way.)

The album is now finished, and hours of editing and putting together the tapes are over. No one really knows if it will sell, which is the ultimate test. However, this is where the Big 3 are, musically, and we hope you have enjoyed listening.

EPILOGUE: SCENE 1

Florida. The Big 3 are on stage. Jim and Tim are tuning. Cass is starting the introduction to Silkie.

Cass: This is a song about a young girl in Norway. She has a son by a creature who is a man on the land and a silkie, a silkie being a seal, on the sea. The son is the same peculiar combination as the father. Some years later the girl marries a hunter . . . actually, he's a proud young gunner, to be accurate . . . and the first shot he shoots after his marriage kills both the silkie father and the silkie son by accident. A tragic tale. By the way, this song bears no resemblance to any incidents occuring during the Civil War . . .

SCENE 2

Roy's office in New York.

Roy: (On the phone) What do you think of the album? Um huh . . . uh huh . . . yeah . . . um huh . . . Yeah, I think so too. Hey, it's a great album!

SIDE A		TIME
1. **I May Be Right** — Writer: R. Weissman *Bermer Publishing Corp.* — BMI		2:24
2. **Anna Fia (Feher)** — L. Wood-N. Rock *Fall River Music Inc.* — BMI		2:44
3. **Tony and Delia** — H. Carey — A. Wood *Hari Pep Music Inc.* — BMI		2:30
4. **Grandfather's Clock** — T. Rose — R. Bowers *Manger Music Inc.* — BMI		1:50
5. **Silkie** — C. Elliot — J. Hendricks — R. Bowers *Manger Music Inc.* — BMI		3:20
6. **Ringo** — H. Carey — A. Wood *Hari Pep Music Inc.* — BMI		2:13
SIDE B		
7. **Down In The Valley** — T. Rose — R. Bowers *Manger Music Inc.* — BMI		2:08
8. **Wild Women** — C. Elliot — T. Rose *Manger Music Inc.* — BMI		3:01
9. **All The Pretty Little Horses** — T. Rose — J. Hendricks — C. Elliot — J. Butler *Manger Music Inc.* — BMI		2:40
10. **Glory Glory** — C. Elliot — T. Rose — J. Hendricks — R. Bowers *Manger Music Inc.* — BMI		2:14
11. **Come Away Melinda** — F. Hellerman — F. Minkoff *Appleseed Music Inc.* — ASCAP		3:10

Produced by Roy Silver, under the Musical Direction of Bob Bowers and the Engineer was Frank Kulaga.
Recorded at Gotham Studios, N. Y. C.
Cover Photo: Frank Gauna
Cover Design: Moskof-Morrison, Inc.

and The Original Folk Jazz Trio. In April 1964, Tollie Records ascended to become the second largest record distributor in the country, chiefly due to carrying The Beatles. But this prominence was too late for The Big 3 because the folk craze was precipitously fading, and the trio began to fragment under the pressure of its powerful personalities and spirited voices. Musical arranger Jim Butler said of Tim and Cass, "You really had two potential stars there. But with Cass, no one else was going to be the star."[410] Rose says, "There was a lot of duality. For a small group there was a lot of intrigue. We all thought three different things were happening. We all got very large egos."[411] Paul Colby at the Bitter End concurred: "Cass was Tim's female counterpart, and together they could grab an audience by the throat. But the volatile nature of their personalities wasn't a good glue. Cass and Tim Rose? You put them together in the same room, and eventually there had to be murder."[412] Butler concluded, "There is no way not to be number two if Cass is around. That was the bottom line. Cass was another step beyond. That had to go hard on Tim. Tim could play, but of course Cass was going to get the attention."[413]

Different directions and competing temperaments ultimately unraveled the group. Around this time, Cass recorded some solo numbers at the Bitter End with Roy Silver and Bob Bowers, including the Scottish traditional "Love Henry" made famous by Judy Henske. Bowers says Silver didn't like the idea of Cass going solo "and that was the end of it."[414] Bowers also remembers the group wanted to move in the direction of jazz: "I wrote an arrangement of 'Another Autumn' in a Four Freshman/Hi-Lo's vein, and we recorded it. But Roy said, 'I don't think we're ready for that.'"[415] Rose wanted a new sound for the group, saying, "After the first album I wanted to add a bass, drums and go electric," claiming that Cass declared she would never sing with an electric guitar and drums.[416] In actuality, Cass and Jim had similar inclinations, but the group was simply not cohering anymore. Instead, Cass and Jim began to explore that kind of sound with producer Erik Jacobsen, who was just beginning his decorated recording career in 1964. Jacobsen recalls, "I hung out with Cass and we smoked reefer together many times at the Albert,"[417] Experimenting in the studio, he laid down several impromptu electrified folk tunes with them and other restless folkies like Jerry Yester and Henry Diltz of the Modern Folk Quartet.

The Erik Jacobsen recordings from 1964 included electrified versions of "Tom Dooley," "Oh Susanna" (sounding very much like The Big 3's "Banjo Song"), "Fun Fun," and "Hold Still." The first two tracks are early folk rock, while the latter are two straight rock and roll. Cass is clearly heard on some of these recordings, as is Zal Yanovsky, although there is some dispute whether it is him or Tim Rose. Tim denied recording these songs, saying, "Cass and Jimmy connected with that crowd but I never did. I always thought they were all a bunch of ponces."[418] Others on the tracks have been identified as Henry Diltz, Jerry Yester, John Sebastian, and Jim Hendricks, although like the Yanovsky-Rose discrepancy

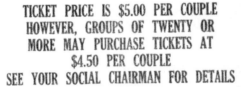

THE CLASS OF 1965 PRESENTS

The First Spring Houseparty

Concert

FEATURING

FOUR SEASONS
FOUR LADS
BIG THREE

TICKET PRICE IS $5.00 PER COUPLE
HOWEVER, GROUPS OF TWENTY OR
MORE MAY PURCHASE TICKETS AT
$4.50 PER COUPLE
SEE YOUR SOCIAL CHAIRMAN FOR DETAILS

Grace Hall

Friday, April 24, 1964

DANCING WITH JOHNNY AND THE HOLIDAYS FOLLOWING THE CONCERT

it's a murky identification at best. None of those living particularly remember the sessions, which were demo-type recordings made by Jacobsen who was developing his chops as a producer. Some of them were first made public in 1998. All were made available by Jacobsen online in 2021.[419]

Despite the schisms and scissures, The Big 3 were persevering and spreading their sound with success as late as April 1964. At Lehigh University, they appeared with The Four Seasons and The Four Lads, and were extolled for their superior showmanship compared to the other acts. "The large woman in the overflowing crimson sack-dress, Cass Elliot, boomed out a big voice with Judy Henske undertones," wrote one reviewer, reporting, "The group's set list that night included 'excellent' performances of songs from both albums," which "swung into a folk rhythm without theatrics." The writer also observed that "mood tunes" like "Winken Blinken Nod," "Down In the Valley," "Ringo," "Nora's Dove," and "Rider" showcased "the group's interpretation of melancholy without maudlinity," while "The Banjo Song," by contrast, was "comic and fresh."[420]

Just a week or so later, while playing during the Indianapolis 500 in May 1964, The Big 3 officially dissolved. Upon learning of their secret nuptials, Rose remembers, "I had found out they were married, and I said, 'Well I think that's it guys.'"[421] Hendricks also recalls, "That's when we told him we had married. We had been to Canada and the prospects of a new group were brewing."[422] Several dates after the Indy were scheduled in Boston, New York, and Winnipeg, but these were likely engagements set and advertised before the group broke up. Some of the billings for these late dates were described as "Cass Elliot & The Big 3," which indicates it was more likely performed by Cass and Jim, along with their friends Denny Doherty and Zal Yanvosky. Similarly, several radio programs also aired live performances in April and May that were recorded before the group split.

Tim recalled going to see Roy Silver after the Indianapolis breakup and being abruptly questioned: "I'm managing Cass and Jimmy. What are you going to do?"[423] Rose wasted little time forging ahead with his solo career. In addition to recording many solo records in the late 1970s—his performance of "Hey Joe" has long been credited as an harbinger to Jimi Hendrix's well known recording of the song—Rose went on to earn a college degree and work as a Wall Street stockbroker. His career came full circle in the 1990s, when he found a second life as a rather celebrated indie rocker in London, where he frequently performed until his sudden death in 2003.

Once The Mamas & The Papas were famous, The Big 3's records were reissued in 1968 by Roulette Records, which had acquired FM's holdings. Roulette unabashedly and almost mawkishly cashed-in on Cass Elliot's fame and name recognition. The Big 3's photograph from their second album was used on a single of "Nora's Dove"/"Grandfather's Clock" with a proclamation, THE BIG MAMA. The 1968 reissue album, with a grouping of songs from both original albums, depicted a cartoonishly drawn and decoupaged image of Cass

in paisley, surfeited with flowers and the lettering of MAMA CASS twice as large as The Big 3. Roulette apparently also fell heir to a stockpile of the group's original albums, because many copies of those were sold in later years with a round, bright orange sticker affixed to the front cover which read: "Featuring Cass Elliot "The Big Mama" from The Mama's & The Papa's [sic]."

Roulette Records' story is now well-known, with the label and its notorious owner Morris Levy mixed up with Mafia misdeeds. Any remuneration from these sales was never seen by the members of the trio. A similar compilation record, titled *Distant Reflections*, resurfaced in 1982 on the obscure Accord label, with the cover also boasting "The Big 3 featuring MAMA CASS." This record too ended up involved in litigation, but the fact remains, as Rose said, there has been continually abiding interest in The Big 3 because of its antecedent role to The Mamas & The Papas.

One of the ads for their final appearances perhaps best described The Big 3 as such: "A unique trio. Neither reverent, doctrinaire, nor spuriously iconoclastic!"[424] In other words, they were about the music. Cass Elliot was fueled and propelled by her emergence from The Big 3, and her time with that group set her on her course as much as any experience in the years before The Mamas & The Papas. "I felt at the time, and I haven't changed my mind in thirty years, she was the finest voice of her generation, " Jim Butler reflected in 1998. "There is no singer at that time who impressed me then or since. You can hear it at the time of The Big 3 with 'Wild Women' and 'Come Away Melinda,' but years later with 'Disney Girls' and 'California Earthquake.' She just grew."[425]

While Cass outgrew The Big 3 in about a year, she soon sashayed with different partners, towards a different dance figure and a new kind of music she made her own.

Thundering and Met with Stunned Silence: The Mugwumps

"Really a tragedy." That's how Cass Elliot once described The Mugwumps to Johnny Carson. She was probably unduly critical of what she also boasted was "the first folk-rock group ever."[426] Cass's hyperbole notwithstanding, The Mugwumps was a pivotal connection in the link between folk and rock music. Cass qualified her characterization by saying the group's tragedy was not musical in nature. It was, she thought, "in a time warp. Just too much before it's time."[427] Bandmate Denny Doherty concurred, saying, "The Mugwumps... What were they like? I still don't know. I still don't know."[428]

Of all the groups that preceded The Mamas & The Papas, The Mugwumps is perhaps the most fascinating because it represents the interstitial, caterpillar-like stage of the metamorphosis from vocal and folk groups to the fully-winged folk rock of The Mamas & The Papas, as well as The Lovin' Spoonful.

The transition from folk music to the danceable, more rock and roll sound of The Mugwumps occurred in 1964, at the meeting point of a most curious ensemble: Cass Elliot, her legal husband Jim Hendricks, Denny Doherty, and Zalman Yanovsky.

Cass and Jim had been in The Big 3, a progressive folk outfit colored by blues, country, and gospel. Just months earlier, Cass Elliot and Jim Hendricks were experiencing wild, sudden success in The Big 3, highlighted by live performances, TV appearances, commercial jingles, and a Midwest hootenanny tour, before being pulled apart by personality differences, poor label support and corrupt business practices. These factors, along with the seismic changes in popular music as the British Invasion swept over the nation, accelerated The Big 3's denouement. Sticking together with Jim and Cass through their split with bandmate Tim Rose was manager and producer Roy Silver. As Jim recalls things, "Roy was always a part of the formation of The Mugwumps. After Cass and I got married, Roy was the only one who knew about it. Then we all knew something that nobody else did. That kept on going, so Roy was always a part of everything we did. We never kept anything from him."[429]

One of the things the pair shared with Roy was the fact that they were toying with the idea of some new group that would include their Canadian friends Denny Doherty and Zal Yanovsky, whose folk group The Halifax Three had also just ended at the beginning of 1964. "Folk music started to die out," Denny summated. "It was overexposed. Hootenanny tours beat it to death, and the music took a big turn after the British Invasion." [430] When The Halifax Three played their last engagement in January in Toronto, followed by the fizzling out of a prospective new venture on the West Coast, Denny and Zal found themselves in Washington, D.C.

From Arlington, Virginia, a drive across the Potomac River on the Francis Scott Key Bridge into Washington, D.C., lands one squarely below the spires of Georgetown University. The bridge empties into M Street, a thoroughfare which in the early 1960s was peppered with numerous nightclubs, bars, and eateries frequented by college students and townies alike. The Halifax Three and The Big 3 had played in several of these establishments, as had The Journeymen.[431]

Mac's Pipe & Drum

Denny and Zal landed in a club in Georgetown on M Street called Mac's Pipe & Drum, which plainly proclaimed in one ad: "Beer – Wine – Pizza." Mac's had been a convenient watering hole for Georgetown students for years. Owner Jack Boyle also owned a number

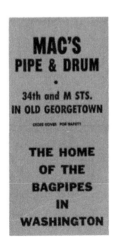

MAC'S
PIPE & DRUM
•
34th and M STS.
IN OLD GEORGETOWN

CROSS OVER FOR SAFETY

THE HOME
OF THE
BAGPIPES
IN
WASHINGTON

Fred Wheary, part of the Mac's Pipe & Drum band in Spring 1964

. . . AND

AFTER THE GAME

SEE YOU AT

MAC'S

Mac's Pipe & Drum
34th & M St., N.W.

In Georgetown

of clubs in Georgetown, such as The Crazy Horse and The Bayou, before going on to start Cellar Door Productions, as a tremendously successful concert promoter into the 1980s. "We got into rock and roll through that," Denny said of the unassuming venue's significance. "Zal and I played in an instrumental band in a beer bar, and in between serving beer we'd play a set."[432]

Fred Wheary was a freshman at Georgetown from Wisconsin who played guitar, mandolin, and banjo. One winter afternoon in late January or early February, he was intrigued by the guitar and drum kit he could see set up through the window at Mac's. Since it was daytime and the place was nearly empty, Wheary wandered in and picked up the guitar and started to play it a bit. Later, he says "a young guy walked in that I didn't know and started playing the snare drum set up." The two began to "fool around" musically, as Wheary recalls, and then "it wasn't long after that Zal Yanovsky and Denny Doherty came in and Zal picked up an instrument and just started jamming." Soon Denny had a bass in hand and Wheary can remember the first song they all tried together: "Searchin'," the 1957 hit by The Coasters. They all knew the fairly standard rock and roll tune, and Denny and Zal started singing together. "As soon as Denny sang, I went nuts in my head over his voice," says Wheary."[433]

From that impromptu afternoon jam session, the four became the unnamed house band for Mac's Pipe & Drum. Zal and Fred would alternate with lead and rhythm guitar duties, Denny played bass guitar, and Ted Hamm was their drummer. "Zal was playing mostly fingerstyle when we first met," recalls Wheary, "but quickly adapted to the flat picking for the rock stuff." Their repertoire was rock and roll and surf material, and in addition to "Searchin'," Wheary remembers them playing "Walk Don't Run," "Johnny B. Goode," and "Hi Heel Sneakers." "Our method was simply someone would start playing something and the rest would follow with stops and starts as needed to clarify chords and phrasing," he says. "Over several weeks the set list grew and evolved. We'd usually futz around with stuff in the afternoon on weekdays at Mac's when it was slow."[434]

Their chosen material and individual playing talents contributed to their sound, but it was also their equipment that helped them succeed. "Zally had a beautiful twelve-string guitar that he told me had been given to him by the Guild Guitar Company when he was with The Halifax Three," says Wheary. It seems that the largesse was not just limited to that bequest. Wheary also remembers the owner of Mac's Pipe & Drum giving Denny and Zal an electric Gibson guitar and bass. Zal spoke of this generosity, telling a local paper how he "met an electric guitar and people said they would give him things if he played it."[435] He went on to boast about "thousands of dollars" and "bins full of assorted electrical musical equipment."[436] Their benefactor also let Denny and Zal take up occupancy upstairs at Mac's for free. Zal described it as "a fat pad with four telephones."[437] Wheary doesn't recall the four phones, but he does remember their living space as being ample and the headquarters

for some revelry and hijinks, especially after nightly shows. "Zal was a wild man," he says. "Denny seemed like the more grounded of the two."[438]

"As thick as thieves," is how Wheary describes the closeness between Denny and Zal during this time, whom he also recalled had "their own kind of look." He was impressed with their devotion to each other and even recalls one representative happening at Mac's: "We were horsing around one afternoon and a voice called, 'Zal, there's a phone call for you.' So Zal went to the phone and waved me over after a few minutes. As I approached him I could hear his side of the conversation and him saying, 'I appreciate the call... I appreciate the offer, but I'm going to turn it down... I don't want to leave Denny.'" Afterwards, Wheary learned that producer and manager Albert Grossman had been on the other end of the call, inviting Zal to be Odetta's accompanist on a European tour.[439]

Zal stayed and the band maintained their beer bar residency for a while in the early spring of '64, when Wheary recalls they played five nights a week and some matinees. By late April, Wheary was facing exams and heading home. When he returned in the fall semester, he saw an advertisement for his friends' latest incarnation: The Mugwumps.

From Denny and Zal's perspective, their last days at Mac's were more dramatic and punctuated. While performing in nearby Georgetown that spring, comedian Hugh Romney, later known as "Wavy Gravy," supplied Denny and Zal with some marijuana. The story goes that drummer Ted Hamm imbibed to the point of being out of control. As Denny and Zal told it, Ted was a member of the Hamm's Brewery family, who Denny claimed was living at the Argentine Embassy, and they received very clear instruction from his attorney father to leave town at once.[440]

That Hugh Romney came to town and supplied pot is more than likely. That Denny and Zal were "avid mischief makers," to quote an old friend from the era, and that they shared some of the stash with Ted Hamm is also hard to dispute.[441] It's probably equally true that young Mr. Hamm got in over his head. The rest of the account is without corroboration, so it's difficult to know what exactly transpired. There does not appear to be a younger generation of the Hamm's Brewery family so named (nor a Hamm presence in Washington) that would support that part of the story. But others remember him too and whoever Ted Hamm was, his father may have been a lawyer and must have been persuasive enough to scare Denny and Zal back to New York, where the end of The Big 3 was imminent. As fate would have it, the Canadians found their friends Cass and Jim at the Hotel Albert.

"We sort of joined forces" is how Denny described it. "Everybody was sitting around in New York scratching their heads."[442] As The Big 3 and The Halifax Three began to disintegrate, he, Zal, Cass, and Jim were spending time and making music together. Cass and Jim had previously visited their friends in Canada and the four had already spent time together at their home base in Greenwich Village. The Hotel Albert was "a skid row

flophouse" according to one observer.[443] Built in the late 1800s, it was a 410-room structure in Greenwich Village, which had seen the likes of Mark Twain, Jackson Pollock, and Robert Louis Stevenson in its glory days. By 1964 it was a haven for the folkies who were in between tours or jobs. Jerry Yester of The Modern Folk Quartet recalled how "the aroma of pot smoke wafted throughout the place twenty-four seven."[444]

Yester, who hung out with the embryonic group, recalls the spring of 1964. "They all stayed in this one room in the Albert. It was nuts being around them. It was like the 'Mad Tea Party.' Lots of noise, Cass baking weird and wonderful smelling illegal baked goods, Zally with no shirt, running around the place joking, playing pranks—the definition of glee."[445] "Lots of weird stuff happened at the Albert," recalls Hendricks. "It was just a melting pot of everybody. There was a magic kind of a thing when Cass and Denny and I sang. Everybody wanted to join in and sing. ["Eve of Destruction" singer] Barry McGuire was there, and he wanted to do it. Felix Pappalardi [of Mountain]. Everybody."[446]

Simultaneous to all the morphing at the Albert, some recordings were made. Erik Jacobsen had played with the folk trio The Knoblick Upper 10,000, and he knew Denny and Zal through intersecting gigs, before quitting the group to experiment with recording.

Denny Doherty and Zal Yanovsky: Dee and Zee or The Noise,
and their dance surf song "The Slurp"

As Jim Hendricks remembers it, Jacobsen was "trying to figure out how to make records and getting his friends to sing for that purpose." He lived at the Albert with Henry Diltz of the Modern Folk Quartet, and they lived next door to John Sebastian. Jacobsen would collar his pals and say, "Hey, go in and sing something." Hendricks can remember then hearing playbacks of the sessions.[447]

In May, Jacobsen played around with some zany "dance-surf" songs with Denny and Zal, akin to their Mac's material. They called themselves alternatively, "The Noise" and "D & Z" (or "Dee and Zee"). Their songs, "The Slurp," "Slurp It," "Slurpin'," "I Got the Word," and "Slurp With Me," had onomatopoeic sound effects from a trombonist named Tony Studd, who had played with the Gil Evans Trio on jazz recordings, and went on to play with Quincy Jones. But this "super sound effect," as Jacobsen called it, was part of the gimmick of the song. Jacobsen claims "The Slurp" created a dance craze, although the record was never released.[448] Curiously, the songs were copyrighted by Erik Jacobsen in the summer of 1964, but the credits for the words and music to the songs are attributed to Jonathan Talbot, the former flamenco guitarist who played with The Halifax Three the previous year in Fort Lauderdale.[449] Talbot only vaguely recalls writing the songs but he does recall them being recorded in the studio with Zal and Denny.[450]

The Bigger Big 3

As they experimented in the basement of the Albert, a new identity began to materialize for the four remnants of two folk trios. The Big 3 was the nucleus of The Mugwumps, which was part of the nuclear fusion that exploded in The Mamas & The Papas. In particular significance to their chemistry was how Denny's three-octave lyrical tenor joined the force-of-nature that was Cass's voice, a blend which was forever emblazoned in The Mamas & The Papas canon a few years later. "Just magical," is how Roy Silver described that sound.[451]

At first it was simply "Bigger Big 3," as Denny put it, but then it was "Cass Elliot & The Big 3," which made four, and this assemblage finished out The Big 3's live commitments.[452] Producer and songwriter Felix Pappalardi joined in on some of the group's rehearsing in the basement, which evidently had decent acoustics.[453] Pappalardi had previously sung with Fred Neil, and would later co-lead Mountain, in addition to producing both The Youngbloods and Cream's *Disraeli Gears*. Jim Hendricks says, "I remember opening the door in the basement of the Albert, and hearing Felix working on Fred Neil's 'Tear Down the Walls.' Felix helped us and, as a matter of fact, he sang with us while we worked on it. We sang the fire out of that song." [454] In addition to writing the song, Fred Neil was an early influence on Bob Dylan, among others, and wrote "The Other Side of This Life," covered by The Lovin' Spoonful and Jefferson Airplane, as well as "Everybody's Talkin'," which appeared in the film *Midnight Cowboy* and won a Grammy in 1969.

In June, they played the Night Owl and the Bitter End in Greenwich Village, still as Cass Elliot & The Big 3, where critics noted "internal changes."[455] Electric reworkings of familiar songs sounded different, and at this particular point they were adding some political song choices such as "Red Flowers," an anti-war song written by Fred Neil about the atomic bombing of Japan, and "Oh Freedom," which Joan Baez had sung at the 1963 civil rights March on Washington. The changes garnered positive, if not prophetic, feedback from one critic, who said they "should easily be one of the lasting acts to come out of the folk movement." The switch-up from the look of a conventional folk threesome was not lost on the observer: "While as a trio the group was already a standout, the addition of another gent with a wildly sonorous fender bass has given new dimension and depth to the whole crew." But the group's focal point commanded the most commentary. "Putting Cass out front was a stroke of genius," the critic raved, calling her "a totally professional performer. Her ability to ad lib is remarkable and her distinct vocal timbre leaves no doubt as to who is in charge." More than one review called her "uninhibited." The "brilliant" group's "pacing" was deemed "exciting and fresh."[456]

CASS ELLIOT & THE BIG THREE
Songs
30 Mins.
Bitter End, N. Y.

Cass Elliot and The Big Three may not be so much a new act, as a "rearranged" act. The new group, headed by Miss Elliot, a good, hefty belter, is an outgrowth of what was originally called The Big Three. Latter included Cass and two lads, one of whom, Jim Hendricks, holds over in the new

As The Halifax Three and The Big 3 cross-pollinated at the Hotel Albert, the foursome continued to metamorphosize and coalesce. Soon they gained a group name as enigmatic as the individuals. Jim Hendricks attributes the name to Erik Jacobsen, who upon hearing the crew rehearse at the Albert, declared: "You sound like a bunch of thundering mugwumps."[457] But Denny maintained that the name came from his Newfoundland grandmother, explaining, "A mugwump is a critter who sits on a fence and can't make up its mind: mug on one side, wump on the other. That was us. Neither folk nor rock, and a year too early for folk rock to even exist."[458] As one DJ characterized it, "The Mugwumps was a crazy name for a crazy group of people."[459]

The group even developed their own Mugwump dialect.[460] They based the vernacular partly on affectionate imitations of folk-blues artists Sonny Terry and Brownie McGhee in a sort of inebriated or thick tongued manner, with a lisp-like "th" added to the end of many words. Hendricks explains, "It was something crazy. Stoned out talk. Basically, Zal started it with Sonny Terry. He thought that Brownie and Sonny were the greatest. He would start out with his hand against his face, covering his eyes, because Sonny was blind. And he would talk this crazy stuff."[461] For instance, in Mugwump Denny became Dennis and was pronounced "Demuth." Years later, Cass and Denny memorialized "spoken Mugwump" with their bantering in the closing seconds of The Mamas & The Papas' recording of "Dancing in the Street." And Jim and Denny still teased each other forty years later in spoken Mugwump.

Thundering at The Shadows

With these changes and accolades, the group was ready in July to start a longstanding gig Roy Silver arranged for them in Washington, D.C. with his cohort Bob Cavallo at the Shadows. Denny attributed that attainment to Cass: "That was all her management."[462] Cavallo knew Cass and Jim because he had auditioned The Big 3 with Roy the previous year at The Shadows, on M Street. Stretching from July to November 1964, the group's Shadows residency defined "The Mugwump era," piquing the interest of both Warner Brothers Records and the FBI along the way.

The Mugwumps' live debut was boldly touted in newspaper advertisements: "New and Exciting Summer Policy at The Shadows, Starting Monday July 13, DANCING to the live, thunderous, and electrifying sound of the MUGWUMPS & Discotheque."[463]

"That was a good club while it was going," remembered Cass of the Shadows. "It had the greats and the near greats." The group sang "for $50 a week," according to Cass, "and had to pay our own bar bills. I worked in the office as a secretary in the daytime. I got paid more being a secretary than I did singing there."[464] The pianist at the club, John Eaton, simultaneously played a jazz repertoire in the cocktail lounge during the evenings while The Mugwumps played the main stage. He recalls the club as an ambitious project by

"THE MUGWUMPS" IS— HERE at the shadows
3125 M St. Georgetown
337 3714

COMPLIMENTS OF
BOB CAVALLO and FRANK WEIS
MEMBERS OF CLASS OF '62

STARTING MONDAY JULY 13th NEW AND EXCITING POLICY at the

shadows

DANCING TO THE
LIVE THUNDEROUS
ELECTRIFYING SOUND
OF THE MUGWUMPS
AND DISCOTHEQUE
NO COVER
3125 M St., Georgetown
For Reservations Call 337-3714

young owners who managed to land big-time acts such as Josh White and Stan Getz.[465] "The Shadows was like a real swanky place with jazz," was Jim Hendricks' impression.[466] The Georgetown University newspaper, *The Hoya*, declared at the time, "The avowed purpose of The Shadows' young management is to present a variety of folk-slanted entertainment without becoming too closely identified with the over-popular sport-shirted-trio type of act. They have achieved notable success with off-beat, ethnic groups…A fortunate if not entirely planned arrangement of overlapping engagements provides something new in the lineup of performers nearly every week."[467]

The entrance to the Shadows was on the side of the building and one walked up to the second floor to enter the cocktail lounge. From there, one entered the showroom, rather dramatically, by descending an interior stairway which "took you right in front of the bandstand," recalled Eaton.[468] *The Washington Post* helped paint the picture: "Oriental rugs, hung on the walls, break the flatness of the wood paneling…Behind the stage is a brick wall, not accidental but built on purpose and acoustically contoured."[469] Pianist Eaton played jazz upstairs with a hypnotist, while The Mugwumps entertained below. Eaton was fascinated by the way the band looked and what they were singing, saying, "These were people from another planet—in dress and in their hybrid singing style."[470]

During the months The Mugwumps performed at The Shadows in Washington, D.C., Cass did secretarial work at the club during the day. One former associate recalled comic

Mort Sahl stopping by and Cass showing him around the neighborhood by walking him around the block.[471] At least part of the time, The Mugwumps lived in Arlington Towers apartments where they were seen practicing their material by the swimming pool.[472] Sometimes they would visit Cass's mother's house in nearby Alexandria. Cass's younger brother Joe remembered, "Whenever those guys came around it was like a cloud of smoke. In and out fast."[473] According to Cass's FBI file, "The Cohen's oldest daughter did not reside at the Cohen residence but was continuously over there late at night and early in the morning with a crowd of her friends whom she generally described as 'Beatniks' and this group continued to make noise into the early morning hours by singing and partying."[474] Partying was a component of The Mugwumps' attitude. One veteran claimed the group partook of amyl nitrite before or while performing,[475] and another friend at the time remembers Cass casually remarking about "doing methadone" when they "played for the kids."[476] And of course marijuana use was on the rise in youth and music culture.

The existence of an FBI file on Cass raises questions. While the file was accessed in the mid-1980s, it no longer exists. It spans from these Mugwump days across the next decade, including some of her anti-war activities in the early 1970s. A sizable portion of the file was redacted and much of that is from the 1964 accounts. It is possible that Zal Yanovsky, who was Canadian and whose father was a communist political cartoonist, was a fellow subject of interest, but there is no known FBI file on him. Another possibility is that Cass's longtime friend Harrison Pickens "Pic" Dawson III, whose father held a high ranking position in the State Department, was of interest to the Bureau. Dawson, who died in 1986, has no records at the FBI now, but he became a notorious narcotics dealer in L.A. in the late 1960s and was participating in that scene in Washington in 1964, where he was caught smuggling marijuana by way of the heel of his boot.[477] Cass had known him from the area since 1961 or 1962 when one friend from the era recalled she was "wandering around the Bohemian sections of Baltimore and was introduced to marijuana which helped to chill her out, because a doctor put her on uppers to help lose weight which jazzed her up too much."[478] Pic and Cass were often together in Greenwich Village as well. Whatever the redacted portion concerned, it is noteworthy that Cass was on the Bureau's radar at this early date.

The makeup of The Mugwumps was not just a fusion of elements of The Big 3 and The Halifax Three. They had a young black drummer, Art Stokes, who was reportedly the nephew of jazz great Art Blakey and a New York jazz drummer who was a member of the "traveling unit of The Mugwumps or when a rhythm section [was] needed. Described as the only male Mugwump who was clean shaven, Stokes's fate is mysterious.[479] Denny Doherty believed he died of a drug overdose but any further musical endeavors are indiscernible.[480] John Sebastian was also known to join the group on harmonica. As Denny said, "When we went to D.C., John was not going to let us leave without him."[481] Hendricks credits Cass's

Pic Dawson, 1964

John Sebastian , 1964

hand in Sebastian's addition, saying, "John was an instrumentalist when we met him. He had played harmonica behind Freddie Neil. With The Mugwumps, he stood over on the right-hand side of the stage playing harmonica. Cass loved his harmonica playing—we all did—and so we said, 'Hey come along with us.'"[482] As Sebastian remembers it, "They were trying to make this transition into folk rock. Cass had known Denny and Zalman longer than I had. Very soon thereafter I got a phone call saying, 'Would you come and bring us a pound of pot and play music for a couple of weeks. We have these wonderful hotel rooms just outside of D.C. and we're kind of living it up so get over here.' I did that and the next thing I knew, I was playing harmonica with The Mugwumps."[483] While Sebastian appeared on stage with the group, he did not make any recordings with them.

Bob Cavallo clarifies that Sebastian's time with the group, although oft cited, was actually very brief, saying, "John was brought in to play with The Mugwumps and to add some character. Zal was a great guitarist and when they started playing together, he started talking to John and I saw Zally going into the blues. 'We're never going to make it in this direction,' I thought."[484] When John and Zal started horseplaying on stage, Roy Silver was not pleased either. He confronted Sebastian, who recalls Roy's words: "We're going to have to let you go because you're a bad influence on Zal Yanovsky. Every time you play something, he'll play it across the stage. Or he plays something, and you do it, and you guys are deviating from the arrangement."[485] Cavallo continues the story: "I had promised John three weeks of work. After the first week, I paid him for one week and then gave him the pay for the other two weeks." The conversation was amicable enough that part of John's response was, "Hey would you want to hear my music?" To this, Cavallo agreed and, as he recalls, "with Sebastian's reverb turned on, one light on him on the stage, with the janitor mopping the floor, Sebastian began to play." With that, Cavallo said, "Would you want to work for me?"[486] Sebastian has a similar recollection, saying, "I had no bad feelings. That evening I sat around with an old piano player in the sort of 'Get Drunk Room' of the Shadows, and Zal and I began doing the Bessie Smith catalog. It seemed like I knew all these tunes and he knew all these tunes. Bob Cavallo, after hearing this said, 'Would you come down here on the stairs with me for a minute?' He said 'If you ever do need any kind of representation, I wish you'd call me.' At which point I said, 'Yeah, yeah. I'm not ready.' And years later Bob Cavallo would repeat the story and say, 'I never talked to any talent ever that said, 'I'm not ready.' But he did make a very good impression."[487]

In between his sets of standards upstairs, house pianist John Eaton would meander down the Shadows stairway and sit in the back of the room. "There I was, a Yale graduate, in my Brooks Brothers suit and army issued glasses and crewcut. And there they were, in their garb doing a totally different thing." Eaton listened to them almost nightly. While he was worlds away from them musically, he attributes this time and The Mugwumps as a pivotal moment in his career: "As a Yale graduate pursuing this musical career at the time, I thought I was rebelling. But these people were in another type of rebellion and almost rejecting me on other grounds. The world was changing fast. Music changed. Attitudes had changed. If you had to sum up the '60s in one year, 1964 was the real watershed year." Eaton credits The Mugwumps with exemplifying that in every way.[488]

That summer, *The Washington Daily* observed that the Shadows changed up its music programming to keep with the times. "Discotheques—fashionable juke joints—are springing up all over the ritzy neighborhood [of Georgetown]," it reported, while specifying that the fare at the Shadows was "not pure discotheque," because it offered a live band in addition to spinning records. The article continued:

> The 'live' music is purveyed by a highly charged, free swinging group of fellows and a single girl who call themselves The Mugwumps. Cass Elliot, the girl is a rotund, hearty creature with a frenetic voice and seemingly the head Mugwump. Though the idea is for everyone to get up and dance to The Mugwumps as well as The Platters no one ventured onto the floor the other night. Evidently the sight and sound of Miss Elliott [sic] fractured them to such an extent they decided to sit and stare. Not so when the stereo hit the speakers. The floor was filled to overflowing in a matter of minutes with every pelvis getting a play.[489]

But there was dancing to The Mugwumps too. Denny once summed up the whole period by saying, "We did dance steps for six months."[490] Added one reporter, "A dancing instructor is around occasionally to demonstrate various steps."[491] A local rag described a new dance based on the band's gyrations and named it in their honor. Reportedly, the youngsters "noticed various hand motions the Mugwumps were making. The teens incorporated these into the dances they already were doing and had a new dance, the Mugwump."[492]

"I remember they seemed very flamboyant," recalls one eyewitness to their performance at the Drive-In in Rockville, Maryland. Some remember them playing atop the snack bar there at a Battle of the Bands event: "I remember they were hanging out in and near their 1964 red Pontiac convertible and even though it was in late August, I vividly recall Mama Cass wearing a huge, gaudy mink coat."[493]

The Washington Post said the group was "attempting a new sound."[494] Another review described Cass as a "large young gal dressed in a leopard-skin muu muu."[495] The description continued of the guys in the group: "One wore his hair combed forward over his brow a la a Beatle. Another looked like you or me except for sideburns which grew at least halfway to his chin. Another looked like Paul of Peter, Paul, & Mary fame." As they played, the critic noted, "the men plucked glistening electric guitars with great vehemence and the one with the Beatle mop moved his head back and forth like a Dupont Circle pigeon spying a crust of bread."[496]

The reference to Dupont Circle was apropos, as the group played a different kind of gig there later in the fall when they sang at a Democratic Party rally with the United States Postmaster General and Skip Humphrey, son of vice presidential candidate Hubert Humphrey.[497] The younger Humphrey, even half a century later, recalls Cass's voice particularly.[498] This was not the only political figure the group encountered. A Georgetown freshman, Bill Clinton also saw the group during that time, writing in his 2004 autobiography, "Sometimes the Cellar Door [a sister club to the Shadows also owned by Bob Cavallo] opened on Sunday afternoon, when you could nurse a Coke and listen to the Mugwumps for hours for just a dollar."[499] Clinton may have been there in early October when the group was advertised as: "TEEN DAY at THE Shadows – Calling All Teenagers! COME SEE and HEAR 'THE MUGWUMPS' Every Saturday 2 to 5 p.m. Admission $1.50 DANCE! DANCE! DANCE!"[500] "They came on stage, and you could not stop looking at them," recalled Cass' sister Leah, who was a teenager at the time. "They were so amazing – especially Zal – his big bushy hair, this big Beatles haircut, but it was like a Beatles haircut done by Fellini. They were complete cut ups on stage. They would take turns lying down. At one point I remember Cass lying down and Zal with one foot on her stomach, playing a solo."[501] One of the few photographs that exist of the group, and the only one of them

in performance, shows similar antics with Cass's hand over Denny's mouth in the middle of playing a number.

This push for afternoon shows was picked up by the press, which said the Shadows was "trying to give more teen-agers an opportunity to see them."[502] Hendricks' memory confirms this. "The Shadows was normally an adult nightclub scene. The Saturday afternoons was an attempt to get kids there."[503] Commensurate with this, seven local fan clubs cropped up in the area and the group played at least two high school concerts in Maryland, including a performance at Albert Einstein High School, ten miles outside of Washington, D.C.[504] An alumnus recalled: "I think they played for our homecoming dance, which was held in the cafeteria. We walked to the gym to listen to them. There were a number of students who had some connections with the Georgetown scene."[505]

"I couldn't believe our Teen Club dance had this group play at our school," remembers then-high schooler Rita Perfater. "They were incredible. I am quite sure I stood, looking and listening with my mouth hung open. I have thought of it many times over these long years. I do remember not liking their name but it wouldn't stop me from seeing them again. Unbelievable. Right in the corner of our gym were what would become The Mamas & The Papas. Did they later remember with wonder at their tours of high schools until they 'made it'?"[506]

Even in this setting, Cass Elliot's voice made an impact. Perfater recounts, "I remember when Cass opened her mouth to sing, I stopped in motion. I couldn't believe the voice."[507] Another classmate recalls it too: "When Mama Cass came out from between the curtains in a leopard print muumuu you could hear the snickers all over the gym. Then she began to sing and you could hear a pin drop."[508]

There was definitely fan hype as the group sold copies of their single at the high school and gave autographs. Girl fans reportedly retrieved Zal's soft drink bottle in yet another parroting of Beatlemania.[509]

"The Mugwumps were real folk rock," states John Sebastian. "That is, not really with a foot in either camp firmly."[510] "We were the first folk group to use electric instruments, long before the Byrds were a germ in anybody's brain," insisted Cass years later.[511] "Picture this group," Denny recalled: "Zalman Yanovsky, freelance Jew; me from Halifax, the weird Irishman playing bass; this 300-pound Cass; we've got Art Stokes, black kid on drums; Jim Hendricks on guitar; John Sebastian sometimes sitting on a stool playing harmonica; and we called ourselves The Mugwumps. We went electric a year before Dylan. Everybody went, 'What? Get out of here.'"[512] At the time, Cass said, "There's usually stunned silence for the first number we do, and after that they begin to dig us."[513] Referred to as Cassie Dol, she went on to point to their collective musical talent: "Most rock and roll groups are gathered together for their playing ability. We didn't do it that way. We wanted to make sure our personalities were compatible and not only our musical abilities."[514] As their recording producer Alan Lorber saw it, "There were three leads of the group: Cass, Denny, and Zal. Each lead had their own personality and thus were cast accordingly. Zal was more R&B influence, out there. Zally was so young and so talented a guitarist who never achieved what he should have as an instrumentalist. Jim lent perfectly to the near blood harmonies of the other three leads." Blood harmonies is a phrase Lorber used to describe "a group's tight and natural harmonies, as if they instinctively breathed and phrased the same." He attributed his experience of the like in earlier work with many black artists.[515]

The Mugwumps' thundering performance of Felix Pappalardi's "Do You Know What I Mean?" was "deafening" to one critic, who was "reminded of an Indian war chant with the braves getting in the mood to raid the stockade in the valley below. But then came the shocker. No sooner had this number ended than the three guitarists and the gal glided soulfully and with fine harmony into 'Earth Angel.' This change of tempo was stunning to say the least. It was fully expected that they would continue attempting to tear down the walls with more of what they began with."[516] They ended that particular night with an original song called "Rock and Roll Is Here to Stay" "while the crowds leaped to the dance floor to wiggle again."[517] Rock and roll was a main dish for what The Mugwumps were serving up. In addition to "Searchin'," Bo Diddley's "You Can't Tell a Book by Its Cover"

TV PREVIEWS
Allan Sherman
To Host Mugwumps

was "part of the act," recalls Hendricks.[518] Along with that, Cass was noted for being "a comic of sorts," with "that flexible type of voice most anybody would enjoy hearing."[519]

Within the month, The Mugwumps were thundering in D.C. and New York. John Sebastian remembers, "They had a nice little pocket of success in Washington, D.C.," and he agrees that as a club, the swanky Shadows was "very uptown."[520] On August 2, 1964, The Mugwumps made a color television appearance on *The Tonight Show* with fellow guests Allan Sherman, Bill Cosby, and Stefanie Powers, which has likely been lost forever like so many *Tonight Show* episodes from this era.[521] Back in D.C., *The Washington Post* reported, "They've got the Shadows jumping," and the singing was captured on tape.[522]

Subsequent sessions generated a handful of stylistically progressive tracks. "Actually a demonstration tape," remarked Cass about the recordings, which resonate with the early fusion of hers and Doherty's voices in all their contrapuntal greatness. This collection of songs, which would eventually become their "posthumous" self-titled album, is a serendipitous vocal snapshot of the short-lived but seminal group. "We had played five sets the night before," Cass remembered, "and then driven 200 miles to go make a demonstration tape, made the tape, and turned right straightaway around and came back to work our gig."[523] The demo tape was recorded at Bell Sound Studios in New York on August 13 and 14, and produced by Alan Lorber, who had seen the group at the Shadows, at the behest of Warner Bros. Records, Roy Silver, and Bob Cavallo. It was likely Lorber whom a newspaper referred to as "a spy from the Warner Brothers record department apparently sneaked in one night and heard them and now they'll be immortalized on wax next week with their first album."[524] Arthur Mogull, the major record executive who had signed Bob Dylan to a publishing deal with Warner Bros, also "pacted" (or signed) The Mugwumps at this time and the deal was reported in several trade publications.[525] Mogull was to be their A&R representative in sessions and several other labels were reportedly "bidding" for the contract.[526]

WB Pacts Mugwumps

WB Inks Mugwumps

Representation seems to have been top-heavy for the group, with Roy Silver and Bob Cavallo managing their live performances at the Shadows and the Cellar Door in Washington, as well as the Village Vanguard in New York. They were also listed as producing the first single, with Alan Lorber's name somehow ingrained in their recording sessions for Warner Bros. and Mogull was enlisted by the label to further their reach in terms of listening audiences. The multiple press accounts from August 1964 concerning Mogull referred to "signing,"[527] "negotiations,"[528] and "ink,"[529] indicating some sophistication in the level of the deal. *The New York Daily News*, however, reported on Roy Silver's "acquisition" of the group in September.[530]

Whoever was at the helm, the promise of a recording deal prompted some photo sessions. A number of publicity shots taken that August showed the group in the recording studio in New York. Another photo op took place in Georgetown, with Stephen Hirsch—later known as DJ Edward Bear of San Francisco underground radio station KMPX—behind the lens. Hirsch was managing a club called the Scene in New York, but went to D.C. to photograph The Mugwumps. "I borrowed a $12,000 ebony statue from a Georgetown antique shop. I told the shop 'I gotta have this.' And the shop said, 'Okay—if it's for The Mugwumps.'" The statue, as described by one of the group, looked like a bust of a faun or Lucifer himself. While few of these images have surfaced, Hirsch laments that no shots from a particular stunt seem to have survived. As he remembers it:

at the
shadows

THE
THUNDEROUS
ELECTRIFYING
SOUND OF THE
"MUGWUMPS"
AND DISCOTHEQUE
no cover

3125 M St. Georgetown
337-3714

> I photographed this absurd, beautiful thing right around the highways of Washington, breaking the laws, speeding, the four of them jammed into a little MG. The main part of the photo shoot was with me hanging out of the back of a car with Cass and the guys following in the MG, doing different things to look interesting or goofy, or anything that would look like fun or make an eye-catching cover. I can't remember if we got help from the cops or not, though, of course, we should have and probably could have if we tried. We might have. The MG wasn't built to handle four and, at times, we were speeding to get the proper windblown effect, so it would have been good to have a police car helping us. What I do remember is that it was a fun-filled day, and we all had a great time. Cass was great to be with and the guys were always good sports.[531]

The Beatles, The Beach Boys and the FBI

Watching movies was a favorite pastime of The Mugwumps. Cass and John Sebastian reminisced about watching movies "all night long" together,[532] and Sebastian says they had a habit of offering commentary and sardonic criticisms of the movie aloud, while it was playing.[533] About this time, they went and saw the new feature film by The Beatles, *A Hard Day's Night*, which was released in early August. Cass "grabbed" Denny, to hear him tell it, and "dragged me to the theater and we sat there from the time the matinee started around 2 o'clock until we had to go back to the club. After the gig that night we got the last flight out of Washington back to New York to go wake our managers up to tell them: 'WE HAVE TO DO THIS. WE HAVE TO DO THIS NOW!'"[534]

Their recordings confirm the group was aiming at the Beatlesque. Since Beatlemania hit Canada earlier than the United States, Jim Hendricks credits an unusually early Beatles influence on Zal and Denny. "Denny and Zal would talk about The Beatles when we talked on the phone," remembers Jim.[535] "Cass was a groupie about the whole Beatles thing." John Sebastian concurs, saying, "And Cass was like the lady on the steamship who makes sure everybody's having a good time."[536] In February 1964, she had enticed Sebastian to meet Zal by claiming Ringo Starr was with her. (The physical likeness between Starr and Yanovsky was not completely without basis). The three ended up watching The Beatles on *The Ed Sullivan Show*. An historic connection was made as Sebastian describes it: "Once Yanovsky and I had played together that night, by the next day it was like signed in blood, both of us knew, 'Whoever the hell that guy is I gotta learn more about him.' This was the origin point from which Sebastian and Zal would ultimately form The Lovin' Spoonful.[537]

The impact of the Fab Four on the formulating four Mugwumps was clear. "When The Beatles finally hit the US," says Hendricks, "we were already doing it." Working out the Beatles influence, the folkies were veering more towards rock and roll. They recorded their own electric rock and roll version of The Coasters' "Searchin'," which Denny and Zal had played at Mac's Pipe & Drum. History would reveal that The Beatles recorded the tune in an audition for Decca in 1962. To say that The Mugwumps were in sync with the British Invasion understates their ingenuity. "We dig [rock and roll] more," Zal simply declared of their moving away from the folk direction.[538] Denny had done his time in the late '50s with his downright rock and roll band The Hepsters. In retrospect Cass agreed, calling The Mugwumps "the closest I ever got to Rock and Roll."[539]

Years after The Mugwumps, Cass acknowledged that the group was "influenced by The Beatles"[540] and, to be sure, Lorber "tried to mix in their existing repertoire with some hit British writers to call radio-attention to the then British invasion influence."[541] One such number was "I'll Remember Tonight," written by British songwriter Chris Andrews for London group The Roulettes. "I really liked The Mugwumps version of the song," Andrews says decades later, "especially Mama Cass in the middle eight."[542] Lorber's efforts gained some traction. In late August 1964, the UK music newspaper *Record Mirror* termed The Mugwumps as Warner Bros.' "answer to the Mersey groups."[543]

Because the group was as original as they were, they did not rely solely on others' works. The Beatles effect was but a part of The Mugwumps sound. They were comfortable forging their own way with their own material, either in songwriting or interpretation. To this day, manager Bob Cavallo says he was never skeptical of their talents, believing it was the lack of stronger material that was a fatal flaw for The Mugwumps. "If we had a great songwriter, we would have made a million bucks," he recalls. "They were good but there was no hit song."[544]

After hearing the results of their first recording session in New York, Hendricks remembers feeling it was overproduced: "We said, 'You know, that ain't us. That's not what we're about. Then Cass and I started writing some songs."[545] Sitting together on the dance floor of the Shadows during rehearsal, Cass and Jim wrote two of the best and most genuinely folk rock numbers the group recorded: "Here It Is Another Day" and "Everybody's Been Talkin'." Jim explains, "I wrote the music and melody, while Cass would go off by herself, write a couple of lines and come back, and we fit it to the melody." Interestingly, these are some of the only extant published songs that Cass wrote during her life. Hendricks asserts they were actually recorded at the Shadows, corroborated by the lack of brass and "bigger production" heard on some of the other tracks.[546]

Everybody's been talking
You don't love me no more
I don't wanna believe them
I've heard that before

My friends just ignore me
They laugh and call me the fool
I smile and say they're all mistaken
You couldn't be so cruel

I'm not wise in the ways of the world
Especially when you're not here
But when you hold me, the maze of the world
Is suddenly clear[547]

"Everybody's Been Talkin'" was covered by at least two other groups: in 1965 by Curt Boettcher's Summer's Children and in 1966 by Group Therapy. Denny also performed it in his 2003 off-Broadway musical, *Dream a Little Dream*. With its strong harmonies, robust drumming, and catchy tune, it is the most folk rock of the Mugwumps recordings and, as Denny said "You can hear the sound of The Mamas & The Papas in it."[548]

There are two similar unpublished compositions by Cass from this time archived at the Library of Congress, which reveal more of her songwriting abilities. "Bright Day" and "Happy Baby" are long lost specimens of The Mugwumps catalog.[549] At least one fan remembers "Happy Baby" being sung live, and these songs are illustrative of the kind of material the group was doing.

These Cass compositions, the D & Z Slurp recordings and Erik Jacobsen's initial dabbles in recording in 1964, all capture some of the spirit of those original sounds. They are a link within the Mugwumps link to The Mamas & The Papas. They encapsulate the moment when folkies in Greenwich Village were electrifying, responding to the British invaders, and innovating a new American sound.

That September, the group played with the Beach Boys in Alexandria, Virginia. Denny recalled the event as being swarmed with girls clawing their way into The Beach Boys' limousines and Beach Boy Mike Love being particularly enamored by the young female fans.[550] Jim recalls it as "wild" and a "big deal" as well, with The Mugwumps brought up

Handbill from concert with The Beach Boys at Alexandria Roller Rink

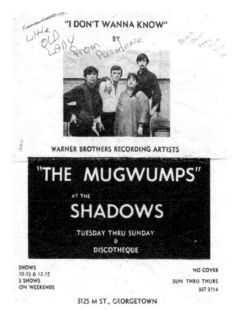

Newcomer Picks

I DON'T WANNA KNOW (2:07) [Gil BMI—Beecham, Rowberry]
I'LL REMEMBER TONIGHT (2:06) [Gill BMI—Andrews]
THE MUGWUMPS (Warner Bros. 5471)

Here's another group with a wild tag, the Mugwumps, that can be an important topic of teen conversation in the weeks to come. It's a frenzied pounder, dubbed "I Don't Wanna Know," that takes a hard beat thump-a-rhythm ride. Artists' potent wailing's backed by a terrific Alan Lorber arrangement. Undercut's an inviting cha cha rocker that can also step out.

in limos surrounded by screaming teenagers.[551] A Mugwumps fan club started in nearby Arlington. Their single "I Don't Wanna Know/I'll Remember Tonight" was released around the same time as this concert. It was a "Newcomer Pick of the Week" for *Cash Box*—just below The Beach Boys' new releases—which said, "Here's another group with a wild tag, The Mugwumps, that can be an important topic of teen conversation in the weeks to come." The review went on, "It's a frenzied pounder, dubbed 'I Don't Wanna Know' that takes a hard beat thump-a-rhythm ride. Artists' potent wailing's backed by a terrific Alan Lorber arrangement."[552] With that lead vocal by Zal Yanovsky and strong tight backgrounds by the others, Denny pointed out decades later, "You can hear The Mamas & The Papas and The Spoonful there.'"[553]

Of the single's tamer B-side, *Cash Box* remarked, "Undercut's an inviting cha-cha rocker that can also step out."[554] Like *The Washington Post* critic noted a month earlier, the group's ability to segue from thunder and frenzy to something exquisite and beautiful was apparently surprising and impressive. Another review of the single said The Mugwumps had "a real sound" with "a lot of talent" and that both sides or their record had an "appeal in the current groove."[555] The range and variety of The Mugwumps had begun in The Big 3 and would be perfected with The Mamas & The Papas.

One music business magazine pegged the record as one of the country's "hottest singles" based on airplay in Washington D.C.[556] A Canadian report indicated a radio executive had "fingers crossed" for the record's success even into late October.[557] The group's live performances were buttressing the positive response to the record. Washington's *Evening Star* reported, "The Shadows plans no immediate change in fare because of the great summer reception accorded to the Mugwumps who have revived business beyond all expectations."[558]

The British pressing of the single was released in October and continued to make news well into the fall, with one UK publication noting the record with approbation as a "quick 45."[559] There seemed to be some momentum with this little American sortie. "I find the rhythm irresistible," UK disc jockey Peter Aldersley wrote for *Pop Weekly*, calling the record "an attractive beater from an American group," and adding, "It would seem that the British pop influence is being felt by American groups because the whole tone and style of this one could well be that of one of our own groups." He even commented on the songwriting and execution of the piece: "The composition and performance are both well up to today's idiom. This is good group work on an above average piece of writing."[560] That the group made a splash overseas—and had records manufactured in England shows Warner Bros.' belief in them. Even "after the fact" in January 1965, *16* magazine picked up the theme in their "Last Minute Flashes" column, writing, "Not to be outdone by England's out-pouring of way-out groups, Warners has come up with The Mugwumps – who happen to be darned good!"[561]

The FBI also speculated on their success and drew parallels with The Beatles. An excerpt from Cass's FBI file from October 19, 1964, read:

> The Mugwumps will perhaps continue playing at The Shadows in Washington D.C. until they have made a hit record. When and if they do, they will probably go on a tour of the United States which tour will be sponsored by the Warner Brothers. The purpose of this tour will be to build up The Mugwumps in the eyes of the youth in the United States similar to the buildup given The Beatles until their growing power will become sufficiently strong to warrant the Warner Brothers making a picture featuring them.[562]

The Mugwumps at the SHADOWS

But Lorber's, Aldersley's, and the FBI's expectations were unrealized. The single went nowhere in sales. As Cass put it, "We were doing very sophisticated folksy stuff but obviously 1964 wasn't the year for it."[563] Denny adds, "Even the way we looked was before our time."[564] Radio DJ Stephen Hirsch shares the reckoning: "The Mugwumps came and went. They were too good, too early."[565]

In November they played their last weekend at The Shadows and performed at Mountaineer Weekend at West Virginia's Monticola College, which promoted them as "a brand-new variety singing quartet from New York City."[566]

They returned to New York for a swansong performance. "The Mugwumps need[ed] to branch out. They ended up getting an opening gig for Joey Dee & The Starliters—a ferocious twist band—at the Peppermint Lounge," recalls John Sebastian.[567] "The Peppermint Lounge— that was like Frank Sinatra," remembers Hendricks. "It was a real adult crowd."[568] Adds

Sebastian, "Now that's really getting away from that polite folk music, so much so that they began their set and the audience quickly just turned their backs and kind of halfheartedly danced until it was over, to minimal applauses." While this hasn't been confirmed, the story goes that after that night, the Peppermint Lounge was closed down for good.

Another last straw, Hendricks recalls, was a push from management or Warner Bros.' for the group to continue sans Cass, because with her they didn't fit the bill visually. Denny recalled this as well. The optics of The Mugwumps was startling to those with a narrow image of what a pop act looks like. This, as much as the newfangled folk rock sound of the music, may have been why The Mugwumps were ahead of their time. "That was the winding down," says Jim. "What seemed to be happening at that point—it was that teenybopper crowd, and they were not accepting Cass at all. When The Beatles came out, all the little girls were screaming and hollering after boys. 'What are you going to do with the fat girl in the middle there?' the record and club guys would ask. It just wasn't working. We got together and we said to the powers that be, 'Listen, we're not going to continue this if Cass can't be a part of it.' And we just drifted off."[569] The Mugwumps were waning and they knew it. "We couldn't even get arrested," says Denny.[570] "They came away from that," remembers John Sebastian, "they were staying at the Albert Hotel and I just heard their sad tale: 'Boy, I don't know. This may not be the thing.' And of course I'm trying to look disappointed, but in my secret heart of hearts I'm thinking, 'Yes…Yanovsky is mine.'"[571]

"At that point," adds Hendricks, "Zal and Sebastian were getting together."[572] Indeed, Bob Cavallo was earnest in developing The Lovin' Spoonful and would ultimately lead and manage them in their many successes.

As The Mugwumps began to disintegrate, Silver believed he still had the essence of The Mugwumps' sound, and reportedly took Jim, Cass and Denny to Columbia to audition. The record label declined them, and so The Mugwumps halted.

According to Michelle Phillips, "The Mugwumps were a cult after the event."[573] She and John forever memorialized them in their lyrics of The Mamas & The Papas' 1967 hit "Creeque Alley," which chronicled the group's history.[574] The group really only came to the fore after The Lovin' Spoonful and The Mamas & The Papas were famous. *The Mugwumps - An Historic Recording*, the album that was put together with nine of their recordings from 1964, wasn't issued until 1967, in the Summer of Love, when both of the later groups were enjoying huge success. A companion single with "Searchin'" and "Here It Is Another Day" came out as well, but it's fair to say that in 1967 these records were more of a curiosity cashing in on then big names than bona fide releases of group that had disbanded three years earlier. Still, *Billboard's* retrospective review for the single listed it as its first "Best Bet" and suggested "The Mugwumps could really go places with this bouncy, infectious love ditty. Keep tabs."[575]

THE MUGWUMPS · WS 1697

STEREO

← STEREO →

An Historic Recording

Late Summer of '64. A young quartet met in Manhattan and recorded nine songs. Their sound was born too early. Too few ears were ready. So, the Mugwumps went their own ways. Zal, Jim, Cass, and Denny moved on to other groups, other kicks. Each eventually entered that weird world of sudden hits, royalties, Aston-Martins. What The Mugwumps left behind is this series of nine historic recordings. Recordings that are the grassroots of today's pop sound. Recordings that, today, sound even better.

WARNER BROS
RECORDS
1697

THE MUGWUMPS

① ZAL YANOVSKY
② JIM HENDRICKS
③ CASS ELLIOT
④ DENNY DOHERTY

WS 1697

AN HISTORIC SAVE!
THE NINE SONGS RECORDED BY
ZAL, JIM, CASS & DENNY
ONCE KNOWN AS

THE MUGWUMPS

SIDE ONE

SEARCHIN'
(2.52)
I DON'T WANNA KNOW
(2.07)
I'LL REMEMBER TONIGHT
(2.00)
HERE IT IS ANOTHER DAY
(2.12)
DO YOU KNOW WHAT I MEAN
(1.56)

SIDE TWO

YOU CAN'T JUDGE A BOOK
BY THE COVER
(2.50)
EVERYBODY'S BEEN TALKIN'
(2.26)
DO WHAT THEY DON'T SAY
(2.13)
SO FINE
(2.35)

The fragments are precious few. You look at hasty 8x10s snatched in a Manhattan recording studio. The faces softer. The eyes younger. Like seeing yourself posed with the rest of Ninth Grade Miss Nancy Jackson's graduating class.

Three years becomes a long time. The Mugwumps were there, were important, and dissolved. Cass and Denny wind up as Mamas and Papas. Jim moves up to Laurel Canyon above Hollywood, involving himself in a new group called The Lamp of Childhood. Zal becomes key to The Lovin' Spoonful.

Behind, a legacy of nine songs. Hence, an album of nine songs, undilluted. Damn lucky to have those.

A Mugwump is a bird that sits on a fence with its Mug on one side and its Wump on the other. A Mugwump is also a long way to "Creeque Alley."

A Mugwump is four persons once in love and still loving.
— Stan Cornyn

PRODUCED BY ROY SILVER & BOB CAVALLO
In association with Alan Lorber / A Cavallo & Silver Production /
Art Direction Ed Thrasher

WARNER BROS. RECORDS, INC., A SUBSIDIARY AND LICENSEE OF WARNER BROS. PICTURES, INC.
4000 WARNER BOULEVARD BURBANK, CALIFORNIA. 321 W. 44TH STREET, NEW YORK, NEW YORK.
MADE IN U.S.A.

185

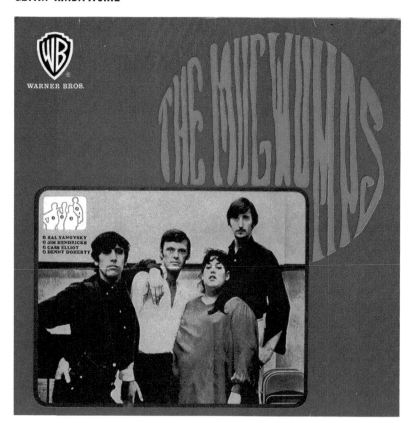

the Mugwumps???

Un nome nuovo, piuttosto originale e complicato, che alla maggior parte di voi non dirà niente, ma... osservando attentamente la foto dei suoi componenti parecchi di voi avranno certo riconosciuto volti tutt'altro che sconosciuti, volti legati a nomi ormai conosciuti nelle più alte sfere della musica leggera: LOVIN' SPOONFUL, LAMP OF CHILDHOOD e MAMAS AND PAPAS!!!!

Vi presentiamo i MUGWUMPS:

ZAL
del LOVIN' SPOONFUL

JIM
del LAMP OF CHILDHOOD

**MAMA CASS
PAPA DENNY**
dei MAMAS AND PAPAS

Uno storico incontro, una storica registrazione, destinata purtroppo a rimanere isolata poiché dopo questo disco il gruppo si sciolse ed ognuno dei singoli componenti prese una strada diversa alla ricerca di nuovi suoni, nuove canzoni, nuovi modi di esprimersi ed affermarsi. Ma di questo eccezionale incontro è rimasta viva testimonianza in questo disco, che senza ombra di dubbio può essere considerato uno dei più validi e nuovi nel campo del «BEAT SOUND» americano.

**SEARCHIN'
HERE IT IS ANOTHER DAY**

DISTRIBUZIONE MESSAGGERIE MUSICALI - MILANO - ROMA

Stampato in Italia su licenza Warner Bros Records, U.S.A. da Compagnia Generale del Disco - Milano

THE MUGWUMPS—
Warner Bros. WS 1697.
The name of the group will not be familiar, although its members will. The success of this album will not result in a followup release because the quartet has disbanded. Its members are (were) Zal Yanovsky, late of the Lovin' Spoonful, Jim Hendricks (the Lamp of Childhood) and Cass Elliot and Denny Doherty (a Mama and a Papa). Among the more interesting cuts: "So Fine," "Searchin'."

To further complicate things, and add to the apocryphal qualities of the group, there were some singles issued by a different group named The Mugwumps on the Sidewalk label in 1966 and 1967. This group also had songs on the soundtracks of *Riot on Sunset Strip* and *Mondo Hollywood*. Even more confusing was the fact that one of the songs they recorded was "Jug Band Music," a Lovin' Spoonful tune written by John Sebastian, and another was Donovan's "Season of the Witch," a tune covered by Jim Hendricks' 1966 group The Lamp of Childhood. The layers of obfuscation are myriad.

Veyler Hildebrand, of the "latter" Mugwumps explains that his band came together on the West Coast, with some high school cronies who named themselves without knowing of the 1964 group.[576] Fellow bandmate Vince Melamed recalls, "I was studying for an American History exam, late 1965, and read about the Mugwump Party around 1876 in our US History and loved the name. We were originally the Catalina Happenings formed in '65 as a teen act to represent Catalina Sportswear as the "Youth of 1965" and play shows at Catalina fashion events."[577] After their first records were issued, these Mugwumps received a cease-and-desist letter from Warner Bros. with respect to the name use, and accordingly they adjusted their handle to "The Mugwump Establishment." In a postscript irony, Hildebrand played on tour with John Sebastian a decade later. He and other members of the band went on to play with artists like Kim Carnes, Bobby Womack, and Bonnie Raitt.

"The fragments are precious few," as Stan Cornyn wrote for the back of their posthumous album. The Mugwumps were short lived, but groundbreaking and influential.[578] They embodied the primordial sound of The Mamas & The Papas and The Lovin' Spoonful, but for their own sake they were prochronistic because folk-rock was just not fully hatched.

We Were the Crossroads: The New Journeymen

The folk revival was waning in the summer of 1964. Not only was the musical landscape transforming, but in the wake of the Kennedy assassination, American culture was changing too. The Vietnam war was heating up, the Civil Rights Act was signed, and the World's Fair in New York was a testimonial to mid-century optimism and consumerism with the theme "Peace Through Understanding," dedicated to "Man's Achievement on a Shrinking Globe in an Expanding Universe."

The Tarriers. Marshall
Brickman, center

During this "Last Innocent Year in America," as one author describes it, John Phillips was engineering a new musical entity out of his all-male folk trio, which included his wife Michelle.[579] Rather than scupper the now broken-up Journeymen's schedule for the upcoming year, not to mention its profits, he innovated.

One trade publication reported, "The Journeymen recently took on a new look when one of their male members left the group and was replaced with an attractive girl singer who greatly increased the variety in their repertoire."[580] At the same time that The Mugwumps sprouted and then sputtered in Washington, D.C. and New York, The New Journeymen were hitting campuses nationwide with a "joltingly different" group featuring John's new male-female arrangements.

In the latter part of 1964, The New Journeymen was composed of John and Michelle, along with Marshall Brickman. Brickman had played in The Tarriers, which he calls "one of the first [racially] integrated folk groups," and who, like The Journeymen, were moving around the collegiate and coffeehouse circuit in 1963.

In the magic circle that led to The Mamas & The Papas, the Shadows in Georgetown recurs in almost all of the groups' stories. It was at the Shadows that Brickman and John Phillips had a conversation speculating about being in a group together one day, which augured The Journeymen's new configuration. This discussion most likely happened in mid-July 1963, when The Journeymen followed The Tarriers' two-week engagement at the Shadows with their own fortnight of appearances. "John was very charismatic," Brickman recalls. "He was almost like a salesman. He was very seductive and we hit it off. He was

the guy who talked mostly while everybody tuned up, and I was that guy in The Tarriers. He was also the force behind his group."[581]

Seeds were sown, but both men proceeded with their respective group's itineraries for the better part of a year before this concept germinated. The Tarriers went on hiatus in April 1964 and The Journeymen played their last shows in May.

"Then at some point, after I left The Tarriers, John said he was going to form a new group called The New Journeymen and asked if I would like to join, and I said yes," remembers Brickman, whose genial affect worked well with John and Michelle. Brickman recalls, "Michelle was kind of the best and worst thing that ever happened to John. She drove John a little crazy and he was crazy for her. Back then she was a knockout and…a little wild."[582]

Michelle recalled a financial incentive for John to change the group's makeup too: "I was modeling teenage lingerie. John said 'You can make even more money singing.' I was making $600 a week as long as I was in New York. But what was happening is that I was on the road with John a lot. I was an enormous economic burden to us. His natural conclusion was that I should join the group because there would be more money and less expenses. A very pragmatic man."[583]

Picking up where The Journeymen left off, The New Journeymen began in earnest with their new constitution. "John decided that we had to go somewhere that we could put together an act and develop some songs. So we went out to San Francisco," Brickman remembers. "I remember getting on a plane with a hundred instruments. John and Michelle were already there. We rented a house, a spec house in the hills above Sausalito. We had this kind of regimented summer and that's how we put together our act." Brickman's memory is that the house was austerely furnished with some "silverware and beds." The Spartan existence did not stop with their setting. "John was like a drill sergeant. He got us up in the morning. We did the Royal Canadian Air Force exercises and then each of us had a training session with a vocal coach named Judy Davis."[584] Michelle backs up that memory: "None of us could sing. I was studying with Judy Davis in San Francisco and Bert Block in New York, depending on where we were.[585]

Davis was "a legend" as Brickman puts it.[586] *The New York Times* concurs, having called her "The Stars' Vocal Coach" in her 2001 obituary.[587] Davis had trained Judy Garland, Frank Sinatra, and Barbra Streisand, and her skill and point of emphasis was in vocal projection and breathing, as well as enunciation and strengthening a singer's vocal cords. She is quoted as having said, "I'm just a vocal plumber. I fix pipes."[588] Both Marshall and Michelle recall driving over the Oakland Bay Bridge to Davis's for their vocal sessions. "Michelle could hardly sing and I could hardly sing," acknowledges Brickman. "She was not a trained singer, but not many members of the folk groups were trained singers." With Davis's expertise and some coaching by John as well, Brickman affirms, "Michelle did sing solos. I took the middle parts so I could hide behind whoever was doing the lead."[589] In addition to the more familiar folk fare, John incorporated songs from Michelle's Mexican childhood to the repertoire. "I was singing 'Guantanamera,'" Michelle recalls. "It was nice to throw that into the set because I am fluent in Spanish."[590]

By summer's end, the trio had taken shape and "through John's good offices," Brickman relates, "his agent got us booked into a bunch of venues around the country."[591] One final detail The New Journeymen had to address was Brickman's draft status. To remedy the situation, Michelle's sister Russell Gilliam's assistance was requested. At this time, married men were exempt from the draft. Just as Cass Elliot had married Jim Hendricks to shield him from being drafted, Russell became Mrs. Marshall Brickman on August 26, 1964. One year later to the day, by executive order, marriages no longer served as a draft exemption and such sham marriages disappeared.

Marriage Certificate of Marshall Brickman and Russell Gilliam, Michelle Phillips' sister.

"They Were Very Mellow"

The new group played a healthy amount of college campuses, as well as clubs. Many were return or similar locations to those that The Journeymen had played over the previous three years. The New Journeymen's first public performance was at East Carolina University in early September, fittingly, as part of the college's Freshman Orientation. "That's the first time I was ever on stage in my life," remembers Michelle.[592] After a "battle with the bugs and stadium lights" they inaugurated a new portable stage in the outdoor stadium with a fast paced program. Brickman took the honors of interweaving anecdotes between songs like "Jesus Met a Woman," "Glorious Kingdom," and a singalong to "Whistling Gypsy Rover."[593]

The fall continued with a steady schedule. Playing with jazz acts like Count Basie and The Oscar Peterson Trio, the group was clearly hitting a more sophisticated stride. With over twenty documented performances, The New Journeymen were not just an ad hoc assemblage. At the *Folk and Jazz Wing Ding* at La Crosse State University, an article described the trio: "The New Journeymen is composed of two composers and a former television model who prefers to sing." The piece continued, "The New Journeymen claims to be the only folk group that does its own arrangements and features old songs seldom heard and new songs." Of Michelle, it particularly noted that the "former model for television commercials has contributed to the repertoire songs she learned in Mexico where she spent five years of her childhood."[594]

FORD CARavan of Music

PRESENTS

the lively ones

oscar peterson TRIO

CPC Presents: Dad's Day Concert

saturday, november 14

8 p.m., iowa memorial union

Tickets Now on Sale at the Union, Iowa City

the new journeymen

New Journeymen Set At Troy With Basie

The New Journeymen will appear with Count Basie, Beverly Wright and Lou Nelson Sept. 19 at Hobart arena in Troy.

The singing trio has appeared on television's Hootenanny four times in six months, with Johnny Carson twice, Steve Allen twice and will be seen with Dinah Shore soon.

But "the folk scene [was] like deathsville," as Roy Silver, manager of The Mugwumps, put it at the time. Despite this demise, Silver astutely discerned, "The good acts will last, of course, and it's good for the field that some of the no talents are falling away."[595] The New Journeymen were among the survivors. Venues, especially coffeehouses, Silver also observed, were drying up: "There just aren't enough worthwhile showcases left."[596] This may be why most of The New Journeymen's concerts were at colleges. Marshall Brickman points out another advantage to the primarily collegiate set: "Back then, the saying among folk groups was 'College audiences were the best. They were so discriminating.' The fact is they were not discriminating. They loved everything, which was great for us. There was not hard criticism."[597] Along with their college gigs, he believes The New Journeymen recorded some commercial jingles, or background singing for ads.

Brickman paints a picture of his experience being on the road and performing with Mr. and Mrs. Phillips: "We would get to a place, say Cleveland or whatever, and I have a degree in music from the University of Wisconsin, so I was heavily into writing charts." With his musical abilities, Brickman busied himself bolstering the group's material. "Wherever we went, we would try and hire a local bass player to fill out the sound and that bass player would work better if the guy had a chart in front of him of what we were doing." This was a solitary effort. "John and Michelle—neither of them could write the music. I would stay at the motel and be writing out bass charts for the performance. Meanwhile, John and Michelle would go out and they'd buy motor scooters and ride around the countryside and come back in time for the performance." A half-century later, Brickman recalls the state of affairs matter-of-factly with no bitterness. "They were very cool. Never uptight at all. They were very 'mellow' was the word at the time. I was trying to hold the thing together with scotch tape but when we got on stage it seemed to be OK. Once on stage, we really pulled it together."[598]

NEW JOURNEYMEN CONCERT TO FOLLOW PARENTS' DAY REGULAR ACTIVITIES

THE NEW JOURNEYMEN

Pair Becomes Trio

There was one happening Brickman recalls, however, that illustrates why, in due course, he moved on from The New Journeymen. "We did have a gig in one of the Carolinas, on campus, in a football stadium to like 12,000 people. John and Michelle had a little tiny apartment in the Village and I was living on the Upper East Side. We were supposed to meet at LaGuardia and take the flight. I got to the airport, and they weren't there. And we had a concert that night, so I called them and woke them up. And I got on the plane for some reason. But I don't believe I did anything solo. I explained when I got there that I couldn't have gotten on and done something by myself."[599]

Brickman says "this sort of informed a little bit" of the experience and his limited time with the trio. "The whole thing was enclosed in a nice haze. They were heavily into the drugs. It wasn't hard drugs, but a lot of grass. Being an obedient Jewish kid from Brooklyn, I stayed away from that as much as I could."[600]

In December Brickman decided to leave. He did so amicably, saying later, "It was too crazy. Too much missing sessions. Too many drugs. It was like a ride on The Wild Mouse: a ride on Coney Island where you get spun around." Yet his loss of drive went deeper than those reasons. "After I left John and Michelle, I was walking along West 57th Street and there was a storefront that had a mirror on the front of it, but it was one of these wavy mirrors that you would see at a carnival, that distorts you. I was carrying three or four instruments because at that time in my life I was doing recording gigs around New York. Folk music was popular for advertising stuff like beer and cars for upwardly mobile young audiences. They wanted to be hip and cool, and they would always try to get folk music behind their pitches and jingles." That's when Brickman had an epiphany. "I looked in this mirror and saw myself carrying these instruments and I looked like a circus geek. I said to myself, 'Did my father escape from Poland in 1922 so that I should wind up playing 'Michael Row the Boat Ashore?' I really made a decision to stop and I was out of folk music forever."[601] Brickman moved on to work as a writer for *The Tonight Show* and *Candid Camera*, eventually earning an Academy Award for Best Screenplay with Woody Allen for the film *Annie Hall*.

Deviled Egg Madness

As John and Michelle planned for a Christmastime engagement, in which they would share the program with Bill Cosby at the Shoreham Hotel in Washington, they needed to fill Brickman's shoes quickly. They had heard that a friend from the previous year's *Hootenanny USA* tour was looking for work. Michelle recalls, "We put the jungle drums out in the Village to try to find Denny Doherty because we knew he was a terrific tenor and if he was out of a job, maybe we could snag him. And that's exactly what happened. We were looking for Denny Doherty and a few days later he called us."[602] As Cass said, "The Mugwumps were hungry. We cleaned Denny up and sent him over to John. He got the job and supported us."[603] Jim Hendricks similarly recalled, "Denny and Cass had no idea what they were doing."[604] According to Denny, "I took the gig because the rest of The Mugwumps were over at the Albert Hotel broke and owing."[605] That propitious dispatch resulted in the new version of John and Michelle's trio.

Denny recalled the madcap method by which he was brought up to speed to learn The New Journeymen's repertoire: "I went over to John and Michelle's apartment and John said, 'Here, take these. We're going to rehearse.' Something called Eskatrol—a diet pill. John was very friendly with the chemist on the corner. We had to come up with twenty-eight pieces of material I had to learn in two days. I gobbled fistfuls of the prescription amphetamines from John's medicine bag, and rehearsed for seventy-two hours straight." Hysterically mimicking a bid caller, he boasted, "I could have led an auction after that."[606] As Michelle described him at the time, Denny was "really too much. He's a very funny, intelligent guy and a gas to work with."[607]

The three fulfilled the commitment at the Shoreham and there were at least a half-dozen other dates that had been scheduled based on the near four-year head of steam of The Journeymen. "They had a lot of bookings," was Denny's memory. "It was money to be gone and picked up—do the performances and finish the gigs."[608] According to Michelle back then, "We do college concerts all over the country," claiming the group was booked throughout the spring.[609] Along with Doherty's mellifluous leads, The New Journeymen

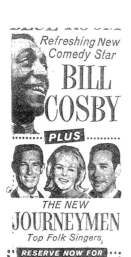

showcased Michelle's dulcet voice, and a new sound emerged. She remembered, "All of a sudden my seemingly very light soprano had a place in the group, with Denny's tenor and John's baritone."[610] This blend is clearly heard in the group's 1965 version of Bob Dylan's "Mr. Tambourine Man" on a recorded radio program, which coincided with The Byrds' groundbreaking rendition. On the same radio show, in Tom Paxton's "Last Thing on My Mind," Denny soars above John and Michelle in a breathtaking harmony arrangement that verges toward the soon-to-come arrangements of The Mamas & The Papas.

With the absence of Brickman's musical chops, John beefed up the group's mix. Eric Hord, who knew John, and Denny from when he had accompanied The Halifax Three, wrote chords for The New Journeymen and played with them too. Hord's widow described the call from John: "Hey man, what's happening? Would you dig coming back here and playing with Mich, myself, and Dennis? We'll be the New Journeymen. We have club and concert dates already booked."[611]

John and Michelle lived with "Maude," their beloved pet poodle, in what Michelle described as "a six room apartment in the East Village with fireplaces in the bedroom and the dining room, dark hardwood floors, kitchen, et cetera. A beautiful place."[612] Michelle was working on her musical skills too. She took guitar lessons from Artie Traum and continued her vocal lessons with Bert Knapp, who she considered "the greatest vocal coach

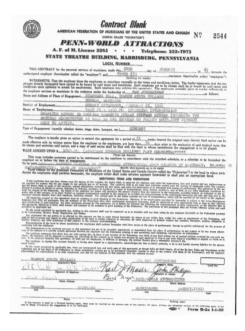

in the city." She wrote to a friend at the time, "John and I have been writing some songs together."[613] It was at this time that John penned, or submitted the copyright for "Me and My Uncle," a longstanding standard first sung by Judy Collins and taken-up perpetually by The Grateful Dead.[614] "John wrote tons of good songs and lyrics, but his chords were never good," relates Molly Hord. It was Eric who would "sit up with him night after night and go through chord charts of various tunes. 'How do you make this chord? How do you make this note? What's the fingering on this position?' Eric was a right-hand man, consultant, and mixer of the drinks."[615]

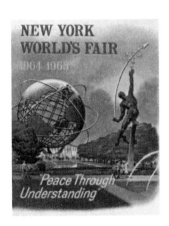

Drinks were not the only thing in the mix. LSD was still legal in early 1965. At the Phillips' apartment about this time, a now fairly famous rendezvous took place between John, Michelle, Denny and his old friend Cass Elliot, when the four future Mamas and Papas dropped acid together. Michelle considers it a milestone because she took LSD for the first time and met Cass on the same night. "We kept hearing about this 'Capse' ['Cass' in Mugwump language] from Denny because he was always on the phone with her. I had never seen her before, and I did now know what she looked like." Nonplussed with the new drug up to this point, Michelle describes opening the door to the astonishing vision of Cass with flip hair, long lashes, pink angora sweater, white pleated skirt and white go-go boots just as the sugar cube laced with LSD kicked in. As the sight of Cass and the acid high converged, Michelle recalls thinking "Wow! This is an amazing drug." For her, that night was the true point of origin of The Mamas & The Papas.

Hord recalled another night with The New Journeymen needing a break from rehearsing and all of them taking LSD, after which, "Suggesting complete madness, John said 'Let's go to the World's Fair.'"[616] Scott McKenzie was working in the RCA pavilion, demonstrating how television images were put together for home viewers. Hord continued, "Everybody got into the car. I was in a small Volkswagen with no room to spare. They pulled out of Eastside Drive at sixty miles an hour, past the U.N. building, and on to the fair, which was just closing." The RCA pavilion with 250 color TV sets was quite the spot for the "deviled egg madness," Hord and the others began to sense[617] from the LSD. Reminded of the trip, Michelle laughs: "I remember it. We were all on acid, but other than that I have never remembered why we were at the World's Fair." These offbeat larks would become almost phantasmagorical once The Mamas & The Papas materialized. Characterizing the circus-like culture that developed, Denny exclaimed, "It was carny!"[618]

In another longer lasting adventure, the trio went to the U.S. Virgin Islands with Hord and a few other friends and stayed for ten days at the Grand Hotel. Whetting their appetite for a longer stay, the group returned home resolving to soon return.

With Denny, The New Journeymen not only continued to perform but they also recorded. They appeared on Oscar Brand's radio show *The World of Folk Music*. In March, Michelle

wrote to a friend, "We'll be recording our first album next month," which seems to have been aspirational.[619] They made two television appearances on the Canadian show *Let's Sing Out*, a program not unlike *Hootenanny* in the United States, in that it was filmed at a university and involved multiple performers, in their case Jesse Colin Young, Bob Carey, and The Travelers. With her blonde hair prettily coiffed in a beehive bun atop lengthy locks, the camera hovered on Michelle's stunning beauty as she performed with John and Denny in a sleeveless dress. Michelle points out, "If you look very closely at this performance, and don't blink, you'll see Marshall Brickman playing guitar behind us. It's really funny and it's unmistakably him. He was doing us a big favor because we needed another guitar which we didn't have."[620]

There was one other element the burgeoning trio was missing. Amidst the intricacies of John's harmonic arrangements, these recordings present a first-time glimpse of the embryonic Mamas & Papas sound, of John, Michelle and Denny, sans electricity and the powerhouse of Cass's voice.

Cass had remained in the D.C. and New York music scenes after The Mugwumps. "I was down in Washington, D.C., working as a single and working as a secretary in the daytime in the club that I was singing in."[621] "She did a jazz thing," Jim Hendricks remembers. "Somebody playing piano and she was singing jazz."[622] Bob Cavallo remembers, "I broke up The Mugwumps with Roy Silver. John Sebastian was my guy. I took The [Lovin'] Spoonful, and Roy kept Bill Cosby. As I was helping to break in the Spoonful, I thought I had a good idea. And it was Cass's idea too. The idea was [for her] to do the Great American Songbook with a jazz emphasis. So I got a really good group of musicians together."[623] A friend at the time also recalls, "[Cass] was singing sort of swing, blues and show stuff at the Shadows with Martin Segal on piano and there was a bass and even drums perhaps.[624] This was her arrangement at the Shadows, where some remember her dynamic song styling as late as June 1965, but Cass was keeping her foot in the door in the New York scene too.

Erik Jacobsen also recalls her efforts to that end in New York: "Bob Cavallo was managing Cass and saw her as a stand-up chanteuse. I went uptown with her several times to her vocal lessons with a famous vocal coach. I remember the walls there being covered with mirrors."[625] Indeed, Cavallo worked to get Cass an important engagement at Bon Soir—the toniest, most sophisticated supper club in Greenwich Village—which had launched the likes of Barbra Streisand and Kaye Ballard. But stage fright got the best of Cass on her opening night. Cavallo recalls, "The rehearsals were good but she was definitely afraid. She cut it short and walked off the stage."[626] As Jacobsen put it, "That career direction faltered after a few gigs."[627]

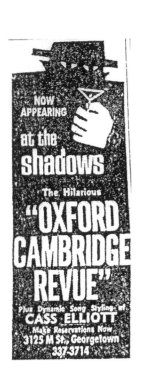

Sometime that spring—around the same time that her former fellow Mugwumps, Zal Yanovsky and John Sebastian recorded "Do You Believe in Magic" in their new incarnation as The Lovin' Spoonful—Cass recorded Sebastian's composition "Didn't Want to Have To Do It" with Alan Lorber at the recording helm and Sebastian on autoharp. The hauntingly beautiful performance is an interesting post-Mugwump timepiece, because it is contemporary and not the standard-type work she was doing at the time.

The New Journeymen's live appearances dropped precipitously in 1965. In April they replaced The Kingsmen on a last minute basis at Hartwick College as they "had just received a club cancellation." They played to over 1000 and were praised for their "amazingly fine blend of musicianship."[628] Yet other reviews grew in criticism of their lack of timeliness, and performances that were increasingly off.

Their last documented appearance was at Firestone High School in Akron, Ohio in mid-May. They were favorably received and one alumnus remembers that the group had been told they could use the boys locker room to prepare for the concert. The track team was dressing out for an out-of-town meet which meant, "It was quite a surprise when Michelle walked in."[629] Another attendee, Jeff Foust, recalled, "Once they arrived they were incredibly open, relaxed, ready to share of themselves, as well as willing to help us in any way they could." During their break between sets Foust and his mother drove in a convertible with The New Journeymen through a shopping center "trying to drum up business" and giving out publicity fliers as the concert was a fundraiser. "Despite not generating much money, the time with John, Michelle and Denny was an incredible gift and life experience. It turned out to be a very intimate personal experience with amazing people."[630] Foust remembers the group talking about taking a break and heading to the Caribbean.

What was probably one of the final endeavors of The New Journeymen was an unusual one. In 2019 a May 1965 newspaper article was discovered that indicated John Phillips had written a song for the Zionist labor organization Pioneer Women (now called NA'AMAT) called "Showing the Way." A nationwide search began to see if this effort had been recorded by Pioneer Women. A copy of not just the recording, but an accompanying film for which the song was written, was found. There is footage of various scenes in Israel, as well as of The New Journeymen singing about the work of the Pioneer Women. John, Michelle, and Denny are in fine vocal form but appear a bit rawboned. Each singer sings different lines in the unusual tune and the three harmonize as well. "Showing the Way" is indubitably John's, and it may be his most overtly political work with some of the most sociological lyrics he ever composed, such as: *Israel, built of dreams and prayers, Women half a million strong.*[631] Denny once said of John's songwriting capabilities, "God did a dance around his cradle," and his deftness with such an esoteric subject bears this out.[632] One can imagine local Pioneer Women chapters projecting and presenting the film at meetings in multiple locations, and the

satisfaction brought by hearing this "au courant" folk group sing about their work. When she watched the film after its uncovering, Michelle recalled it well. "The agency called John: 'Listen, you want to make some extra money and do a commercial?' It was like what The Journeymen had done with Armstrong Tile and Schlitz Beer."

"Showing the Way" is most likely the last recording of The New Journeymen before they became The Mamas & The Papas. It is a fitting valediction to the story of The New Journeymen as pioneers themselves, into the new sphere of folk rock.

In spring 1965, Michelle claimed "in July we're all going to Mexico City."[633] That plan was amended to another southerly destination: the Virgin Islands. It was here that The New Journeymen informally added a fourth member—Cass Elliot—and the primordial sound of The Mamas & The Papas began to meld.

"We were the crossroads, the intersection between being folkie and hip," Marshall Brickman says of The New Journeymen's legacy.[634] Their end came quickly. As late as July 1965, Capitol Records was quoted as "betting" the group would be "smart talk on campus" in the upcoming fall semester.[635] Curiously, they were even listed in an end-of-the-year directory as Capitol artists that also included a new group on Dunhill Records named The Mamas & The Papas.[636] The times could not keep up with the changes happening. For a short-lived group that recorded very little, The New Journeymen were the final junction on the road to The Mamas & The Papas.

Epilogue

Several weeks after Michelle, John and Denny performed their last engagement as a trio, they found themselves wandering along a beach with Cass Elliot, "into the exotic beauty of St. John's Caneel Bay" in the Virgin Islands. As Michelle recalls it 55 years later: "We made bonfires on the beach at sunset, wrote love songs, and sang to John's sweet guitar."[637]

Rather poetically, a new fire started just as the sun set on their preceding journeys. When these four individuals came together in song and friendship, they created a paradisiacal vocal sound unlike any other. The Mamas & The Papas first fully converged and coalesced personally and vocally in that summer of 1965. Their sound was breathtaking and groundbreaking, as their future producer Lou Adler fittingly said, "if you could believe your eyes and ears." They began a journey as a group that typified American folk rock.

When that flame ignited, the sun set on the horizon of a huge body of music performed during the previous seven or eight years. From the floor shows of The Smoothies, to the college crowds of The Journeymen, to the humor-laden Canadian harmonies of The Halifax Three, to the bold, sexually integrated sounds of The Big 3, to the offbeat unconventionality of The Mugwumps, and the tamer but mixed vocal sound of The New Journeymen, there was a gloaming twilight on all those little combinations that kindled into the Fantastic Four.

Ground was tilled when a young songwriter first led a vocal quartet into Decca records in the 1950s. When a Canadian teenager stood up on a dare to sing a Pat Boone song, the mic dropped with reverberating echoes into the United States. Seeds were sown as thousands of college students across the country heard the harmonies of intricate, beautiful arrangements performed by a folk trio. Boundaries were broken when the fat girl, who people were tempted to dismiss "until they heard her sing," won critics and crowds over in Manhattan and the Midwest. And a ball started rolling when the young beautiful model suddenly became a marital and vocal partner with a gifted songwriter. All these years and all these happenings were part of what made The Mamas & The Papas a "fixture" in American music, as Cass characterized them.[638]

"When it's all over," Cass boasted in 1967, "we're the ones who will have the legend."[639] The Mamas & The Papas legend is full of personal triumphs, heartbreaks, and stories of California dreamin' and coming to the canyon. The lore of this group from 1965 to 1968 is a story in itself. Yet, part of the legend that belongs to The Mamas & The Papas, as one of those folk groups sang, "lies in yesterday."[640]

CREEQUE ALLEY

by John and Michelle Phillips,
Annotated and Explicated[641]

Creeque Alley (or Creque's Alley) is an alcove on St. Thomas in the U.S. Virgin Islands once frequented by pirates. In 1965, the alley was home to Duffy's, a club where Cass, John, Michelle, and Denny first truly sang together publicly. The proper Americanized pronunciation is "creaky."

John and Mitchie were gettin' kinda itchie
Just to leave the folk music behind

John and Michelle Phillips were attuned to the demise of the American Folk Revival. John had played in it constantly from 1961 to 1964 and Michelle had been married to him for over half that time. With the British Invasion, and particularly the arrival of The Beatles, popular music was turning the page, and they were keen to be a part of it.

Zal and Denny workin' for a penny
Tryin' to get a fish on the line

Denny Doherty had played in The Colonials and The Halifax Three, and in the latter group had enlisted the help of Zal Yanovsky, who sometimes made The Halifax Three a foursome. "Fish on the line" is an expression meaning trying to get work and also plays well into the maritime origins of group, as Denny's hometown of Halifax, Nova Scotia is a harbor town on the North Atlantic. These two were also angling to get on with things and go beyond the traditional folk in which they began.

In a coffee house Sebastian sat
And after every number they'd pass the hat

Another peer, John Sebastian, had been playing as a background harmonica for Valentine Pringle, an African American folk singer with a deep baritone voice, who was discovered by and wrote songs for Harry Belafonte. He went on to have an acting career before he was murdered at age 62. Sebastian and Pringle were playing in clubs like the Shadows in Washington and the Village Gate in New York, following an almost identical arc in time and pace as Cass Elliot's group The Big 3, in terms of fame and momentum. The custom in folk clubs was to "pass the hat" or take up a collection for the performers by way of a hat or basket.

McGuinn and McGuire just a gettin' higher
In L.A., you know where that's at

Roger McGuinn was one of the lead members of The Byrds, another of America's cutting edge folk rock groups. He had lived at the Earle Hotel in New York for some of the same time as John and Michelle Phillips. Barry McGuire had sung with The New Christy Minstrels and lived at the Hotel Albert in New York at the same time as Cass and Denny. In mid 1965, both McGuinn and MGuire were in Los Angeles and were ascending the charts with some of the first nationally popular folk rock songs: McGuinn with The Byrds' hit version of "Mr Tambourine Man" and Barry McGuire with "Eve of Destruction. "Getting' higher" may have double or triple entendres. In addition to the "higher" success each man was having in his respective sphere, McGuinn's group was first named The Jet Set in 1964 and changed to The Byrds later that year (both names could connote flying high); and there's the perennial chemical drug insinuation from "higher."

And no one's gettin' fat except Mama Cass

Perhaps because of her size, or perhaps because Cass had a decent amount of success with The Big 3 and her brief solo run, she managed a modicum of success as a single in Washington, D.C. and New York. At this point, while others cast about for the next gig, Cass was landing on her feet more frequently than not.

Zally said Denny, you know there aren't many
Who can sing a song the way that you do,
    let's go south
Denny said Zally, golly, don't you think that I
    wish I could play guitar like you

Once The Halifax Three broke up by the beginning of 1964, Denny Doherty and Zal Yanovsky stuck together. The two headed south from not only Canada, but also New York, and wound up working in a Washington, D.C. beer and pizza establishment named Mac's Pipe & Drum. There they played as part of the "house band" and the symbiosis of the two was palpable, with Zally's guitar playing and Denny's singular voice.

Zal, Denny and Sebastian sat (at the Night Owl)
And after every number they'd pass the hat

After furnishing some marijuana to an unwitting bandmate at Mac's Pipe & Drum, and being threatened by that bandmate's father, Zal and Denny high-tailed it back to New York. In the late spring of 1964 they fooled around with some surf-dance songs made under the names " D & Z" and "The Noise." One song was called "The Slurp" and was not a success. They, along with their pal John Sebastian, found themselves yet again playing hootenanny nights in local coffeehouses, such as the Night Owl, and trying to figure out what came next as the British Invasion hit the music scene hard and other artists started to leave Greenwich Village for California

McGuinn and McGuire still a gettin' higher
In L.A., you know where that's at
And no one's gettin' fat except Mama Cass
When Cass was a sophomore, planned to go to Swarthmore
But she changed her mind one day
Standin' on the turnpike, thumb out to hitchhike
Take me to New York right away

Rhyming scheme aside, Ellen Cohen had some notion (or her family did) to go to medical school. Her family was populated with learned and educated individuals in medicine, law and theology. In fact, as a sophomore at George Washington High School in Alexandria, Virginia (the same high school attended by John Phillips, and later by Jim Morrison of The Doors) she was a member of the Caduceus Club, a sort of pre-med organization named for the physician's symbol. Swarthmore was not the actual likely destination but rather, it has been said, it was Goucher College in Maryland. In the summer of 1959, Cass was bit by the show business bug, taking over a part in a local theater production of *The Boy Friend*, sparking her ambition to go to New York and try her hand on Broadway. She did not hitchhike but drove a Volkswagen. Eventually, she assumed the stage name Cass Elliot, which she first used in a traveling production of *The Music Man* in the summer of 1962.

When Denny met Cass he gave her love bumps
Called John and Zal and that was the Mugwumps

Denny Doherty and Cass Elliot met in the summer of 1963 when Cass's folk group, The Big 3, were regularly appearing at the Bitter End, and Denny's group, The Halifax Three, was in and out of New York as home base for their gigs up and down the East Coast. Cass was immediately smitten with Denny and while the feeling was not exactly mutual, the two developed a fast friendship. When their respective folk groups ran their course, they, along with Zal Yanovsky, Jim Hendricks and sometimes John Sebastian, formed The Mugwumps, what some have called the first American folk rock group, in the summer of 1964.

McGuinn and McGuire couldn't get no higher
But that's what they were aimin' at
And no one's gettin' fat except Mama Cass
Mugwumps, high jumps, low slumps, big bumps
Don't you work as hard as you play
Make up, break up, everything is shake up
Guess it had to be that way

In 1964, The Mugwumps played in Washington, D.C. and New York. In addition to being ahead of their time musically, they were zany and partied like it was already the Summer of Love, often while they played. They showed some real promise, hinting at the trajectories of popular music and the group's members, but despite "making" it on television, opening a concert for The Beach Boys, and issuing a record, they broke up before the year's end.

Sebastian and Zal formed the Spoonful
Michelle, John, and Denny gettin' very tuneful

Out of the breakup of The Mugwumps, Zal Yanovsky and John Sebastian formed The Lovin' Spoonful. Simultaneously, at the end of 1964 and into the first part of 1965, Denny Doherty replaced Marshall Brickman in The New Journeymen, a trio with John and Michelle Phillips which was finishing the last engagements of John's earlier group, The Journeymen.

McGuinn and McGuire just a catchin' fire
In L.A., you know where that's at
And everybody's gettin' fat except Mama Cass

By the summer of 1965, Roger McGuinn and Barry McGuire were new rock stars, livin' large in Los Angeles. Their records were taking flight on the charts "catchin' fire." With The New Journeymen gainfully employed, and Cass on her own but not necessarily making it big, all of the parties involved were "gettin' fat" and making progress, if not success , while Cass remained more static in her singing career.

Broke, busted, disgusted, agents can't be trusted
And Mitchy wants to go to the sea
Cass can't make it, she says we'll have to fake it
We knew she'd come eventually

The New Journeymen had run their course by spring 1965. They had been fulfilling old contract dates, but their sustainability and viability was limited, and ultimately the group was out on their ear because of that. Restless to change musical styles and with an appetite for adventure, the threesome and an entourage of a dozen people including John's five-year old daughter Mackenzie and the French poodle Maude, traveled to the Virgin Islands. The story goes that Michelle Phillips was blindfolded and "landed" on this location on a map, of any place in the world, to go. With dogs and motorcycles in tow, they also took camping equipment. Michelle recalls Cass arriving a few weeks after the rest of the group. "We saw an indecipherable dot on the beach moving closer." When Denny realized it was Cass he leapt up, ran to her, and they hugged and squealed and fell on the sand in mirth. While this group all bought one-way tickets to St. Thomas,

Cass Elliot had the foresight to buy a roundtrip ticket and joined them after they arrived.

Greasin' on American Express cards
Tent's low rent, but keeping out the heat's hard
Duffy's good vibrations and our imaginations
Can't go on indefinitely

The Virgin Islands party was living on The Journeymen's American Express credit card. "Greasin'" refers to cheating or accomplishing something in a non-standard, usually underhanded way. Migrating to the smaller island of St. John, they set up camp in the National Park there, but as the last campers to arrive, their location was far from paradise. In fact, they were next to a mosquito bog and nicknamed their encampment Camp Torture. Quickly, it was decided to return to St. Thomas, the main island, where they landed a job as the house band at Duffy's, a bar on Creques Alley where the group sang country, folk, pop, and surf tunes like The Ventures' "Walk, Don't Run," and the Everly Brothers' "Like Strangers" as they figured out their new musical direction. While the other three musicians played onstage, Cass was waiting tables at Duffy's, harmonizing with them from the restaurant floor.

And California dreamin' is becomin' a reality

After their brief stint at Duffy's, The New (Fangled) Journeymen were beginning to fatigue. There is one account of the son of a government official on the island getting a little too mixed up in the partying, and the group being issued an ultimatum to leave the island. Moreover, the financial underpinnings of The Journeymen's credit card was also beginning to deteriorate. As the group started looking homeward they faced the quandary of having only bought one way tickets (except for Cass). Eventually they made their way back to New York, but California was the desired destination. When they returned to Greenwich Village their impression was that everyone had gone to the West Coast. John, Michelle, and Denny drove a rental car across the country, arriving in L.A. during the Watts Riots of August 1965. Cass was already there. Starting as The Magic Circle, the four quickly became The Mamas & The Papas, and their California Dream was actualized.

Notes

1   The Big 3. Come Away Melinda, 1963.

2   Gilliland, John, and John Phillips. Pop Chronicles Interviews #91 - John Phillips. Pop Chronicles. Bel Air, California, May 8, 1968. https://digital.library.unt.edu/ark:/67531/metadc1692060/.

3   Gilliland, Pop Chronicles.

4   Elliot, Cass. "Audience Rap." Don't Call Me Mama Anymore. Mister Kellys, Chicago, Illinois, 1973.

5   Gilliland, Pop Chronicles.

6   Elliot, Cass. "Interview with Mama Cass." Promotional Disc Jockey Record Issued with White Label Promotional Versions of A Gathering of Flowers, 1970.

7   Surratt, Paul. Unpublished Video Interview with John Phillips, April 26, 1986. Private Collection of Author.

8   Phillips, John. "How I Write Songs." Hit Parader, January 1967.

9   Gabbard, Krin. Jammin' at the Margins: Jazz and the American Cinema. University of Chicago Press, 1996.

10 Gilliland, Pop Chronicles.

11 Whelan, Barbara Nutwell. Private Interview with Author, 2009.

12 Phillips, "How I Write Songs."

13 Johnson, L.A. Interview with John Phillips and Scott McKenzie. Forrest Gump: Music, Artists & Times. CD-ROM, 1995.

14 Johnson, Forrest Gump: Music, Artists & Times.

15 Surratt, Interview with John Phillips.

16 Boran, Michael. Private Interview with Author, 1998.

17 Whelan to Author, 2009.

18 Boran to Author, 1998.

19 Johnson, Forrest Gump: Music, Artists & Times.

20 Boran to Author, 1998.

21 Boran to Author, 1998.

22 Wiest, Molly and Jack Kugell. Private Interview with Joel Wiest and George Wilkins.

23 McKenzie, Scott. Private Interview with Author, 1998.

24 Boran, Christine. Private Interview with Jean Wyss.

25 Johnson, Forrest Gump: Music, Artists & Times.

26 Surratt, Interview with John Phillips.

27 Phillips, John Edmund Andrew. "Golden Hair," as part of "Songs for Jeff; no. 1-4." Unpublished work, Library of Congress, 1959.

28 Boran to Author, 1998.

29 Straight Shooter: The Mamas and The Papas. VHS. Hallway Productions/Rhino Video, 1989.

30 Straight Shooter: The Mamas and The Papas.

31 Boran, Mike, Bill Cleary and Scott McKenzie. Online Discussion, 2010. https://www.facebook.com/groups/johneaphillips/posts/10150120054373039/?mibextid=6NoCDW

32 Surratt, Interview with John Phillips.

33 Detroit Free Press, December 1, 1959, Detroit Free Press, December 15, 1959. The Windsor Star, December 12, 1959.

34 Eagle, Jack, Frank Mann, and John Phillips. "Ring A Ding Ding," Unpublished work, Library of Congress, 1961.

35 McKenzie, Scott, Bill Cleary and Mike Boran. Online Discussion, 2010. https://www.facebook.com/groups/johneaphillips/posts/10150120054373039/?mibextid=6NoCDW

36 Cleary, Bill and Scott McKenzie. Online Discussion, 2010. https://www.facebook.com/groups/johneaphillips/posts/10150120054373039/?mibextid=6NoCDW

37 Phillips, "How I Write Songs."

38 Detroit Free Press, December 20, 1960.

39 Bacas, Harry. "Top Tunes." The Sunday Star, June 9, 1960.

40 McKenzie, Scott. Online Discussion, 2010. https://www.facebook.com/groups/johneaphillips/posts/10150120054373039/?mibextid=6NoCDW

41 Bacas, "Top Tunes."

42 Boran to Author, 1998.

43 "Singin' Sweet and Smooth - The Smoothies." Hit Parader, January 1961.

44 Surratt, Interview with John Phillips.

45 Boran to Author, 1998.

46 Johnson, Forrest Gump: Music, Artists & Times.

47 Rose, Tim. Private Interview with Author, 1998.

48 Boran to Author, 1998.

49 Phillips, Johnny. "Ride, Ride, Ride." Northern Music Corp, 1960.

50 McKenzie, Scott. Online Discussion, 2010. https://www.facebook.com/groups/johneaphillips/posts/10150120054373039/?mibextid=6NoCDW

51 Phillips, Johnny. "Softly" Northern Music Corp, 1960.
52 Bacas, "Top Tunes."
53 Bacas, "Top Tunes."
54 Cash Box, June 18, 1960.
55 Billboard, October 17, 1960.
56 Boran to Author, 1998.
57 Johnson, Forrest Gump: Music, Artists & Times.
58 Johnson, Forrest Gump: Music, Artists & Times.
59 "Sing Along with John, Scott and Dick." The Dalhousie Gazette, February 13, 1963.
60 "Sing Along with John, Scott and Dick."
61 Johnson, Forrest Gump: Music, Artists & Times.
62 Surratt, Interview with John Phillips.
63 "Sing Along with John, Scott and Dick."
64 The State Journal, December 8, 1960.
65 Boran to Author.
66 Johnson, Forrest Gump: Music, Artists & Times.
67 Brand, Oscar. Private Interview with Author, 2003.
68 Johnson, Forrest Gump: Music, Artists & Times.
69 Gilliland, Pop Chronicles.
70 Surratt, Interview with John Phillips.
71 Weissman to Author, 1998.
72 McKenzie to Author, 1998.
73 Weissman, Dick. Private Interview with Author, 2003.
74 Weissman to Author, 2003.
75 Johnson, Forrest Gump: Music, Artists & Times.
76 Penton, Edgar. "'Hootenanny' Spotlights U.S. Folk Music." The Post Crescent, March 31, 1963.
77 "Hootenanny." The Record, March 19, 1960.
78 Seidenbaum, Art. "Who Gives a Hootenanny." The Los Angeles Times, September 1, 1963
79 "Hootenanny Set at Valley College." The San Bernardino Valley Sun, October 15, 1963.
80 Nelson, Bob. "Seattle Folksingers: Those Who Led the Way: Don Firth." Pacific Northwest Folklore Society. http://pnwfolklore.org/SeattleFolksingers-ThoseWhoLedTheWay-DonFirth.html.
81 Weissman to Author, 1998.
82 Johnson, Forrest Gump: Music, Artists & Times.
83 The Ottawa Citizen, June 3, 1961.
84 Costello, Ed. "Kingston Trio Shadow Fine." The Spokesman-Review, November 16, 1961.
85 Weissman to Author, 2003.
86 Weissman to Author, 1998
87 Surratt, Interview with John Phillips.
88 Weissman to Author, 2003.
89 "Curious Song." Chess.com. https://www.chess.com/forum/view/off-topic/curious-song.
90 Surratt, Interview with John Phillips.
91 Pearce, Lewis. "So You Like the Brothers Four?" Stillwater News-Press, November 19, 1961.
92 Wedman, Les. "TV - The Glass Eye." The Vancouver Sun, May 29, 1961.
93 The San Francisco Examiner, July 9, 1961.
94 Richmond, Dick. "It's All Happening At Once For Michelle." St. Louis Post-Dispatch, November 28, 1977.
95 Here I Am: Denny Doherty and The Mamas & The Papas. Bravo TV (Canada), 2010.
96 Straight Shooter: The Mamas and The Papas.
97 Young, Patrick. "Journeymen Combine Humor and Harmony." Linton Daily Citizen, January 29, 1962.
98 Cash Box, September 23, 1961.
99 Odell, Rod. "Record Review." The Herald News, September 20, 1961.
100 Billboard, September 18, 1961.
101 Weissman to Author, 2003.
102 "The Journeymen Are On Their Way." Capitol Records Promotional Brochure, 1961.
103 The Journeymen. Coming Attraction - Live! 1961.
104 "Their 'Sound of Music' Most Enthusiastic." Latrobe Bulletin, January 18, 1963.
105 "The Journeymen Are On Their Way."
106 Cash Box, January 6, 1962.
107 Arganbright, Frank. "Listening on Records." Journal and Courier, February 10, 1962.
108 Odell, "Record Review."
109 Weissman to Author, 2003.
110 "German Club Reports Concert a Success." Hampden-Sydney Tiger, March 9, 1962.
111 "Delhi Tech Hears Journeymen." The Oracle, December 11, 1963.
112 "Hootenanny Set at Valley College."
113 Weissman to Author, 2003.
114 Weissman to Author, 2003.

115 Weissman to Author, 2003.
116 Lambert, Philip. To Broadway, to Life!: The Musical Theater of

Bock and Harnick. Oxford University Press, 2010.

117 Lambert, To Broadway, to Life!

118 Harnick, Sheldon. Letter to Author, October 1, 2003.

119 Harnick, Letter to Author.

120 Smith, Charles L. "Folksinging is Praised." Daily Reveille, April 1964.

121 Private Recording of Concert at West Virginia University, May 9, 1964.

122 "Campus Enjoys Spring Finals In Spite of Fickle Weather." The Flat Hat, May 17, 1963.

123 Markunas, Christine. "Journeymen Exhibit More Enthusiasm Than Talent." Old Gold and Black, September 30, 1963.

124 West, Hedy. Private Interview with Author, 2003.

125 Johnson, Forrest Gump: Music, Artists & Times.

126 Weissman to Author, 2003.

127 Haskew, Jerry. Private Interviews with Author, 2003, 2022.

128 Yon, Jim. "The Journeymen." Smoke Signals, Fall 1962.

129 Billboard, September 15, 1962.

130 Cash Box, September 22, 1962.

131 McCord, Merrill. "Vocal Groups Grind Out New Discs." Louisville Courier Herald, September 30, 1962.

132 Pollock, Barry. "12 Points Discussed." The Eagle, December 7, 1962.

133 Laffler, William. "Turntable Topics." The Fresno Bee, May 27, 1962.

134 Cash Box, April 14, 1962.

135 Billboard, September 1, 1962.

136 Weissman to Author, 2003.

137 Phillips, Michelle. Letters to Sue Lyon, February 8, 1963, March 3, 1965.

138 Phillips, Letters to Sue Lyon.

139 Surratt, Interview with John Phillips.

140 Lomax, Alan. "The Folkniks and the Songs I Sing." Sing Out, 1959.

141 Denny Doherty. Dream A Little Dream, 1999.

142 Surratt, Interview with John Phillips.

143 Johnson, Forrest Gump: Music, Artists & Times.

144 "Their 'Sound of Music' Most Enthusiastic." Latrobe Bulletin.

145 Surratt, Interview with John Phillips.

146 Weissman to Author, 2003.

147 Cash Box, March 30, 1963.

148 Private Recording of Concert at West Virginia University, May 9, 1964.

149 Weissman, to Author, 2003.

150 Weissman to Author, 2003.

151 McKenzie, Scott. Online Discussion, 2010. https://www.facebook.com/groups/johneaphillips/posts/10150120054373039/?mibextid=6NoCDW

152 Markunas, "Journeymen Exhibit More Enthusiasm Than Talent."

153 Lamb, Bob. "Folk Singer Borrows Pair of Pants So That Show Can Be Held at Mercer." The Macon News, October 12, 1963.

154 Billboard, August 24, 1963.

155 Cash Box, September 28, 1963.

156 Weissman to Author, 2003.

157 Phillips, Michelle. Private Interview with Author, 2002.

158 "TV Plug Cited." Intelligencer Journal, May 28, 1965.

159 Arganbright, Frank. "Listening on Records." Journal and Courier, October 26, 1963.

160 Campbell, Mary. "Records." The Sumter Daily Item, September 9, 1963.

161 "Promo Journey for Journeymen." Cash Box, October 12, 1963.

162 Surratt, Interview with John Phillips.

163 Powers, Chuck. "Folksinger's Blues, I Gotta Be Travelin' On." Kansas State Collegian, November 22, 1963.

164 "Hootenanny is All American Entertainment." The Daily Iberian, November 17, 1963.

165 "Hootenanny in Lafayette November 19." The Daily Iberian, November 5, 1963.

166 Powers, "Folksinger's Blues, I Gotta Be Travelin' On."

167 LaCroix, Patrick. Private Interview with Author, 1998.

168 Powers, "Folksinger's Blues, I Gotta Be Travelin' On."

169 Phillips, M. to Author, 2022.

170 Cash Box, December 14, 1963.

171 "Folk Groups Sing at Carnegie Hall; Glenn Yarbrough is M.C. Before 1,200." The New York Times, December 2, 1963.

172 "Delhi Tech Hears Journeymen."

173 "Who's Who In the World of Music." Billboard, December 28, 1963.

174 Wright, Danny. "Journeymen Give Variety in Unique, Creative Manner." The Daily O'Collegian, April 2, 1964.

175 Smith, "Folksinging is Praised."

176 Wright, "Journeymen Give Variety in Unique, Creative Manner."

177 M. Phillips to Author, 2023.

178 Gilliland, Pop Chronicles.

179 Gilliland, Pop Chronicles.

180 "Long Rough Road To The Top, But There's Always a Crowd."

The Gazette, February 17, 1962.
181 Doherty, Denny. Private Interview with Author, 1985
182 Doherty to Author, 1985.
183 "Long Rough Road To The Top, But There's Always a Crowd."
184 Doherty, Denny, Greg Godovitz, and Bob Reid. Rock Talk. Newstalk Radio 1010, 2006.
185 Doherty, Rock Talk.
186 Sheehan, Richard, Greg Godovitz, and Bob Reid. Rock Talk. Newstalk Radio 1010, February 10, 2007.
187 Sheehan, Rock Talk.
188 Doherty to Author, 1985.
189 Sheehan, Rock Talk
190 Doherty to Author, 1985.
191 "Long Rough Road To The Top, But There's Always a Crowd."
192 Sheehan, Rock Talk.
193 Documents from Rodeo Records. Beaton Institute Archives, Cape Breton University, Nova Scotia.
194 LaCroix to Author, 1998.
195 LaCroix to Author, 1998.
196 Cash Box, March 25, 1961.
197 Documents from Rodeo Records.
198 LaCroix to Author, 2019.
199 Doherty to Author, 1998.
200 LaCroix to Author, 1998.
201 Doherty to Author, 1998.
202 Doherty to Author, 1998.
203 Doherty to Author, 1998.
204 "Long Rough Road To The Top, But There's Always a Crowd."
205 Doherty to Author, 1998.
206 Doherty to Author, 1998.
207 "Iris Paul at Black's." The Gazette. January 31, 1962.
208 Doherty to Author, 2003.
209 LaCroix to Author, 2002.
210 LaCroix to Author, 2002.
211 "Iris Paul at Black's." The Gazette.January 31, 1962.
212 Doherty to Author, 1985.
213 "Long Rough Road To The Top, But There's Always a Crowd."
214 LaCroix to Author, 2002.
215 Doherty to Author, 1998.
216 LaCroix to Author, 2002.
217 LaCroix to Author, 2019.
218 Morgan, Bob. Private Interview with Author, 1998.
219 Billboard, December 8, 1962
220 Berman, Shelley. Private Interview with Author, 2002.
221 LaCroix to Author, 2002.
222 Liner Notes, The Halifax Three, 1963
223 Matthews, Pete. "Pete's Platters." The Calgary Albertan, September 28, 1963.
224 Doherty to Author, 1985.
225 LaCroix to Author, 2019.
226 Doherty to Author, 1985.
227 LaCroix to Author, 1998.
228 Gardiner, Sandy. "Platter Patter and Idol Chatter." The Ottawa Journal, March 23, 1963.
229 Morgan to Author, 1998.
230 "Gag Played on Mitch Turns Into Hit Record." Somerset Daily American, March 15, 1963.
231 The Halifax Three. "The Man Who Wouldn't Sing Along With Mitch," 1963.
232 "Walter Winchell In New York." The Columbus Ledger-Enquirer, March 2, 1963.
233 Billboard, February 23, 1963.
234 "Newspaper Strike, Gag Lead to Sing-Along Novelty Single on Epic." Cashbox, February 9, 1963.
235 Doherty to Author, 1998.
236 Billboard, February 23, 1963.
237 "Don Wilson's Disk Derby," Frederick News Post, April 17, 1963.
238 Billboard, February 23, 1963.
239 Billboard, March 9, 1963.
240 Saimo, Daveen Koppel. Private Interview with Author, 2022.
241 LaCroix to Author, 2002.
242 Untitled Newspaper Review. Personal Archives of Pat LaCroix.
243 Carlin, George. Last Words. Simon & Schuster, 2009.
244 Talbot, Jonathan. Private Interview with Author, 2022.
245 LaCroix to Author, 2002, 2019.
246 Talbot to Author, 2022.
247 Doherty to Author, 2002.
248 Doherty to Author, 1998.
249 Talbot to Author, 2022.
250 Talbot to Author, 2022.
251 LaCroix to Author 2019
252 LaCroix to Author, 2002.
253 Doherty to Author, 1998.
254 "Don Wilson's Disk Derby." Frederick News Post, April 17, 1963.
255 LaCroix to Author, 1998.

256 Duff, Morris. "Halifax Three Improve." The Toronto Daily Star, 1963.

257 Doherty to Author, 1985.

258 Morgan to Author, 1998.

259 Winters, Paul. Private Interview with Author, 2022

260 Migliore, Fred, and Denny Doherty. FM Odyssey. WFIT, April 2003.

261 "Show on TV to Kick Off UGF Drive." The Evening Star. October 1, 1963.

262 Thwaites, Jim. "Hootenany-CUCND Style." The Varsity Review, October 18, 1963.

263 "Gale Sets Hoot Acts." Billboard, August 31, 1963.

264 LaCroix to Author, 1998.

265 Doherty to Author, 1985.

266 LaCroix to Author, 2002.

267 "Good Hootenanny Fails to Draw Crowd in Wichita." The Wichita Eagle, November 21, 1963.

268 Miller, Dave. "Hoot 'n' Rock? Hootenanny Performances Ranges From Excellent to Miserable." The Advertiser, November 20, 1963.

269 LaCroix to Author, 1998.

270 Migliore, FM Odyssey.

271 "All The Good Times Have Passed and Gone." Traditional.

272 "Presenting Hootenanny Hair Do's." HairDo Magazine, December 1963.

273 Ruhlmann, William. "Peter, Paul and Mary: A Song to Sing All Over This Land." Goldmine Magazine, April 12, 1996.

274 "Mama Cass." Biography. A&E, 2003.

275 "Boy Friend Held Over." The Baltimore Sun, August 23, 1959.

276 Gardner, R.H. "New Revue at Hilltop." The Baltimore Sun, September 15, 1959.

277 Henderson, Skitch. Interview with Cass Elliot. Skitch & Co., Army Reserves Radio Program, 1973.

278 Browning, Norma Lee. "No More Mama For Cass." The Chicago Tribune, November 12, 1972.

279 Paulsen, Don. "The 15 Year Silence of Cass Elliott [sic]." Hit Parader, January 1967.

280 Browning, "No More Mama For Cass."

281 Copley, George. "She Knew Herself." The Shreveport Journal, August 6, 1974.

282 Sander, Ellen. Trips: Rock Life in the Sixties. Scribners, 1973.

283 Rivers, Joan. "Mama Cass Elliot." E! True Hollywood Story, February 19, 2001.

284 The Tonight Show, Spring 1970.

285 The Tonight Show, Spring 1970.

286 Paulsen, Hit Parader.

287 Leah Kunkel, Rex Rawsthorne Reports, Radio Show, 1980

288 "At Pocono Playhouse 'Music Man' Tops in Musicals." Pocono Record, July 11, 1962.

289 Galle-Van Buren, Myrna. Private Interview with Author, 2016.

290 Opsasnick, Mark. Private Interview with Author, 2022.

291 Elliot, Don't Call Me Mama Anymore.

292 Elliot, Cass. Taped discussion with Cass Elliot in preparation for her 1973 TV special. Private Collection of Author.

293 Paulsen, Hit Parader.

294 Boran to Author, 1998.

295 Moore, Jaye. "Who Will Be The Father of My Baby," Motion Picture, August 1967.

296 M. Phillips to Author, 2006.

297 Rose to Author, 1998.

298 Rose to Author, 1998

299 Rose to Author, 1998

300 Kloman, William. "Sink Along with Mama Cass." Esquire, June 1969.

301 Rose to Author, 1998.

302 Brown, John. Private Interview with Author, 1999.

303 Brown to Author, 1999.

304 Brown to Author, 1999.

305 Kloman, "Sink Along with Mama Cass."

306 Elliot, 1973 Interview.

307 Brown to Author, 1999.

308 Elliot, 1973 Interview.

309 Brown to Author, 1999.

310 Brown to Author, 1999

311 Rose to Author, 1998.

312 Brown to Author, 1999.

313 The Gateway, February 22, 1963.

314 Fort Collins Coloradoan, March 16, 1962.

315 "Case of The Crooked Ear." My Omaha Obsession. https://myomahaobsession.com/2020/04/27/case-of-the-crooked-ear/

316 Hendricks, James. Private Interview with Author, 1998.

317 Rose to Author, 1998.

318 "Who Will Be The Father of My Baby?"

319 Hendricks to Author, 1998.

320 "District 66 Teacher Turns Hobby Into Full-Time Job." Omaha World-Herald, March 24, 1963.

321 Philadelphia Daily News, October 24, 1963.

322 Rose to Author, 1998.

323 Silver, Roy. Private Interview with Author, 1998.

324 Rose to Author, 1998.

325 Silver to Author, 1998.

326 Rose to Author, 1998.

327 Sander, Trips: Rock Life in the Sixties.

328 Hendricks to Author, 1998.

329 "District 66 Teacher Turns Hobby Into Full-Time Job."

330 The Village Voice, May 9, 1963

331 Kozero, John. "'Big Three' Scores A Hit." Lehigh University Brown and White, May 1, 1964.

332 "Weintraub Whirling Into World of Folk." Billboard, May 25, 1963.

333 "Weintraub Whirling Into World of Folk."

334 Colby, Paul, with Martin Fitzpatrick. The Bitter End: Hanging Out at America's Nightclub. Cooper Square Press, 2002.

335 Colby, The Bitter End.

336 "Weintraub Whirling Into World of Folk."

337 Nassour, Ellis. Dream a Little Dream of Me. Liner Notes, 1973

338 Hendricks to Author, 1998.

339 "Summertime Talent Show Starts Today." The Post Crescent, July 2, 1963.

340 Rose to Author, 1998.

341 Kozero, "'Big Three' Scores A Hit."

342 Kozero, "'Big Three' Scores A Hit."

343 Bowers to Author, 1998.

344 Hendricks to Author, 1998.

345 Bowers to Author, 1998.

346 Butler, Jim, Private Interview with Author 1998

347 Bowers to Author, 1998. .

348 Bowers to Author, 1998.

349 Kozero, "'Big Three' Scores A Hit."

350 Bowers to Author, 1998.

351 The Big Three. Oscar Brand World of Folk Music, Episode #148. Radio Show, 1964.

352 Bowers to Author, 1998.

353 Colby, The Bitter End.

354 Cash Box, September 14, 1963.

355 Billboard, October 5, 1963.

356 "New Vee Jay Regime Broadens Horizons." Billboard, September 7, 1963.

357 Ramone, Phil, with Charles Granata. Making Records: The Scenes Behind the Music. Hyperion, 2009.

358 Bowers to Author, 1998.

359 Colby, The Bitter End.

360 Guest Star, Radio Show. United States Savings Bonds, May 1964.

361 Hendricks to Author, 1998.

362 Guest Star, Radio Show.

363 Bowers to Author, 1998.

364 Bowers to Author, 1998.

365 Bowers to Author, 1998.

366 Bowers to Author, 1998.

367 Bowers to Author, 1998.

368 Rose to Author, 1998.

369 Winters, Paul. Private Interview with Author, 2022.

370 The Hartford Courant, October 14, 1963.

371 Lugsdin, Nancy. "1500 Sing Clap, Folk Groups Lead Detroit Hootenanny." The Windsor Star, October 26, 1963.

372 Stern, Harold. "After Theater," The Brooklyn Daily Eagle, June 8, 1963.

373 Harrington, Frank. "Linkletter Hootenanny Hit in S.F." Argus Leader, October 19, 1963.

374 "Folk Song Fans Delighted With Young Quartet." Syracuse Post Standard, November 17, 1963.

375 "Gill, Alan. "Television and Radio News and Views." Steubenville Herald Star, July 9, 1963.

376 "Folk Stars Featured." The Windsor Star, October 16, 1963.

377 McKinnon, Raun. Private Interview with Author, 2021.

378 Ingram, Bob. Private Interview with Author, 2000.

379 Silver to Author, 1998.

380 Hendricks to Author, 1998.

381 Hendricks to Author, 1998.

382 Hendricks to Author, 1998.

383 Hendricks to Author, 1998.

384 Moren, Marilyn. Private Interview with Author, 2023.

385 Bowers to Author, 1998.

386 "Interview with Mama Cass," A Gathering of Flowers.

387 "'The Big Three' does their 60-second version of the new 1964 Ballantine radio jingle." Ballantine News, February 1964.

388 "How an Expensive Jingle Gets That Way." Sponsor Magazine, February 4, 1964.

389 Hendricks to Author, 1998.

390 Hendricks to Author, 1998.

391 Bowers to Author, 1998.

392 Music Vendor, April 11, 1964.

393 "Vee Jay Records Unveil New Tollie Label." Billboard, March 7, 1964.

394 Billboard, December 5, 1964.

395 Rose to Author, 1998.

396 Wildes, Shel. Private Interview with Author, 2019.

397 Billboard, April 11, 1964.

398 The Big 3. Come Away Melinda, 1963.

399 Hendricks to Author, 1998.

400 Philadelphia Daily News, October 24, 1963.

401 Sebastian, John. Private Interview with Author, 2022.

402 Bowers to Author, 1998.

403 Hendricks to Author, 1998.

404 Rose to Author, 1998..

405 Travers, Mary. Private Interview with Author, 2002.

406 Bowers to Author, 1998.

407 Herve, Gusti. Private Interview with Author, 1998.

408 Cass Elliot, Jim Hendricks, Tim Rose, Wild Women, Manger Music, Inc. 1964. Lyrics used with permission.

409 Bowers to Author, 1998.

410 Butler to Author, 1998.

411 Rose to Author, 1998.

412 Colby, The Bitter End.

413 Butler to Author, 1998.

414 Bowers to Author, 1998.

415 Bowers to Author, 1998.

416 Rose to Author, 1998.

417 Jacobsen, Erik. Private Interview with Author, 1998.

418 Rose to Author, 1998.

419 https://www.allabouterik.com/musical-journey/early-productions

420 Kozero, "'Big Three' Scores A Hit."

421 Rose to Author, 1998.

422 Hendricks to Author, 1998, 2000.

423 Rose to Author, 1998.

424 "Big Three on Hootenanny Card Wednesday." Burlington Hawk Eye, April 13, 1964.

425 Butler to Author, 1998.

426 The Tonight Show.

427 The Tonight Show.

428 Doherty to Author, 2003.

429 Hendricks to Author, 1998.

430 Migliore, FM Odyssey.

431 Doherty to Author, 1985.

432 Doherty to Author, 2003.

433 Wheary, Fred. Private Interview with Author, 2021.

434 Wheary to Author, 2021.

435 "Would You Believe - Still More on the 'Ever Lovin" Spoonful!" The Hoya, April 7, 1967.

436 "Would You Believe - Still More on the 'Ever Lovin" Spoonful!"

437 "Would You Believe - Still More on the 'Ever Lovin" Spoonful!"

438 Wheary to Author, 2021.

439 Wheary to Author, 2021.

440 Doherty to Author, 2003

441 Rosel, Roxanna. Private Interview with Author 2021

442 Migliore, FM Odyssey.

443 Bowers to the Author 1998.

444 Yester, Jerry. Private Interview with Author, 1998.

445 Yester to Author, 1998.

446 Hendricks to Author, 1998.

447 Hendricks to Author, 1998.

448 Jacobsen to Author, 1998, 2021. https://www.allabouterik.com/musical-journey/early-productions

449 Talbot, Jonathan. "The Slurp," "Slurpin'," "Slurp With Me," "Slurp It." Unpublished compositions, Library of Congress. Used and reprinted by permission of Jonathan Talbot.

450 Talbot to Author, 2022.

451 Silver to Author, 1998.

452 Doherty to Author, 1985.

453 Hendricks to Author, 1998.

454 Hendricks to Author, 1998.

455 "Night Club: Big Three, Turtles, Joan Toliver Bitter End, N.Y." Music Business, June 27, 1964

456 "Night Club: Big Three, Turtles, Joan Toliver Bitter End, N.Y."

457 Hendricks to Author, 1998.

458 Doherty to Author, 1985.

459 Hirsch, Stephen. Private Interview with Author, 2020.

460 Oberman, Ronnie. "The Mugwumps." Washington Star, October 24, 1964.

461 Hendricks to Author, 1998.

462 Doherty to Author, 2003.

463 The Washington Post, July 10, 1964.

464 The Evening Sun, Mar 5, 1971.

465 Eaton, John. Private Interview with Author, 2022.

466 Hendricks to Author, 1998.

467 Singer, Bill. "Phenomenal Growth Distinguishes The Shadows." The Hoya, February 15, 1963.

468 Eaton to Author, 2022.

469 MacArthur, Harry. "After Dark – Atmosphere, The Hard Way." The Washington Post, January 17, 1963.

470 Eaton to Author, 2021.

471 Sanders, Stephen. Private Interview with Author, 2007.

472 Embrey, Robert. "The Mugwumps." D.C. Monuments, 1998.

473 Cohen, Joseph. Private Interview with Author, 1998.

474 Elliot, Cass. FBI File # WFO 140-14271. Federal Bureau of Investigation. Accessed 1987.

475 Silver to Author, 1998.

476 Bowers to Author, 1998.

477 Hallette Dawson, Letter to the Author, 2005.

478 Rosel to Author, 2021.

479 Segraves, John. "The Mugwumps: A Unique Bunch?" The Washington Post, August 13, 1964.

480 Doherty to Author, 1985.

481 Doherty to Author, 1998.

482 Hendricks to Author, 1998.

483 DiMuccio, Don. "Episode 38 – John Sebastian." It's Only Rock & Roll, Podcast, March 20, 2022.

484 Cavallo, Robert. Private Interview with Author, 2022.

485 DiMuccio, It's Only Rock & Roll.

486 Cavallo to Author, 2022.

487 DiMuccio, It's Only Rock & Roll.

488 Eaton to Author, 2022.

489 "Tips on Tables." The Washington Daily, July 14, 1964.

490 Doherty to Author, 1985.

491 Pagones, John. "On the Town: Discotheques Fad Growing Big Here." The Washington Post, July 19, 1964.

492 Oberman, "The Mugwumps."

493 Oropollo, Mark. Private Interview with Author, 2022.

494 Pagones, "On The Town."

495 Segraves, "The Mugwumps: A Unique Bunch?"

496 Segraves, "The Mugwumps: A Unique Bunch?"

497 "This Morning's News on the Campus Fronts - A Rally and a Hootenanny." The Eagle, October 16, 1964.

498 Humphrey, Skip. Private Interview with Author, 2018.

499 Bill Clinton, My Life, Knopf Publishing. 2004.

500 The Washington Post, October 2, 1964.

501 "Mama Cass," Biography.

502 Oberman, "The Mugwumps."

503 Hendricks to Author, 2007.

504 Oberman, "The Mugwumps."

505 Stevenson, Cathi. Private Interview with Author, 2022.

506 Perfater, Rita. Private Interview with Author, 2022.

507 Perfater to Author, 2022.

508 Hill, James. Private Interview with Author, 2022.

509 Oberman, "The Mugwumps."

510 DiMuccio, It's Only Rock & Roll.

511 Paulsen, Don. "The Mama's and The Spoonful's??!! The Lovin' Papa's??" Hit Parader, January 1967.

512 Doherty to Author, 1985.

513 Oberman, "The Mugwumps."

514 Oberman, "The Mugwumps."

515 Lorber, Alan. Private Interview with Author, 2006.

516 Segraves, "The Mugwumps: A Unique Bunch?"

517 Segraves, "The Mugwumps: A Unique Bunch?"

518 Hendricks to Author, 2007.

519 Segraves, "The Mugwumps: A Unique Bunch?"

520 DiMuccio, It's Only Rock & Roll.

521 "Allan Sherman To Host Mugwumps." Dayton Daily News, August 3, 1964.

522 Segraves, "The Mugwumps: A Unique Bunch?"

523 Matthews, Brian. Cass Elliot Interview. BBC, July 1974.

524 Segraves, "The Mugwumps: A Unique Bunch?"

525 Billboard, August 22, 1964. ;

526 "WB Pacts Mugwumps." Cash Box, August 22, 1964.

527 Music Business, August 29, 1964.

528 "WB Pacts Mugwumps." Cash Box, August 22, 1964.

529 "WB Inks Mugwumps." Record World, August 15, 1964

530 Watt, Douglas. "Record Review." New York Daily News, September 20, 1964.

531 Hirsch to Author, 2020.

532 The Mama Cass Television Program. ABC TV, 1969

533 Sebastian to Author, 1998.

534 Migliore, FM Odyssey.

535 Hendricks to Author, 1998.

536 Sebastian to Author, 1998.

537 DiMuccio, It's Only Rock & Roll.

538 Oberman, "The Mugwumps."

539 Matthews, BBC Cass Elliot Interview.

540 Matthews, BBC Cass Elliot Interview.

541 Lorber to Author, 2006.

542 Andrews, Chris. Private Interview with Author, 2006.

543 "The Things We Hear." Record Mirror, August 29, 1964.

544 Cavallo to Author, 2022.

545 Hendricks to Author, 1998.

546 Hendricks to Author, 2007.

547 Cass Elliot, Jim Hendricks. "Everybody's Been Talkin'." Third Story Music, Co. 1965. Manger Music, Inc. 1967. Lyrics used with permission.

548 Doherty to Author, 2003.

549 Elliot, Cass. "Happy Baby," "Bright Day." Unpublished Compositions, Library of Congress.

550 Doherty to Author, 1998.

551 Hendricks to Author, 1998.

552 Cash Box, September 19, 1964.

553 Migliore, FM Odyssey.

554 Cash Box, September 19, 1964.

555 Music Business, September 19, 1964.

556 Music Business, September 26, 1964.

557 Cash Box, October 3, 1964.

558 The Evening Star, September 17, 1964.

559 Atherstone Herald, October 30, 1964.

560 Aldersley, Peter. "DISCussion." Pop Weekly, October 20, 1964.

561 "Last Minute Flashes." 16, Magazine, January 1965.

562 Elliot, Cass. FBI File.

563 Matthews, BBC Cass Elliot Interview.

564 Doherty to Author, 1985.

565 Hirsch to Author, 2020.

566 "Four Saints, Mugwumps To Provide Twin Treat." Daily Athenaeum, November 13, 1964.

567 DiMuccio, It's Only Rock & Roll.

568 DiMuccio, It's Only Rock & Roll.

569 Hendricks to Author, 1998.

570 Doherty to Author, 1985.

571 DiMuccio, It's Only Rock & Roll.

572 Hendricks to Author, 1998.

573 Phillips, Michelle. California Dreamin'. Warner Books, 1986.

574 The Mamas & The Papas. "Creeque Alley." Universal Music, 1967.

575 Billboard, April 27, 1967.

576 Hildebrand, Veyler. Private Interview with Author, 2022.

577 Melamed, Vince. Private Interview with Author, 2022

578 The Mugwumps. An Historic Recording. Warner Brothers, 1967.

579 Margolis, Jon. The Last Innocent Year: America in 1964—The Beginning of the 'Sixties'. William Morrow, 1999.

580 Daily Oklahoman, September 9, 1964.

581 Brickman, Marshall. Private Interview Author, 2022.

582 Brickman to Author, 2022.

583 Richmond, Dick. "It's All Happening At Once For Michelle." St. Louis Dispatch, November 28, 1977.

584 Brickman to Author, 2022.

585 M. Phillips to Author 2022, 2023.

586 Brickman to Author, 2022.

587 "Judy Davis–The Stars' Vocal–81." The New York Times, February 1, 2001.

588 Stein, Ruthe. "Giving Voice to the Famous – Vocal Coach Judy Davis Honored at Bammies." San Francisco Chronicle, March 5, 1995.

589 Brickman to Author, 2022.

590 M. Phillips to Author, 2023.

591 Brickman to Author, 2022.

592 M. Phillips to Author, 2023.

593 "Journeymen Performance Brings Orientation to a Close." East Carolinian, September 11, 1964.

594 "Folk, Jazz Wing Ding Plays Here Friday Night." The La Crosse Tribune, November 7, 1964.

595 Music Business, July 18, 1964.

596 Music Business, July 18, 1964.

597 Brickman to Author, 2022.

598 Brickman to Author, 2022.

599 Brickman to Author, 2022.

600 Brickman to Author, 2022.

601 Brickman to Author, 2022.

602 M. Phillips to Author, 2023.

603 "Who Will Be The Father of My Baby?"

604 Hendricks to Author, 1998.

605 Migliore, FM Odyssey.

606 Migliore, FM Odyssey.

607 Phillips, Letters to Sue Lyon.

608 Migliore, FM Odyssey.

609 Phillips, Letters to Sue Lyon.

610 Phillips, California Dreamin'.

611 Hord, Molly. "Virgin Islands (Beyond the Cosmos)." Molly's Rough Draft, October 23, 2016. https://mollysroughdraft.blogspot.com

612 Phillips, Letters to Sue Lyon.

613 Phillips, Letters to Sue Lyon.

614 Phillips, John. Copyright Application for "Me and My Uncle," November 24, 1964. Private Collection of Author.

615 Hord, "Virgin Islands (Beyond the Cosmos)."

616 M. Phillips to Author, 2023.

617 M. Phillips to Author, 2023.

618 M. Phillips to Author, 2023.

619 Phillips, Letters to Sue Lyon.

620 M. Phillips to Author, 2023.

621 "Interview with Mama Cass," A Gathering of Flowers.

622 Hendricks to Author, 1998.

623 Cavallo to Author, 2022.

624 Sanders to Author, 2007.

625 Cass Elliot | All About Erik https://www.allabouterik.com/musical-journey/musical-friends/cass-elliot

626 Cavallo to Author, 2022.

627 Jacobsen to Author, 1998, 2021.

628 "Journeymen Replace Kingsmen," Hilltops, April 9, 1965

629 Bray, Eric. Online discussion. https://m.facebook.com/groups/673594956035655/permalink/1139405739454572/?comment_id=5520043668057402&mibextid=S66gvF.2023

630 Foust, Jeff. Online discussion. https://m.facebook.com/groups/673594956035655/permalink/1139405739454572/?comment_id=5520043668057402&mibextid=S66gvF. 2022

631 Phillips, John. "Showing the Way," 1965.

632 "Behind the Music: The Mamas & The Papas. VH1. 1998.

633 Phillips, Letters to Sue Lyon.

634 Brickman to Author, 2022.

635 "An Envied Few Enjoy College Date Bookings, "Jacksonville Courier." July 9, 1965.

636 Billboard Music On Campus, March 19, 1966

637 Phillips, Michelle. "Caribbean Dreamin'." Letter to the Editor, The New York Times, February 6, 2020.

638 "Interview with Mama Cass," A Gathering of Flowers.

639 Kloman, William. "Touring With The Mamas and The Papas." The Saturday Evening Post, March 25, 1967.

640 The Big 3. "Come Away Melinda." 1963.

641 "Creeque Alley" by John Phillips and Michelle Gilliam, Copyright Universal Music, 1967. Copyright Renewed. All Rights Reserved. Used by Permission. *Reprinted by Permission of Hal Leonard LLC.*

642 Lyrics to Thom McAn and Ballantine jingles used and reprinted by permission of Bob Bowers..

Appendix

SELECTED CONCERTS, LIVE APPEARANCES, AND IMPORTANT DATES OF JOHN PHILLIPS, THE ABSTRACTS AND THE SMOOTHIES

ARNOLD AND THE MUV'S (JOHN PHILLIPS)
Circa 1957 Private Recording/Acetate, 78 RPM, Edgewood
Studios "Muvver"

THE ABSTRACTS
1958/59 Private Recording/Acetate, 78 RPM, Edgewood Studios
"Remember"/ "When You Find Your Love"
1958/59 Private Recording/Acetate, 78 RPM, Edgewood Studios
"Cindy Lou"/ "Comin' Round Tonite"

December 1959 (4 week engagement), Elmwood Casino, Windsor,
Ontario. Referred to as "the vocalizing Abstracts four."
Appearing with comedy teams Mark Antone & Jackie Curtiss,
also Jack Eagle & Frank Mann. Also appeared with Ballroom
Dancers Lawrence & Carroll in "Yuletide Routines with a
chorus."
January 1960, The Town Casino, Buffalo, New York. Appearing with
Jack Eagle & Frank Mann.

THE SMOOTHIES
March 3, 1960, Recording Date, Decca Studios New York, New York.
Recorded, "Softly," "Coming Round Tonight," "Joanie," and
"Twenty Four Hours"
May 10-13, 1960, Annual Cotton Carnival, Memphis, Tennessee.
Stayed in Hotel. Over 100 bands played at the event which hosted
100,000 people. Tim Rose played banjo with them. Described as
a "five-man, one-girl harmony outfit.
Early Summer 1960, "Club Suzanne" at Mount Airy Lodge in the
Poconos, Pennsylvania. Bob Dorough was pianist. Robert
Newman was conductor.
July 2, 1960, Palisades Amusement Park, George Tucker's *Teen Beat*
broadcast. Also appearing: Paul Evans, The Delicates.
July 15, 1960, Recording Date, Decca Studios, New York, New York,
Recorded "Michael Row the Boat Ashore," "Ride, Ride, Ride."
July 23, 1960, billed as "The Smoothies Quartet," Ocean Grove
Auditorium "On Wings of Song" – Presented by the Ocean Grove
Camp Meeting Association and the New York Opera Festival.
Appeared with Josephine Guido, Edward Ansara, Marienka
Michna.
July 25, 1960, *American Bandstand*, performed "Softly", also
appearing: Conway Twitty.
Summer 1960, *The Milt Grant Show*, Washington, D.C. television
dance program.
August 2, 1960, Recording Date, Decca Studios, New York, New
York. Recorded "Lonely Boy and Pretty Girl," "Bile Th' Cabbage
Down," and "The Canal Boat Song."
August 22-September 4, 1960, "Jay Musto's Summertime Spectacular
'Showtime,'" Long Island, New York. Appearing along with
Jimmy Rodgers, Connee Boswell, Henry Youngman, Dorothy
Keller, Will B. Able, and Tony Galento
September 5-10, 1960, Haddon Hall Resort Casino, Atlantic City,
New Jersey.
September 19-26, 1960, billed as "The Four Smoothies," Elmwood
Casino, Windsor, Ontario, with Jimmy Casanova, Jack Madden's
Orchestra, Roller Skating by Terry Taylor. "Softly" referred to in
one press account.
Fall 1960 (possibly September 26-October 1), The Blue Mirror
Restaurant and Cocktail Lounge, Washington, D.C. Appearing
with Mickey Shaughnessy (comedy).
December 18, 1960, Oldsmobile Show, Lansing Civic Center, Lansing,
Michigan, *Community Christmas Concert,* with Florence
Henderson, Johnny Carson, and the Oldsmobile Rocketaires.
December 17- 24, 1960, The Elmwood Casino, Windsor, Ontario,
"Salute to the United Nations Revue," cast of 30, with Pat
Henry (Comedian), The Tumbling Moroccans, Nick Forrest, The
Elmwood Lovelies, Jack Madden's Orchestra, and (by 12/24)
the comedy team of Eagle & Man. Called "The Harmonizing
Smoothies" in 12/24/60 issue of *The Windsor Star* newspaper.

THE SMOOTHIES SESSIONOGRAPHY & DISCOGRAPHY

Joanie (3/3/60; Decca Studios, New York) Matrix # 108799

Softly (3/3/60; Decca Studios, New York) Matrix # 108800

Comin' Round Tonite (3/3/60; Decca Studios, New York) Matrix # 108801

Twenty Four Hours (3/3/60; Decca Studios, New York) Matrix # 108802

Michael (7/15/60; Decca Studios, New York) Matrix # 109366

Ride, Ride, Ride (7/15/60; Decca Studios, New York) Matrix # 109367

The Canal Boat Song (8/2/60; Decca Studios, New York) Matrix # 109368

Lonely Boy And Pretty Girl (8/2/60; Decca Studios, New York) Matrix # 109369

If I Ever Get Aboard That Train (8/2/60; Decca Studios, New York) Matrix # 109370

Bile Tha Cabbage Down (8/2/60; Decca Studios, New York) Matrix #109371

Michel Ruppli, "The Decca Labels: A Discography" (Greenwood Press, 1996); "Discography of American Historical Recordings," UC Santa Barbara Library. According to these sources, these matrixes indicate recordings were issued from the master for the two singles. No recordings were issued from the other masters.

SINGLES

Decca 9-31105   Joanie/Softly (6/60; both sides non-LP)

Decca 9-31159   Ride, Ride, Ride/Lonely Boy And Pretty Girl (10/60)

TELEVISION APPEARANCES

American Bandstand (ABC-TV), filmed 07/25/60

The Milt   Grant Show (Washington, D.C. local dance program), filmed Summer 1960

SELECTED CONCERTS, LIVE APPEARANCES AND IMPORTANT DATES OF THE JOURNEYMEN

February 3, 1961, Billed as "The Modern Folk Three," Caffe Lena, Saratoga Springs, New York.

March 8, 1961, The Second Fret, Philadelphia, Pennsylvania, with Carolyn Hester.

April 11, April 25, 1961, May 4, 1961, Some accounts refer to a two-week engagement. Billed as "The Journeymen III," Gerde's Folk City, New York, New York. Other known acts: The Clancy Brothers, Lightnin' Hopkins, Bob Dylan, Logan English.

May 18, 1961, *Pops Americana* folk music show with Herb Shriner, also appearing Ed Madden's orchestra and singer Patti Pollock, Boston, Massachusetts.

May 26-27, 1961, The Ice House, Pasadena, California.

May 28, 1961, *The World of Music* (Canadian TV Show) with Wally Koster.

June 3, 1961, Mentioned in a press release as the new group Capitol was grooming called "The Journeymen Three"

June 9-10, 1961, The Ice House, Pasadena, California, with Lynn Gold and Alvara Ancona also appearing. June 19-24, 1961, Billed as "The Journeymen III," Kornman's Front Room, Cleveland, Ohio.

July 1, 1961, Billed as "The Journeymen III," The Music Barn/The Potting Shed, Berkshire, Massachusetts.

July 7-16, 1961, at the hungry i, San Francisco, California.

July 21, 1961, Billed as "The Journeymen 3," *Dimensions 3* Television Show on KYW-TV, Cleveland, Ohio, appearing along with Ellie Frankel and her jazz trio.

July 27, 1961, *PM West* Television Show, with Dick Gregory.

August 12, 1961, *Parade* Canadian TV Show with Wally Koster. Show also featured singer Joyce Hahn.

September 4, 1961, Folk Music and Guitar Festival, Grossingers, Catskill Resort Hotel, Liberty, New York.

October 1, 1961, Georgetown University, Rat Race Freshman Mixer, Washington, D.C. with The John Keats Combo and The Collegians.

Summer/Fall 1961, The Joker Club, San Jose, California. Played for six weeks.

November 16, 1961, Spokane Plantation Restaurant, Spokane, Washington.

November 19, 1961, Elks Club, Liberty Lake, Washington.

November 27-December 1, 1961, Malcoff's Stein and Sirloin, Phoenix, Arizona with Meade Lux Lewis. Booked by Joe Glazer of ABC Associated Booking, and canceled after an unknown number of dates.

December 1, 1961, Childress Buick Dealership, Phoenix, Arizona, "Come Meet The Journeymen, Capitol Recording Stars – Come Get Your Free Album."

January 2-14, 1962, The Padded Cell, Minneapolis, Minnesota.

January 1962, The Plantation Restaurant/Club, Spokane, Washington.

January 19, 1962, Indiana State College, Fisher Auditorium, Indiana County Heart Fund with Bobby Hackett, Indiana County, Pennsylvania.

January 29-February 25, 1962, the hungry i, San Francisco, California, with Mort Sahl.

February 17, 1962, The Fairmont Hotel, San Francisco, California, Stanford University Inter Fraternity Council Ball.

March 3, 1962, Hampden Sydney College, Virginia, Midwinters Weekend, sponsored by The German Club, replacing The Brothers Four.

March 16, 1962, Bowdoin College, Campus Chest Charity Weekend, Brunswick, Maine.

March 17, 1962, 2-4 PM, St. Patrick's Festival, Alfred University, Alumni Hall, Wellsville, New York.

March 18, 1962, 8:00 PM, Lewiston High School, Lewiston, Maine.

March 19-24, 1962, The Coffee House Theater, Springfield, Massachusetts.

March 30, 1962, 7:30 PM and 9:30 PM, Ball State College, L.A. Pittenger Student Center, Muncie, Indiana. Two concerts in celebration of the Student Center's 10th Anniversary. Sang "Benny" and "Whistling Gypsy Rover."

March 31, 1962, Atlantic Christian College, Wilson, North Carolina.

April 4, 1962, University of Richmond, 8-10 PM Millhiser Gymnasium. Performed "500 Miles" and "Black Girl"

April 6, 1962, Montclair State University, Bloomfield College Gymnasium, New Jersey. Press reports stated the concert was "to be recorded by Capitol for an album."

April 23-May 6, 1962 at La Fiesta Restaurant, Juarez, Mexico.

May 10, 1962, The University of Alabama, Foster Auditorium, Tuscaloosa, Alabama. Appearing with Juliet Prowse.

May 12, 1962, Clemson University, Clemson, South Carolina, Junior-Senior Dance.

May 19-20, 1962, Junior League Horse Show, Des Moines, Iowa, also appearing Mary Ann Mobley, former Miss America.

July 7-14, 1962, Cape Cod Folk Song Festival, Cape Cod, Massachusetts.

August 19-26, 1962, Freddie's, Minneapolis, Minnesota, also appearing, Josh White. September 10, 1962, The Dalton Saloon, Cleveland, Ohio.

October 13, 1962, Nasson College, Springvale, Maine.

October 19, 1962, University of Tennessee Roundup "Nahheeyayli," Knoxville, Tennessee. Performed "Cotton Mill Girls," 3,000 in attendance.

October 20, 1962, University of Minnesota, Homecoming.

October 25, 1962, Auburn University, Auburn, Alabama.

October 27, 1962, Kansas State College of Pittsburg, Homecoming.

November 3, 1962, Florida State University, Homecoming. Performed "Shape of Things," "Please Papa, Don't Whip Little Benny," "How Mountain Girls Do Love."

November 3, 1962, The Journeymen "Festival of Folk Songs" aired on WCLM radio in Chicago at 7 PM. Performed "Old Joe Clarke Blues."

November 10, 1962, Princeton University, Princeton, New Jersey.

November 16, 1962, State University of New York at Plattsburgh, performing at St. John's Academy.

December 1, 1962, Hollins College, Roanoke, Virginia.

December 2, 1962, American University, Homecoming Weekend, Sunday afternoon performance.

December 8, 1962, Mount Holyoke College, South Hadley Massachusetts.

December 17, 1962, The Shadows, Georgetown, Washington, D.C.

December 21-23, 1962, The Shadows, Georgetown, Washington, D.C., New location. Wedding Reception for John and Michelle Phillips held there December 31, 1962.

Late 1962 or early 1963, The Journeymen, Cleveland, Ohio. John did not show up at this show. Scott and Dick performed as a duo.

Early 1963, The Shoreham Hotel, Washington, D.C. Bill Cosby opened.

Early 1963, The Shadows, Washington, D.C. Bill Cosby opened.

February 7, 1963, Dalhousie University, Halifax, Nova Scotia.

February 9, 1963, 8 PM, Sigma Alpha Mu, Drexel Institute of Technology, Philadelphia, Pennsylvania. Appearing with Raul McKinnon.

February 15, 1963, McGill University, Montreal, Canada, Winter Carnival, Sir Arthur Currie Gymnasium, 3,000 in attendance.

February 16, 1963, St. Lawrence University, New York. Winter Carnival Ball. Also appearing Josh, White, Chris Barber Jazz Band, Jack Peters Band.

February 23, 1963, 2-4 PM, University of Richmond, Virginia, Mid-Winters.

February 28-March 2, 1963, University of South Carolina, Greek Week.

March 2, 1963, St. Anselm College, Practical Arts Auditorium, Manchester, New Hampshire.

February-March 1963, Memorial Hall, Pittsburgh, Pennsylvania. Lenny Litman to present, reported in 12/31/62 *Pittsburgh Post*, may have only been scheduled.

March 8, 1963, with Peter Nero at the Veterans Memorial Stadium, Ohio State University.

March 8, 1963, Hampden Sydney College, Hampden Sydney, Virginia.

March 16, 1963, 2:30-4:30 PM Alfred University, Wellsville, New York, Agricultural and Technical Institute Gymnasium, 31st Annual St. Pat's Festival.

March 17, 1963, Pilgrim Fellowships Rally at Bushnell Memorial Hall, Hartford, Connecticut.

March 20, 1963, Bridgewater College, Bridgewater, Virginia.

March 27, 1963, University of Arkansas, Men's Gym.

March 29, 1963, Emory University, Atlanta, Georgia, Field House.

April 13, 1963, also aired May 3, 1963, from Brown University, *Hootenanny* ABC-TV Show. Performed with Theodore Bikel, Ian & Sylvia, The Rooftop Singers. Performed "I May Be Right," "500 Miles," and "A Mighty Day."

April 18, 1963, Wake Forest University, Lawn Concert, Wake Forest, North Carolina.

April 25, 1963, Westminster College, Fulton Missouri.

April 26, 1963, Culver Stockton College, Canton, Iowa.

April 25-27, 1963, Louisiana State University, Baton Rouge, Louisiana, 10th Annual Southern Universities Student Government Association Conference.

April 27, Randolph Macon Women's College, Lynchburg, Virginia.

April 30, 1963, "Annual H-Day" at Howard College, Birmingham, Alabama (later became Samford University in 1965).

Spring 1963, Junior-Senior Dance at Clemson University.

May 1, 1963, The University of Alabama, Foster Auditorium, Greek Week.

May 2, 1963, Veisha Celebration at Iowa State University Armory.

May 3, 1963, Texas Tech University, Lubbock Texas, Lubbock Municipal Auditorium.

May 4, 1963, Loyola University, Evanston, Illinois.

May 9, 1963, Appalachian State Teachers College, Boone, North Carolina.

May 10, 1963, East Carolina University.

May 11, 1963, The College of William & Mary, Matoaka Amphitheater, Williamsburg, Virginia ("appearing after a successful tour of West Coast colleges and nightclubs").

May 24, 1963, Dade County Auditorium, Miami-Dade Junior College, Miami, Florida.

June 6, 1963, Senior Class Picnic, Southwick Auditorium, University of Vermont, Burlington, Vermont.

June 7, 1963, Boston College, Surf Ballroom, "Night on the Town" with Peter Nero.

June 10-16, 1963, Baker's Keyboard, Detroit, Michigan.

June 28-July 4, 1963, Faragher's, Cleveland, Ohio.

July 6, 1963, 8 PM and 11:30 PM, Alan Shepherd Auditorium, Virginia Beach, Virginia.

July 9-July 22, 1963, The Shadows, Washington, D.C. Opening act: Bill Cosby.

August 27, 1963, The Troubadour, Los Angeles, California.

September 14, 1963, Howard University, Baltimore, Maryland.

September 28, 1963, *The Hootenanny Hour*, CFOX Radio. Program featuring Chad Mitchell Trio, The Easy Riders, The Journeymen, and The Halifax Three

September 29, 1963, *Folkways USA*, KTAR Radio, Phoenix, Arizona. Host Bryan Hickox,

October 1-2, 1963, Southern Methodist University, *Hootenanny* ABC-TV, 5,000 in attendance. Appeared with Theodore Bikel, Dave Astor, Judy Collins, Bob Gibson, Ian & Sylvia, Clara Ward, The Carolina Kloggers, Freddie Powers and his Powerhouse Five, and The Wanderers Three. Later Broadcast on November 9, 1963 and April 26, 1964.

October 11, 1963, Willingham Chapel, Mercer University, Macon, Georgia.

October 12, 1963, Birmingham Southern College, "Southern Accent."

October 12, 1963, Begin a 10-day 7-city tour as reported in *Cash Box* magazine. Cities visited: Boston, New York, Atlanta, Miami, Detroit, Cleveland, Cincinnati.

October 13, 1963, McGill University, Montreal, Canada, "Hootenanny" with Odetta, Ian & Sylvia, and The Tarriers.

October 15, 1963, Possibly at University of Arizona for *Hootenanny* ABC TV

October 18, 1963, Marshall University, Huntington, West Virginia. Sponsored by Huntington Jaycees. Appearing with The Cumberland Singers, The Portland Four, and Kitty & Bill.

October 21, 1963, *Meetin' House* show on Chicago FM Radio WXRT with Jerry Woods and The Brothers Four.

October 24, 1963, Troy State College, Troy, Alabama, Sartain Hall.

October 25, 1963, East Stroudsburg State College, Stroudsburg, Pennsylvania, Fall Weekend.

October 26, 1963, University of Southern Illinois. Also appearing Bud & Travis and Judy Henske. Performed in Edwardsville Junior High School Auditorium.

Hootenanny USA Tour with Jo Mapes, The Geezinslaw Brothers, The Halifax Three and Glenn Yarbrough:

October, 31, 1963, Greensboro Coliseum, Greensboro, North Carolina.

November 1, 1963, 8:30 PM, Dorton Arena, Raleigh, North Carolina.

November 2, 1963, Greenville Memorial Auditorium, Greenville, South Carolina.

November 3, 1963, City Auditorium, Atlanta, Georgia.

November 4, 1963, Municipal Coliseum, Knoxville, Tennessee.

November 5, 1963, Columbus Municipal Auditorium, Columbus, Georgia. 1,100 in attendance. Performed "500 Miles" and "Mighty Day."

November 6, 1963, Jacksonville, Florida. (Scheduled)

November 8, 1963, Township Auditorium, Columbia, South Carolina. Less than 500 people in attendance

November 9, 1963, Bell Auditorium, Augusta Georgia.

November 10, 1963 at Charlotte Coliseum, Charlotte, North Carolina. Approximately 400 in attendance.

November 11, 1963 at Macon City Auditorium, Macon, Georgia.

November 12, 1963 at City Auditorium, Chattanooga, Tennessee.

November 14, 1963 Memphis, Tennessee.

November 15. 1963, City Auditorium, Jackson, Mississippi. Scheduled but canceled. Played at Tougaloo College, Jackson Mississippi instead.

November 16, 1963 at Alabama State, Garrett Coliseum, Montgomery, Alabama.

November 17, Loyola University, Field House, New Orleans, Louisiana

November 18, 1963, McNeese Arena, McNeese State University, Louisiana. Scheduled but canceled.

November 19, 1963, Municipal Auditorium, Lafayette, Louisiana.

November 20, 1963, Arcadia Theater/Wichita Forum, Wichita, Kansas.

November 21, 1963, 7:30 PM, Kansas State University, University Auditorium.

November 22, 1963, KRNT Theater, Des Moines, Iowa. Scheduled but canceled.

November 24, 1963, Orpheum Movie Theater, Springfield, Illinois. Scheduled.

November 25, Miami University, Oxford, Ohio

November 26, 1963, Columbus Veterans War Auditorium, Columbus, Ohio.

November 27, 1963, Washington Coliseum, Washington, D.C.

November 28, 1963, Mosque Theatre, Newark, New Jersey

November 29, 1963, County Center, White Plains, New York, "Campus Type, Folk Music 2-Hour Folk Sing Along."

November 30, 1963, Carnegie Hall, New York, New York, with The Halifax Three, Glenn Yarborough, Joe Mapes, The Geezinslaw Brothers. 1,200 in attendance according to *The New York Times*.

December 7, 1963, University of Tulsa, Oklahoma.

December 10, 1963, SUNY at the Delaware Academy Central School Auditorium in Delhi, New York. Performed twenty songs including "Chase the Rising Sun," "500 Miles," "Waggoner's Lad," "Whistling Gypsy Rover," "Rock Me Lord," "One Quick Martini," "Metamorphosis," "Please Papa Don't Whip Poor Little Benny," "Church Street," "Cumberland Mountain Deer Chase," "All the Pretty Little Horses," "The Shape of Things," "The Complete Anthology of the Blues."

1963-1964, Delta State College, Cleveland, Mississippi.

January 28, 1964, Hootenanny Program at March of Dimes Mothers March, Dallas Memorial Auditorium

January-February 1964, St. Olaf College, Northfield, Minnesota, Winter Sports Week.

February 1, 1964, Virginia Polytechnic Institute, Blacksburg, Virginia, 2nd Annual Civilian Weekend.

February 2, 1964, Bates College, Lewiston, Maine, Winter Carnival. Played "Cocaine" and "Swing Low Sweet Chariot."

February 7, 1964, University of Georgia, Stegman Hall, sponsored by the Inter Fraternity Council, with Flatt & Scruggs.

February 21, 1964, Ohio State University, "The Big Hoot" at St. John Arena, with Josh White and the New Christy Minstrels. 11,000 in attendance.

February 23, 1964, Wisconsin State College, College Fieldhouse, Milwaukee, Wisconsin, Winter Carnival.

February 28, 1964, The Royal Agricultural College in Guelph, Ontario, Canada, *Let's Sing Out* TV program, filmed three episodes. "Fare Thee Well," "Wagoner's Lad," "500 Miles," "Rock Me Lord," "Black Girl," "Little Brown Jug," "Cumberland Deer Chase," "Gypsy Rover." Appeared with Mike Settle, Anita Sheer, The Seaways Singers, and Allan Milles. Taped 3 episodes.

March 6, 1964, University of Florida, Spring Frolics.

March 21, 1964, Richmond Polytechnic Institute (Later Virginia Commonwealth University), Richmond, Virginia.

March 26, 1964 *Let's Sing Out* broadcast.

March 28, 1964, University of Mississippi. Scheduled but canceled.

March 31, 1964, Cameron College, Field House, Lawton, Oklahoma.

April 1, 1964, Oklahoma State University, Stillwater, Oklahoma.

April 2, 1964, Drury College, Missouri.

April 10, 1964, 8:30 PM, University of Houston, Cullen Auditorium.

April 11, 1964, Village Fair Festival, Auburn, Alabama. Also appearing Ian & Sylvia.

April 17, 1964, Louisiana State University, Student Government Folk Fest. Also appearing Ian & Sylvia.

April 18, 1964, 3:00 PM, Vanderbilt University, Nashville, Tennessee, Greek Week.

April 24, 1964, Spring Festival at Hobart & William Smith College.

April 24, 1964, Baldwin-Wallace College, Ohio, Ursprung Gymnasium.

May 1, 1964, *Lets Sing Out* broadcast, Episode 32 with Mike Settle and Anita Sheer.

May 3, 1964, New York Mills High School Auditorium for Utica College, Utica, New York.

May 9, 1964, West Virginia University.

May 17, 1964, Clarkson College, Potsdam, New York.

Unknown Date, *The Ruth Lyon Show*, Cincinnati, Ohio.

Unknown Date, *The Lloyd Thaxton Show*.

THE JOURNEYMEN SESSIONOGRAPHY & DISCOGRAPHY

SESSIONOGRAPHY

500 Miles (03/21/61; Capitol Studios, NY)

Ride, Ride, Ride (03/21/61; Capitol Studios, NY)

Soft Blow The Summer Winds (03/23/61; Capitol Studios, NY)

Cumberland Mountain Deer Chase (03/23/61; Capitol Studios, NY)

Make Me A Pallet (03/23/61; Capitol Studios, NY)

River Come Down (03/24/61; Capitol Studios, NY)

Black Girl (04/05/61; Capitol Studios, NY)

Fennario (04/10/61; Capitol Studios, NY)

Gilgara Mountain (04/10/61; Capitol Studios, NY)

Dunya (04/11/61; Capitol Studios, NY)

Chase The Rising Sun (04/12/61; Capitol Studios, NY)

Rock Me Lord (04/12/61; Capitol Studios, NY)

Environment (04/21/61; Capitol Studios, NY)

The Ballad Of The Shape Of Things (04/21/61; Capitol Studios, NY)

Kumbaya (10/23/61; Capitol Studios, Hollywood)

Oh, Miss Mary (10/23/61; Capitol Studios, Hollywood)

Don't Turn Around (02/27/62; Capitol Studios, Hollywood)

I Never Will Marry (studio version) (02/27/62; Capitol Studios, Hollywood)

Hush Now Sally (02/27/62; Capitol Studios, Hollywood)

Rock Island Line (02/27/62; Capitol Studios, Hollywood)

I Am A Poor And A Ramblin' Boy (live) (06/01/62; The Padded Cell, Minneapolis, MN)

Dark As A Dungeon (live) (06/01/62; The Padded Cell, Minneapolis, MN)

Old Joe Clarke's Blues (live) (06/01/62; The Padded Cell, Minneapolis, MN)

In The Evening (live) (06/01/62; The Padded Cell, Minneapolis, MN)

Metamorphosis (live) (06/01/62; The Padded Cell, Minneapolis, MN)

Waggoner's Lad (live) (06/01/62; The Padded Cell, Minneapolis, MN)

Cotton Mill Girls (live) (06/01/62; The Padded Cell, Minneapolis, MN)

I Never Will Marry (live) (06/01/62; The Padded Cell, Minneapolis, MN)

Gypsy Rover (live) (06/01/62; The Padded Cell, Minneapolis, MN)

Born In Bethlehem (live) (06/01/62; The Padded Cell, Minneapolis, MN)

Jack The Sailor (live) (06/01/62; The Padded Cell, Minneapolis, MN)

Johnny Booker (live) (06/01/62; The Padded Cell, Minneapolis, MN)

One Quick Martini (live) (06/01/62; The Padded Cell, Minneapolis, MN)

Benny (live) (06/01/62; The Padded Cell, Minneapolis, MN)

How Mountain Girls Can Love (live) (06/01/62; The Padded Cell, Minneapolis, MN)

Loadin' Coal (07/06/62; Capitol Studios, NY)

What'll I Do (07/06/62; Capitol Studios, NY)

Tell Ole Bill (07/06/62; Capitol Studios, NY)

Rag Mama (02/13/63; Capitol Studios, NY)

San Francisco Bay (Version 1) (02/13/63; Capitol Studios, NY)

Virgin Mary (03/31/63; Capitol Studios, Hollywood)

Ben And Me (03/31/63; Capitol Studios, Hollywood)

Country Blues (03/31/63; Capitol Studios, Hollywood)

Someone To Talk My Troubles To (04/10/63; Capitol Studios, Hollywood)

All The Pretty Little Horses (04/10/63; Capitol Studios, Hollywood)

Four Strong Winds (04/10/63; Capitol Studios, Hollywood)

It Makes A Long Time Man Feel Bad (04/10/63; Capitol Studios, Hollywood)

San Francisco Bay (Version 2) (04/11/63; Capitol Studios, Hollywood)

Bay Of Mexico (04/11/63; Capitol Studios, Hollywood)

Someday Baby (04/11/63; Capitol Studios, Hollywood)

Ja-Da (04/12/63; Capitol Studios, Hollywood)

Stackolee (04/12/63; Capitol Studios, Hollywood)

Two Hoboes (04/12/63; Capitol Studios, Hollywood)

Mary Wore Three Links Of Chain (04/13/63; Capitol Studios, Hollywood)

I May Be Right (04/13/63; Capitol Studios, Hollywood)

Greenland Whale Fisheries (04/13/63; Capitol Studios, Hollywood)

One Quick Martini (studio version) (04/13/63; Capitol Studios, Hollywood)

SINGLES

Capitol 4625   500 Miles/ River Come Down (09/61)

Capitol 4678   Kumbaya/ Soft Blow The Summer Winds (01/62; A-side non-LP)

Capitol 4737   Don't Turn Around (mono mix)/ Hush Now Sally (04/62; both sides non-LP)

Capitol 4829   What'll I Do (mono mix)/ Loadin' Coal (08/62; both sides non-LP)

Capitol 4943   Rag Mama/ I Never Will Marry (03/63; with picture sleeve – both sides non-LP)

Capitol 5031   Ja-Da/ Kumbaya (edit) (09/63; B-side non-LP)

UNUSUAL FOREIGN EPS

French Capitol EAP-4-1629   The Journeymen (11/61; with front cover photograph of forest)

(TRACKS: 500 Miles; Black Girl;/ Make Me A Pallet; Fennario)

French Capitol EAP-1-20446   More Ballads By The Journeymen (10/62; with front cover photograph of the countryside featuring cattle)

(TRACKS: Dark As A Dungeon; Old Joe Clarke's Blues;/ Loadin' Coal; Johnny Booker)

ALBUMS

Capitol T/ST-1629 The Journeymen (10/61)

(TRACKS: River Come Down; Soft Blow The Summer Winds; Black Girl; Dunya; Fennario; Ride, Ride, Ride;/ 500 Miles; Rock Me Lord; Make Me A Pallet; Chase The Rising Sun; Cumberland Mountain Deer Chase; Gilgara Mountain)

Capitol T/ST-1770 Coming Attraction – Live! (09/62; the mono LP has the words "Coming Attraction" in tan lettering with the word "Live!" in white, while the stereo LP has all of the lettering in white.)

(TRACKS: I Am A Poor And A Ramblin' Boy; Dark As A Dungeon; Old Joe Clarke's Blues; In The Evening; Metamorphosis; Wagoner's Lad;/ Cotton Mill Girls; I Never Will Marry; Gypsy Rover; Born In Bethlehem; Jack The Sailor; Johnny Booker)

Capitol T/ST-1951 New Directions In Folk Music (09/63)

(TRACKS: Stackolee; All The Pretty Little Horses; Two Hoboes; San Francisco Bay [Version 2]; Someone To Talk My Troubles To; Ja-Da;/ Bay Of Mexico; Ben And Me; Someday Baby; One Quick Martini; Country Blues; Four Strong Winds)

Capitol CDP 7 98536 2 Capitol Collector's Series - The Journeymen (May 1992)

(TRACKS: Greenland Whale Fisheries; Oh, Miss Mary; Mary Wore Three Links Of Chain; I May Be Right; River Come Down; 500 Miles; Chase The Rising Sun; Make Me A Pallet; Fennario; Cotton Mill Girls [live]; Dark As A Dungeon [live]; Old Joe Clarke's Blues [live]; Wagoner's Lad [live]; Stackolee; Bay Of Mexico; All The Pretty Little Horses; Virgin Mary; Two Hoboes; Environment; Someone To Talk My Troubles To; Ja-Da; Four Strong Winds; What'll I Do?; Don't Turn Around – all of the tracks have been remixed from the original 3-track master tapes.)

CCM-415-2, Collector's Choice Music   The Journeymen (expanded reissue of ebut album) (February 2003)

(TRACKS: River She Come Down; Soft Blow The Summer Winds; Black Girl; Dunya; Fennario; Ride, Ride, Ride; 500 Miles; Rock Me Lord; Make Me A Pallet; Chase The Rising Sun; Cumberland Mountain Deer Chase; Gilgar Mountain. BONUS TRACKS: Heredity-Environment; The Ballad of the Shape of Things; Kumbaya (Single Version); Oh, Miss Mary; Jack the Sailor (Studio Version); Kumbaya (Mono Single Version). Unlisted Track: Advertisement for Armstrong Tiles.

CCM-416-2, Collector's Choice Music   Coming Attraction Live! (expanded reissue of original album) (2003)

(TRACKS: I Am A Poor And Ramblin' Boy; Dark As A Dungeon: Old Joe Clarke's Blues; In The Evening; Metamorphosis; Waggoner's Lad; Cotton Mill Girls; I Never Will Marry; Gypsy Rover; Born In Bethlehem; Jack The Sailor; Johnny Booker. BONUS TRACKS: Don't Turn Around (Single); I Never Will Marry (Single); Hush Now Sally (Single); Rock Island Line; One Quick Martini (Live At the Padded Cell); Benny (Live At The Padded Cell); How Mountain Girls Can Love (Live At the Padded Cell); Loadin' Coal (Single); What'll I Do (Single); Tell Ole Bill.

CCM-417, Collector's Choice Music   New Directions in Folk Music (Expanded Reissue of Original Album) (2003)

(TRACKS: Stackolee; All The Pretty Little Horses; Two Hoboes; San Francisco Bay Blues; Someone To Talk My Troubles To; Ja-Da; Bay of Mexico; Ben and Me; Someday Baby; One Quick Martini; Country Blues; Four Strong Winds; BONUS TRACKS: Rag Mama; San Francisco Bay Blues (Alternate Version); Makes A Long Time Man Feel Bad; Virgin Mary; Mary Wore Three Links of Chain; I May Be Right; Greenland Whale Fisheries. Unlisted Track: Advertisement for Armstrong Tiles)

RADIO SHOWS

"Veterans Administration Presents Here's To Veterans," 1963. A-side: Program No. 1022 – The Journeymen (Orphans Education Program) (Time 14:30).   Contains John Phillips vocal introductions before the songs "Ja-Da," "Stackolee," "All The Pretty Little Horses," and "Ben And Me." The record was processed and pressed by Columbia Records.

COMMERCIALS

The Journeymen recorded radio commercials for Canada Dry Ginger Ale (1961), a San Francisco bread company (1961), Schlitz Beer (1962-1964), and Armstrong Tile (airing on *The Danny Kaye Show* starting on 09/25/63).

SELECTED CONCERTS, LIVE APPEARANCES AND IMPORTANT DATES OF THE COLONIALS & THE HALIFAX THREE

THE COLONIALS

January 21, 1961, Denny Doherty, *Birt's Bandstand* audition, Canadian Broadcasting Corporation.

March 5, 1961, Capitol Theatre, CBHT Channel 3, CBH, 1340 Radio. Halifax Symphony Benefit Pop Concert. The Colonials perform "They Call The Wind Maria."

April 8, 1961, *Birt's Bandstand,* Canadian Broadcasting Corporation. Sang "The Wind They Call Mariah," "Hold Him Joe," "Scarlet Ribbons," "San Pedro."

June 2, 1961, Sobey's Grocery Store.

July 1961, *Travellin' On Home,* CBHT Television, 16 Episodes.

November 16, 1961, Venus de Milo Room, Montreal, Quebec. Appearing with Dino Vale with Gerry DeVilliers.

December 29, 1961-January 5, 1962, *The Tommy Ambrose Show* TV, CBWT.

January 24, 29, 1962, February 2, 1962, February 9, 1962, Lou Black's Living Room, Montreal, Quebec, with Iris Paul and Liane.

February-March, 1962, Four weeks in Toronto, Ontario.

March 12-18, 1962, The Seaway Hotel, Toronto, Ontario.

March 26-April 1, 1962, The Seaway Hotel, Toronto, Ontario.

April 6, 1962. Two Week Engagement. Fallsway Hotel, Niagara Falls, Ontario.

Early 1962, The Colonial Hotel, Sarnia, Ontario.

THE HALIFAX THREE

Unknown Date, Village Gate, Greenwich Village, New York, New York, with Adam Keefe.

June 23, 1962, *Parade* TV show. Filmed around Metro Toronto with Richard Hayman, Elon Stuart, Ian Tyson, and the Carl Tapscott Singers.

July 8, 1962, House of Hambourg, Toronto, Ontario.

October 6, 1962, House of Hambourg, Toronto, Ontario.

October 13 or 15, 1962, *Juliette Show,* CBWT.

December 7, 1962, *The Tommy Ambrose Show*.

December 28, 1962, The Village Corner, Toronto, Ontario.

January 19, 1963, Plainview High School, Opening for "An Evening With Shelley Berman."

January 29-February 10, 1963, The Fifth Peg, with Bill Cosby. Carolyn Hester fell ill and The Halifax Three replaced her. Reported as "Halifax Three Plus One" (probably with Eric Hord).

February 25, 1963, reports of nightclub tour of Canada that month.

March 1, 1963, Houlton State Armory, Part of Ricker College's annual Snow Ball, Bangor, Maine.

March 8-30, 1963, House of Pegasus, Fort Lauderdale, Florida. Jonathan Talbot accompanying.

March-April 1963, appearing in Fort Lauderdale, Orlando, and Tampa, Florida, as the Triple S Triplets.

April 17, 1963, Rippowam High School, Stamford, Connecticut.

June 3, 1963, The Casino, Washington, D.C. Referred to as Quartet. Appearing with Knoblick Upper 10,000, Judy Lloyd, Don Sherman & Lynn Gold.

June 7, 1963, *The Tommy Ambrose Show*.

Summer 1963, Unknown Date, United Way Fundraiser-Concert, Washington, D.C. Appeared with Judy Collins, Rod McKuen. Robert F. Kennedy, Keynote Speaker.

June 25-29, 1963, Scheduled for American Folk Festival. Asheville, North Carolina.

Summer 1963, Tour with Shelley Berman.

Summer 1963, House of Hambourg, Toronto, Ontario.

July 31 and August 4-11, 1963, The Shadows, Virginia Beach, Virginia. Paul Winter Sextet opened. Zal Yanovsksy played with the group.

August 7, 1963, Palisades Park, New Jersey, with Judy Lloyd.

August 26-September 7, 1963. Faragher's, Cleveland Ohio.

September 3, 1963, *The Mike Douglas Show*, with Ralph Lee Smith, Tom Glazer, Laura Green, Hans Holzer, and Hal March. Also broadcast on September 10, 1963.

September 12, 1963, Garden State Plaza, New Jersey, with Oscar Brand.

September 15, 1963, "Something to Sing About" with Ian & Sylvia, The Raftsmen, Shirley Singer, The Travelers, and Tom Hawken. Celebrating CTV's new Coast-to-Coast microwave relay system. The Halifax Three sang from Peggy's Cove at the entrance of Halifax Harbor. Zal Yanovsky with them.

September 19, 1963. Kiwanis Club Barbecue. Flint, Michigan.

September 21, 1963, Battle Creek, Michigan, W.K. Kellogg Auditorium, "The American Hootenanny Festival" with Elan Stuart, The Talisman Four, Bill Biedler, and Ron Haller. Sponsored by the Birchwood Methodist Men's Club.

September 23, 1963, *The Jerry Lester Show* (1st Episode) on CTV. With Ruth Walker, William Walker, Adam Keefe, and Gene Wood. Sang "The Green Green[sic]" and "Rocky Road."

October 1, 1963, United Givers Fund Rally (Televised), International Inn, Washington, D.C. Appeared with Rod McKuen, Judy Collins and actor David Wayne. Attorney General Robert F. Kennedy was the featured speaker. The Suitland High School band also played at the kickoff-dinner rally.

October 4-5, 1963, Hootenanny Haven, Baltimore, Maryland. Also appearing, Paul "Biff" Rose.

October 17, 1963, *Gazette* television show, CBC. Interviewed by Jim Bennet.

October 18, 1963, "World's Biggest Hootenanny," Maple Leaf Gardens, Toronto, Ontario. Appearing with The Tarriers, Judy Henske, Elan Stuart, The Towne Criers, The Pioneers, The Chanteclers, Dave Wiffin, and Greg Winkfield.

October 26, 1963, Ontario Agricultural College, Mariposa Arts Weekend.

Hootenanny USA Tour with Jo Mapes, The Geezinslaw Brothers, The Journeymen, and Glenn Yarbrough:

October 31, 1963, Greensboro Coliseum, Greensboro, North Carolina.

November 1, 1963, 8:30 PM, Dorton Arena, Raleigh, North Carolina.

November 2, 1963, Greenville Memorial Auditorium, Greenville, South Carolina.

November 3, 1963, City Auditorium, Atlanta, Georgia.

November 4, 1963, Municipal Coliseum, Knoxville, Tennessee.

November 5, 1963, Municipal Auditorium, Columbus, Georgia. 1100 in attendance.

November 8, 1963, Township Auditorium, Columbia South Carolina. Less than 500 in attendance.

November 9, 1963, Bell Auditorium, Augusta, Georgia.

November 10, 1963, Charlotte Coliseum, North Carolina.

November 11, 1963, Macon City Auditorium, Macon, Georgia.

November 12, 1963, City Auditorium, Chattanooga, Tennessee.

November 14, 1963, Memphis, Tennessee.

November 15, 1963, City Auditorium, Jackson, Mississippi. Scheduled but canceled.

November 16, 1963 at Alabama State Garrett Coliseum, Montgomery, Alabama.

November 17, 1963, Loyola University, Field House, New Orleans, Louisiana.

November 18, 1963, McNeese Arena, McNeese State University, Louisiana. Scheduled but canceled.

November 19, 1963, Municipal Auditorium, Lafayette, Louisiana.

November 20, 1963, Arcadia Theater/Wichita Forum, Wichita Kansas.

November 21, 1963, 7:30 PM, Kansas State University, University Auditorium, Manhattan, Kansas.

November 23, 1963, KRNT Theater, Des Moines Iowa. Scheduled but canceled.

November 24, 1963, Orpheum Movie Theater, Springfield Illinois. Scheduled

November 25, 1963, Miami University, Oxford, Ohio.

November 26, 1963, Columbus Veterans War Auditorium, Columbus, Ohio.

November 27, 1963, Washington Coliseum, Washington D.C.

November 28, 1963, Mosque Theatre, Newark, New Jersey

November 29, 1963, County Center, White Plains, New York, "Campus Type, Folk Music 2 Hour Folk Sing Along."

November 30, 1963, Carnegie Hall, New York, last show of tour. 1,200 in attendance according to *The New York Times*.

January 25, 1964, *Radio Hootenanny* with Nick Corvello featuring The Halifax Three and others WYDD FM. May have simply played recordings.

January 1964, Royal York Hotel.

Unknown Date, Grossinger's Catskill Resort Hotel, Liberty, New York.

Unknown Date, *Let's Sing Out*, CTV Television Network.

Unknown Date, *Sing Along with Mitch*, NBC TV.

THE COLONIALS/THE HALIFAX THREE

SESSIONOGRAPHY AND DISCOGRAPHY

As THE COLONIALS (all tracks recorded in an unknown studio in Halifax, Nova Scotia, Canada)

Cora (02/61)

Scarlet Ribbons (02/61)

Passing Through (02/61)

Hold 'Em Joe (02/61)

Blow Ye Winds (02/61)

Kisses Sweeter Than Wine (02/61)

All My Trials Lord (02/61)

Mangwani Mpulele (02/61)

Maria (02/61)

17 Days in the Saddle (02/61)

As THE HALIFAX THREE (all tracks recorded at Columbia Studios, New York, except *)

Something Old – Something New (05/28/62)

Far Side Of The Hill (05/28/62)

Fare-Thee-Well (05/28/62)

Hush Little Baby (06/07/62)

All My Trials (06/07/62)

Headin' On Home Again (06/08/62)

Bull Train (06/11/62)

I Passed By A Stream (06/11/62)

Come On By (06/11/62)

When I First Came To This Land (06/11/62)

Oh Mary Don't You Weep (06/11/62)

Come Down The Mountain Katie Daly (09/05/62)

The Man Who Wouldn't Sing Along With Mitch (01/21/63)

Sing Hallelujah (01/21/63)

A Satisfied Mind (04/14/63, received 04/15/63)

The Great Silky (04/14/63, received 04/15/63)

Little Sparrow (04/17/63, received 04/18/63)

San Miguel (04/17/63, received 04/18/63)

East Virginia (04/18/63, received 04/19/63)

I'm Gonna Tell God (04/18/63, received 04/19/63)

He Call Me Boy (04/18/63, received 04/19/63)

San Francisco Bay Blues (04/21/63, received 04/22/63)

Rocks And Gravel (04/21/63, received 04/22/63)

Rubin Had A Train (04/21/63, received 04/22/63)

All The Good Times (Based on Goodnight Irene) (09/11/63; recorded at an unknown church in New York City with a gospel choir)*

SINGLES

THE COLONIALS

Rodeo 280 They Call The Wind Maria/ All My Trials Lord
   Soon Be Over (02/61)

THE HALIFAX THREE

Epic 5-9560 Bull Train/ Come On By (11/62)
   Epic 5-9572 The Man Who Wouldn't Sing Along With Mitch/
   Come Down The Mountain Katie Daly (02/63; with picture sleeve)
Epic 5-9637 San Francisco Bay Blues/ All The Good Times (Based on
   Goodnight Irene) (11/63; B-side non-LP)

ALBUMS

THE COLONIALS

Banff (A Product of Rodeo Records Ltd.) RBS-1180   Hootenanny
   (1961)
(TRACKS: Cora, Scarlet Ribbons, Passing Through, Hold 'Em Joe,
   Blow Ye Winds, Kisses Sweeter Than Wine, All My Trials Lord,
   Mangwani Mpulele, Maria, 17 Days in the Saddle)

THE HALIFAX THREE

Epic LN 24038/ BN 26038   The Halifax Three (01/63)
(TRACKS: Bull Train; I Passed By A Stream; Something Old –
   Something New; Hush Little Baby; All My Trials; Come On By;/
   Come Down The Mountain Katie Daly; Far Side Of The Hill;
   When I First Came To This Land; Fare-Thee-Well; Headin' On
   Home Again; Oh Mary Don't You Weep)
Epic LN 24060/ BN 26060   San Francisco Bay Blues (07/63)
(TRACKS: San Francisco Bay Blues; Rocks And Gravel; Little
   Sparrow; San Miguel; Sing Hallelujah; East Virginia;/ I'm Gonna
   Tell God; Rubin Had A Train; A Satisfied Mind; The Man Who
   Wouldn't Sing Along With Mitch; The Great Silky; He Call Me
   Boy [sic])
Collectors Choice Music– CCM-298-2   The Complete Halifax Three
   (CD Reissue of both albums and non-LP single track). (2002)
(TRACKS: Bull Train; I Passed By A Stream; Something Old –
   Something New; Hush Little Baby; All My Trials; Come On By;/
   Come Down The Mountain Katie Daly; Far Side Of The Hill;
   When I First Came To This Land; Fare-Thee-Well; Headin' On
   Home Again; Oh Mary Don't You Weep, San Francisco Bay Blues;
   Rocks And Gravel; Little Sparrow; San Miguel; Sing Hallelujah;
   East Virginia;/ I'm Gonna Tell God; Rubin Had A Train; A Satisfied
   Mind; The Man Who Wouldn't Sing Along With Mitch; The Great
   Silky; He Call Me Boy. BONUS TRACK; All The Good Times).

RADIO SHOWS

The World Of Folk Music With Oscar Brand, United States Social
   Security Department, 1963 (Episode #86). Contains brief
   interviews and live performances of "The Man Who Wouldn't
   Sing Along With Mitch" and "When I First Came To This Land."

SELECTED CONCERTS, LIVE PERFORMANCES, AND IMPORTANT DATES OF CASS ELLIOT, THE TRIUMVIRATE, AND THE BIG 3

ELLEN COHEN IN THE BOY FRIEND

August 23-30, 1959, New Hilltop Theater, Owings Mills, Maryland
   ("For the first time in Maryland Summer Theater History a
   production will be held over for a 4th Week"-according to *The
   Baltimore Sun*)

ELLEN COHEN IN PRIOR TO BROADWAY

September 15-20, New Hilltop Theater, Owings Mills, Maryland

CASS ELLIOT IN THE MUSIC MAN

June 26-July 8, 1962, Northland Playhouse, Detroit, Michigan.
July 9-21, 1962, The Pocono Playhouse, Mountainhome, Pennsylvania.
July 23-28, 1962, Ogunquit Playhouse, Maine.
July 30-August 4, 1962, Lakewood Theater, Bangor, Maine.
August 6-13, 1962, Lake Whalom Playhouse, Fitchburg,
   Massachusetts.
August 14-20, 1962, The Lakes Region/Gilford Playhouse, New
   Hampshire.
August 20-25, 1962, Ivoryton Playhouse, Connecticut.
August 27-September 1, 1962, Tappan Zee Playhouse, Nyack, New
   York.

THE TRIUMVIRATE (ALSO BILLED AS THE TRIUMVIRATES)

December 1962, Unknown Christmas Party, Fred Niles Film Studio, Chicago, Illinois.

December 1962, Old Town North, Chicago, Illinois.

December 1962. The Fickle Pickle, Chicago, Illinois.

December 1962, The Rising Moon, Chicago, Illinois.

December 1962, Gate of Horn, Chicago, Illinois.

December 1962, La Cave, Cleveland, Ohio. A June 1963 newspaper listed a Radio Show on WCLV in Cleveland that was going to play "Folk Music in Stereo with The Triumvirate Folk Group recorded at La Cave."

December 1962, *The One O'Clock Club*, Cleveland Ohio Television Show, WEWS.

January 22, 1963, Gate of Horn, Chicago, Illinois.

February 1963, The Crooked Ear, Omaha, Nebraska.

February 22- March 7, 1963, The Third Man Coffee House, Omaha, Nebraska, with James Hendricks opening).

THE BIG 3

May 9, 1963, Gaslight Café, New York, New York. "1st New York Engagement, New Folk Group"; appearing with Len Chandler and John Hammond.

May 25, 1963, *Billboard* magazine referred to Roy Silver and Fred Weintraub managing The Big 3 under the auspices of "New Talent Directions," also one of Weintraub's "picks."

June 8, 1963, The Bitter End, New York, New York. "Making their first professional appearance"; also reported as opening for Bud & Travis, with Bill Cosby.

June-July 1963, The Bitter End, New York, New York.

July 2, 1963, *Arthur Godfrey's Talent Scouts*. One article said they sang "Railroad Man" (possibly "Makes a Longtime Man Feel Bad" or "Rider") and another said they sang "Goodbye, My Honey" (referring to "Nora's Dove").

July 3, 1963, Free Hootenanny Show at Palisades Amusement Park, New Jersey. Appearing with The Callicoats and Casey Anderson. Live 1 ½ hour program each Wednesday night, broadcast on WINS.

July 20, 1963, *Cash Box* magazine "held over for the third time at The Bitter End"; Billboard Magazine indicates FM Records had "already recorded" an album by The Big 3.

July 29-August 11, 1963, The Shadows, Washington, D.C. Valentine Pringle opening.

August 28-September 2, 1963, The Shadows, Virginia Beach, Virginia. Also appearing - Paul Winters Jazz Sextet. Last Act of the Season.

September 1, 1963, Princess Anne Courthouse, Virginia Beach, Virginia. Fraternal Order of Police Lodge Cabaret.

September 6, 1963, Rock-a-Hoot, Hunter's Lodge, Fairfax Virginia. Attended by 500.

Early September 1963, Boston University, broadcast on ABC-TV *Hootenanny*, October 24, 26. Appeared with Woody Allen, The Chad Mitchell Trio, and Jo Mapes.

September 12, 1963, *The Tonight Show* (in color), New York, New York. With Kurt Kasznar, Gene Baylos, Jesse White, and Constance Towers.

September 21, 1963, The Exodus Club, Denver, Colorado.

September 23, *The Tonight Show* (in color), also with Richard Egan, Henny Youngman.

October 10, 1963, *The Tonight Show* (in color), New York, New York, with Al Capp and Dr. Voost Meerloo.

October 12, 1963, Cornell University, Barton Hall, Ithaca, New York, with Lydia Woods, Brooks Jones, Johnny Gil & Bobby, Stan Rubin and the Tigertown Five, The Grandison Singers, and comedian Dick Davey. Sponsored by the Inter Fraternity Council.

A Folk Festival, appearing with Jack Linkletter, Joe & Eddie, Lex Baxter's Balladeers, Raun Mackinnon. Reported as "16 One Night Stands."

October 18, 1963, Sioux Falls, South Dakota. Later broadcast on *Hootenanny*.

October 21, 1963, Capitol Theater, Madison, Wisconsin.

October 22, 1963, Minneapolis Auditorium, Minneapolis, Minnesota.

October 23, 1963, Kiel Opera House, St. Louis, Missouri .

October 24, 1963, Parthenon Theater, Hammond, Indiana. The tour stopped to eat at Mary Ann Restaurant in Spiceland, Indiana "on the way from Hammond to Evansville."

October 25, 1963, Olympia Stadium, Detroit, Michigan.

October 26, 1963, Northwestern University, Evanston, Illinois. Homecoming Jamboree to over 3,500. Played with Paul Winter Jazz Sextet and Jan Murray. (Not a *Folk Festival* appearance).

October 27, 1963, The Showplace, Milwaukee Wisconsin. 3 Shows.

October 30, 1963, Toledo Sports Arena, Toledo, Ohio.

November 1, 1963, Roberts Stadium, Evansville, Indiana.

November 3, 1963, Centennial Hall at Augustana College in Rock Island, Illinois. Along with other members of the *Folk Festival*, appeared with local groups The Bettendorf High River Ramblers and The William Dale Singers. Crowd of 1,500.

November 5, 1963, at Cedar Rapids Memorial Coliseum, Cedar Rapids, Iowa. 700 in attendance.

November 6, 1963, Illinois State Normal University's Horton Field House, Bloomington, Illinois. Audience of 4,000. Performed "Winken Blinken Nod."

November 7, 1963, Veterans Memorial Auditorium, Des Moines, Iowa.

November 8, 1963, Pershing Auditorium, Lincoln Nebraska. Characterized in advance press as "Witty but irreverent."

November 10, 1963, 2:30 and 8:00 PM, Memorial Hall, Kansas City, Kansas.

November 12, 1963 at Fordham University. Sang "Nora's Dove." Appeared with Woody Allen, New Christy Minstrels, Leon Bibb, Will Holt, Joan Tolliver, and the Dukes of Dixieland. Crowd of 850. Broadcast on ABC-TV on November 16, 1963. (Not a *Folk Festival* appearance).

November 14, 1963, Folk Music Festival sponsored by Twin City Junior Chamber of Commerce in St Joseph High School Gymnasium, St. Joseph, Michigan. Audience of 1,200

November 16, 1963, War Memorial, Syracuse, New York. Sang "Dark as a Dungeon" and "Rider." 3,500 people attended

November 17, 1963, Kleinhans Music Hall, Buffalo, New York, 400 people attended.

November 21, 1963, 8 and 10 PM, The Stanton Theater, 514 North Howard Street, Baltimore with Jack Linkletter, Les Baxter's Balladeers.

November 23, 1963, The RKO Flushing Theater. Continuous appearances all day alternating with the "screen attraction." (Canceled?)

November 25, 1963, broadcast on December 4, 1963, *The Danny Kaye Show*, sang "Rider."

December 6, 1963, 7:15 and 9:30 PM, Winter Folk Festival, Richmond Arena, Richmond, Virginia. Appearing with The Virginians, Fanny Hill Singers, Marilyn Moren, Virginia Travelers, and John Bassette. Concert may actually have taken place at The Mosque Theater Auditorium in Richmond

December 8, 1963, American University, Homecoming Concert, Washington, D.C.

December 9, 1963, The Shadows, Georgetown, Washington, D.C.

December 16, 1963. *The Tonight Show* (in color), New York, New York. Performed "O Holy Night."

December 19, 1963, The Shadows, Georgetown, Washington, D.C.

Fall 1963, The Academy of Music, Philadelphia, Pennsylvania.

January 13, 1964, *Meetin' House* show, Chicago FM Radio WXRT with Jerry Woods. Also, Bob Gibson and Peter, Paul & Mary.

January 20, 1964, *The Tonight Show*. Also appearing, Rosemary Clooney, John Bubbles, David Atkinson, Eva Gabor.

January 25, 1964, Indianapolis Armory, Indianapolis, Indiana. Hootenanny sponsored by the Lion's Club, featuring Leon Bibb, Raun McKinnon, and the Stuart Ramsey Trio.

January 27, 1964, *Meetin' House* show on Chicago FM Radio WXRT with Jerry Woods. Also with The Good Time Singers and The Kingston Trio.

February 12, 1964, Recording Second Album.

February 21, 1964, Academy of Music, Philadelphia, Pennsylvania, with Bill Cosby.

March 9, 1964, *The Tonight Show*.

March 6, March 13-15, March 20, 1964, Crossway Airport Inn, Miami, Florida.

March 26, 1964, *The Tonight Show*. Also an Easter Parade fashion show.

April 1, 1964, *The Mike Douglas Show*, with guest Gordon Hall; Hootenanny with Bob Gibson, Walter Slezak, Jerry Lester and Betty Johnson.

The Midwest Folk Festival/Jamboree. Appearing with Jimmie Rodgers, Gale Garnett, The Countrymen, Jeff Espina, The Original Folk Jazz Trio, and The Yeomen.

April 10, 1964, Minneapolis, Minnesota. "The Parkettes Present Midwest Folk Jamboree" at The Minneapolis Auditorium. Newspaper article says The Big 3 and other groups were secured for 16-day, 7-state tour.

April 12, 1964, 7:30 PM, Gym at Manitowoc School of Vocation, Technical and Adult Education, Mantiwoc, Wisconsin. Sponsored by Manitowoc Collegiate Student Union.

April 12, 1964, 8:30 PM, Sheboygan Armory, Sheboygan, Wisconsin. Also appearing with the groups were The New Providence Singers, Sheboygan's Own De Cappas. 2 ½ hour show. Sponsored by the Sheboygan Jaycees.

April 14, 1964, Memorial Auditorium, Burlington, Iowa. Also appearing was Judy Reddick and The Eureka Singers. 300 people attended. Sang "Ringo."

April 15, 1964, L.L. Culver Gymnasium, Culver Stockton College,

Canton, Iowa. Sponsored by the Pan Hellenic Council. Also appearing with the groups were The Bondsmen.

April 16, 1964. Regis Auditorium, Regis High School, Cedar Rapids, Iowa, The Midwest Hootenanny Festival, appearing with the groups were The New Providence Singers.

April 17, 1964, Fremont, Nebraska, Fremont City Auditorium, Hootenanny Festival.

April 21, 1964, Loras College Fieldhouse, Dubuque, Iowa.

April 23, 1964, Austin High School Auditorium, Austin Minnesota. Sponsored by Austin Junior College Yearbook.

April 24, 1964, Grace Hall, Lehigh University, "The First Spring Houseparty" featuring The Four Seasons, The Four Lads, The Big Three.

April 27- May 9, 1964, The Embers, Indianapolis, Indiana. Appearing also, Susan Barrett.

Some of the following appearances may not have materialized. Documentation is for both confirmed and scheduled performances. If they did take place, they likely involved Denny Doherty and Zal Yanovsky, without Tim Rose in a pre-Mugwumps or quasi-Mugwumps assemblage.

May 12-17, 1964, Someplace Else, Boston, Massachusetts. (Reported May 1, 1964.)

May 28-June 3, 1964, The Bitter End, New York. Billed as "Cass Elliot and The Big 3" and "Five Time Winner" on *The Tonight Show*. Appearing with Jim, Jake and Joan, and Joan Tolliver.

June 1964, The Establishment, Winnipeg, Manitoba. (Probably did not occur but reported on May 16, 1964.)

June 10, 1964, "Cass Elliot & The Big 3," Nathan's Gardens, Long Island, New York.

June 20, 1964, "Cass Elliot & The Big 3," The Bitter End, New York, New York.

July 16, 1964, "The Big Three" Atlanta, Georgia, City Auditorium, with Josh White and The Town Criers.

August 24, 1964, "Cass Elliot & The Big 3," Nathan's/Roadside Rest at Coney Island, Part of Oceanside Music Festival. Seated 1,200 under tent. (Announced July 4, 1964 in *The New York Times*.)

THE BIG 3 SESSIONOGRAPHY & DISCOGRAPHY

Rider (09/63; Music Makers Studio, New York)

(It Makes) A Long Time Man Feel Bad (09/63; Music Makers Studio, New York)

Nora's Dove (Dink's Song) (09/63; Music Makers Studio, New York)

Young Girl's Lament (09/63; Music Makers Studio, New York)

Sing Hallelujah (09/63; Music Makers Studio, New York)

Come Along (09/63; Music Makers Studio, New York)

Dark As A Dungeon (09/63; Music Makers Studio, New York)

The Banjo Song (09/63; Music Makers Studio, New York)

Winkin', Blinkin' & Nod (09/63; Music Makers Studio, New York)

Ho Honey Oh (09/63; Music Makers Studio, New York)

Come Away Melinda (09/63; Music Makers Studio, New York)

Come Along (live version) (late 1963)

I May Be Right (02/64; Gotham Studios, New York)

Anna Fia (Feher) (02/64; Gotham Studios, New York)

Tony And Delia (02/64; Gotham Studios, New York)

Grandfather's Clock (02/64; Gotham Studios, New York)

Silkie (02/64; Gotham Studios, New York)

Ringo (02/64; Gotham Studios, New York)

Down In The Valley (02/64; Gotham Studios, New York)

Wild Women (02/64; Gotham Studios, New York)

All The Pretty Little Horses (02/64; Gotham Studios, New York)

Glory Glory (02/64; Gotham Studios, New York)

SINGLES

FM 3003   The Banjo Song/ Winkin' Blinkin' & Nod (10/63)

FM FM-9001 Come Away Melinda (different mix)/ Rider (12/63; A-side non-LP)

FM FM-9004 The Banjo Song/ Winken Blinken Nod (01/64)

Tollie 9006 The Banjo Song/ Winken, Blinken And Nod (03/64)

Roulette R-4689 Nora's Dove (Dink's Song)/ Grandfather's Clock (05/66) (with picture sleeve; shown on label as "The Big Three Featuring Cass Elliot – The Big Momma")

NOTE: "Winkin,' Blinkin' And Nod" was variably spelled on the above releases as well as the albums below.

ALBUMS

FM 307/ SFM-307   The Big Three (10/63)
(TRACKS: Rider; [It Makes] A Long Time Man Feel Bad; Nora's Dove [Dink's Song]; Young Girl's Lament; Sing Hallelujah;/ Come Along; Dark As A Dungeon; The Banjo Song; Winkin', Blinkin' & Nod; Ho Honey Oh)

FM 310   A Rootin' Tootin' Hootenanny (06/64; one live track: "Come Along")

FM 311/ SFM-311   The Big Three Live At The Recording Studio (06/64; copies of this LP pressed after the success of The Mamas & The Papas were issued with an orange sticker stating "Featuring Cass Elliot 'The Big Mama' from The Mama's And The Papa's")
(TRACKS: I May Be Right; Anna Fia [Feher]; Tony And Delia; Grandfather's Clock; Silkie; Ringo;/ Down In The Valley; Wild Women; All The Pretty Little Horses; Glory Glory; Come Away Melinda)

FM 319   The World Of Folk Music (1964; various artists LP with exclusive live version of "Come Along")

Roulette R/SR 25361   The Big Three Featuring Cass Elliot (03/68; reissued 05/68 as Roulette SR 42000)
(TRACKS: Young Girl's Lament; The Banjo Song; Winkin', Blinkin' & Nod; Grandfather's Clock; Come Away Melinda;/ Wild Women; Nora's Dove [Dink's Song]; Come Along; Tony And Delia; Ho Honey Oh; Rider)

Accord SN-7180   Distant Reflections (07/82) (shown as THE BIG THREE FEATURING MAMA CASS)
(TRACKS: Grandfather's Clock; Come Away Melinda; Young Girl's Lament; The Banjo Song; Winkin, Blinkin' And Nod;/ Wild Women; Tony And Delia; Ho Honey Oh; Nora's Dove [Dink's Song]; Come Along; Rider)

Sequel Records - NEM CD 755   The Big 3 Featuring Mama Cass Elliot, Tim Rose and Jim Hendricks (1995 CD Reissue of both albums)
(TRACKS: I May Be Right; Anna Fia (Feher); Tony & Delia; Grandfather's Clock; Silkie; Ringo; Down In The Valley; Wild Women; All The Pretty Little Horses; Glory Glory; Come Away Melinda; Young Girl's Lament; The Banjo Song; Winken Blinken and Nod; Ho Honey Oh; Nora's Dove (Dink's Song); Come Along; Rider; It Makes A Long Time Man Feel Bad; Sing Hallelujah; Dark As A Dungeon)

Collectables - COL-CD- 6216   The Big 3 Featuring Mama Cass (2000 CD Reissue release of all but three tracks from both albums)
(TRACKS: Young Girl's Lament; The Banjo Song; Winken, Blinken And Nod; Grandfather's Clock; Come Away Melinda; Wild Women; Nora's Dove; Come Along; Tony And Delia; Ho Honey Oh; Rider; I May Be Right; Anna Fia (Feher); Silkie; Ringo; Down In The Valley; All The Pretty Little Horses; Glory Glory)

RADIO SHOWS

The World of Folk Music - Starring Oscar Brand - "A Series of Radio Shows Produced By The Department of Health, Education and Welfare, Social Security Administration, Bureau of Old Age and Survivors Insurance." Live Performances of Music and short interviews. Episode #105 "The Banjo Song" and "Winkin, Blinkin And Nod" and Episode #148 ("I May Be Right," "Ringo"). Both Episodes 1964.

Guest Star #897, Treasury Department, Air Date 05/31/64, GXTV 92439. Contains live performances of "Winkin', Blinkin' & Nod," "The Banjo Song" and "I May Be Right" with a brief interview.

DEE AND ZEE SESSIONOGRAPHY & DISCOGRAPHY

The Slurp (05/64)
Slurp It (05/64)
Slurpin' (05/64)
I Got The Word (05/64)
Slurp With Me (05/64)

SINGLE

Providence Records TP-2   The Slurp/I Got The Word (05/64)

SELECTED CONCERTS, LIVE APPEARANCES, AND IMPORTANT DATES OF THE MUGWUMPS

July 13, 1964, Began their long running gig at The Shadows, Washington, D.C. that ran until November 1964. (On July 13, 1964, The Shadows opened as a discotheque with a new dance floor.)

July 16, 1964, Atlanta, Georgia, City Auditorium, with Josh White and The Town Criers (Advertised as "The Big 3).

July 17, 1964, The Shadows, Washington, D.C.

July 25, 1964, The Shadows, Washington, D.C.

August 2, 1964, The Shadows, Washington, D.C.

August 3, 1964, *The Tonight Show* (in color), New York, New York. Appeared with Stefanie Powers and Allan Sherman.

August 5, 1964, *The Steve Allison Show*, WWDC Radio, Washington D.C. "Cass and Dennis members of the 'Mugwumps' now appearing at the Shadows club." Appeared on program with Sylvan Reichgut, director of D.C. Selective Service.

August 12-15, 1964, The Shadows, Washington, D.C.

August 13-14, Bell Sound Studios, Recordings with Alan Lorber.

August 22, 1964, reported to be at The Village Vanguard, New York, New York.

August 24, 1964, Nathan's Gardens, Long Island, New York. (Advertised as Cass Elliot & The Big 3.)

August 26, 1964, Rockville Drive-In Theater, Rockville, Maryland. Played atop the snack bar.

September 6, 1964, The Shadows, Washington, D.C.

September 13-17, 1964, The Shadows, Washington, D.C.

September 23, 1964, Alexandria Roller Rink, Alexandria, Virginia. (Opening for The Beach Boys.)

October 2, 1964, The Shadows, Washington, D.C.

October 3, 1964, "Teen Day at the Shadows," The Shadows, Washington, D.C.

October 9, 1964 "Teen Day At The Shadows," The Shadows, Washington, D.C.

October 11, 1964, The Shadows, Washington, D.C.

October 13-18, 1964, The Shadows, Washington D. C.

October 17, 1964, "Rally and Hootenanny" scheduled by the American University Democrats at Dupont Circle. Appeared with Skip Humphrey, an American University student and son of Senator Hubert Humphrey, and Assistant Postmaster General Richard Murphy, presented at 11 AM.

October 24, 1964, The Shadows, Washington D.C.

October/November, Unknown Date, The Peppermint Lounge, New York, New York. Opened for Joey Dee and the Starlighters.

November 6-7, 1964, The Shadows, Washington, D.C. (*The Washington Post* ad for Mugwumps says "Last Weekend at The Shadows.").

November 13, 1964, West Virginia University. Appearing with The Four Saints. Described in one article promoting their concert ahead of time as a "brand new variety singing quartet from New York City."

Fall 1964, Homecoming, Einstein High School, Kensington, Maryland.

Fall 1964, Montgomery Blair High School, Silver Spring, Maryland.

Unknown Date, 1964, Village Corner, Toronto, Ontario.

THE MUGWUMPS SESSIONOGRAPHY AND DISCOGRAPHY

Searchin' (08/64; Bell Sound Studios, New York)

I Don't Wanna Know (08/64; Bell Sound Studios, New York)

I'll Remember Tonight (08/64; Bell Sound Studios, New York)

Here It Is Another Day (08/64; The Shadows, Washington, D.C.)

Do You Know What I Mean (08/64; Bell Sound Studios, New York)

You Can't Judge A Book By The Cover (08/64; Bell Sound Studios, New York)

Everybody's Been Talkin' (08/64; The Shadows, Washington, D.C.)

Do What They Don't Say (08/64; Bell Sound Studios, New York)

So Fine (08/64; Bell Sound Studios, New York)

SINGLES

Warner Bros. 5471   I'll Remember Tonight/ I Don't Wanna Know (09/64)

Warner Bros. 7018   Searchin'/ Here It Is Another Day (04/67)

ALBUMS

Warner Bros. W/WS 1697
  The Mugwumps: An Historic Recording (07/67)
  (TRACKS: Searchin'; I Don't Wanna Know; I'll Remember Tonight; Here It Is Another Day; Do You Know What I Mean;/ You Can't Judge A Book By The Cover; Everybody's Been Talkin'; Do What They Don't Say; So Fine)

UK Valiant VS 134 An Historic Recording Of The Mugwumps (05/70) (TRACKS: same as above with different graphics that employs the original front cover)

Collectors' Choice Music - CCM 795 An Historic Recording Of The

Mugwumps (CD Reissue of Album) (2007)
(TRACKS: Searchin'; I Don't Wanna Know; I'll Remember Tonight; Here It Is Another Day; Do You Know What I Mean;/ You Can't Judge A Book By The Cover; Everybody's Been Talkin'; Do What They Don't Say; So Fine)

THE NEW JOURNEYMEN APPEARANCES, IMPORTANT DATES AND KNOWN RECORDINGS

September 6, 1964, an article in *The Daily Oklahoman* stated that The New Journeymen "recently took on a new look when one of their male members left the group and was replaced with an attractive girl singer who greatly increased the variety in their repertoire."

September 9, 1964, East Carolina University, concluding Freshman Orientation. Sang "When Jesus Met a Woman," "Metamorphosis," "Glorious Kingdom," and "Gypsy Rover."

September 17, 1964, Western Illinois University, Freshman Orientation.

September 19, 1964, Hobart Arena, Troy, Ohio. Appearing with Count Basie, Beverly Wright, and Lou Nelson.

September 23, 1964, Northwest Missouri University, Lamkin Gym, TKE Fraternity sponsored.

September 26, 1964, Iowa Wesleyan College Chapel. Announcement mentioned their singing of "Amazing Grace" and also billed them as "Capitol Recording Stars."

October 10, 1964, Shepherd College, Shepherdstown, West Virginia. Part of Parents Day. Student newspaper article noted "they have only been together since June."

October 16, 1964, Sweet Briar College, Virginia.

October 17, 1964. Northwestern High School. Washington, D.C.

October 30, 1964, University of Rochester, New York, Palestra River Campus. Appeared with The Modern Jazz Quartet.

October 31, 1964, Lynchburg College, Virginia.

November 13, 1964, LaCrosse State University, Wisconsin, AOPi Sorority, FORD CARavan of Music performing with Oscar Peterson Trio.

November 14, 1964, The University of Iowa, Iowa City. In conjunction with Iowa Dad of the Year Day and the Ford Motor Company.

November 21, 1964, Florida State University.

Fall 1964, Queens College, Charlotte, North Carolina, Panhellenic Weekend.

New Year's Weekend, 1964-65, The Shoreham Hotel, Washington, D.C. with Denny Doherty replacing Marshall Brickman. Appeared with Bill Cosby.

January 19, 1965, The Ryerson Polytechnical Institute in Toronto for Canadian television show *Let's Sing Out.* "Children Go Where I Send Thee," "500 Miles," "Jesus Met the Woman at the Well" (with Jesse Colin Young and Bob Carey). Broadcast on February 9, 1965. Rerun June 22, 1965 and again on August 24, 1965.

February 5, 1965, Muskingum College, Ohio. "Winter Weekend" appearing with Comedian Don Rice.

February 21, 1965, Towson State University, Maryland.

March 1-2, 1965, University of Oklahoma, Holmberg Hall.

March 13, 1965, Radford University, Virginia, Preston Hall. (Two concert dates in January had been canceled.)

March 30, 1965, Ryerson Institute of Technology in Toronto. Oscar Brand hosts The New Journeymen, Bob Carey and Jesse Colin Young. "Bound for Higher Ground," "I'm a Rake and Ramblin' Boy," possibly "Red River Valley" (with The Travelers and Tom Shipley).

April 3, 1965, Hartwick College, Oneonta, New York. (Replaced The Kingsmen). Played to over 1000 people.

May 1, 1965, Westfield State College, Dever Auditorium, Springfield, Massachusetts. Part of the college's 125th Anniversary Celebration.May 8, 1965, Firestone High School, Akron, Ohio.

May 1965, *Showing the Way* film, for Pioneer Women Jewish Women's Organization.

RADIO SHOW

The World Of Folk Music With Oscar Brand, United States Social Security Department, 1965 (Episode # 196) – Contains brief interviews and live performances of "Mr. Tambourine Man" and "The Last Thing On My Mind."

OTHER RECORDINGS OF INTEREST

Also of interest may be the 1999 CD, The Magic Circle...Before The Mamas & The Papas which contains tracks by several of the groups profiled in this work.

Varèse Sarabande VSD 5996   The Magic Circle...Before The Mamas & The Papas (CD) (1999)

(TRACKS: Creeque Alley (Single Version)(The Mamas & The Papas); Ride, Ride Ride (The Smoothies); Lonely Boy And Pretty Girl (The Smoothies); Oh Mary Don't You Weep (The Halifax Three); Rider (The Big 3); The Man Who Wouldn't Sing Along

With Mitch (The Halifax Three); Come Along (The Big 3); I May Be Right (The Big 3); Oh Suzanna (The Banjo Song) (Zal Yanovsky, Cass Elliot, Jerry Yester & Jim Hendricks); Bound for Higher Ground (The New Journeymen); Tom Dooley (Jerry Yester, Cass Elliot, Jim Hendricks & Henry Diltz); Searchin' (The Mugwumps); Mr. Tambourine Man (The New Journeymen); I'll Remember Tonight (The Mugwumps); The Last Thing On My Mind (The New Journeymen); California Dreamin' (The Mamas & The Papas).

Iris Music Group B001257YPQ Here's A Song You Might Have Missed Great Record Finds (2006) also available online http://www.orpheusreborn.com/iris/i040.html

Contains Two Versions of "Didn't Want to Have to Do It" by Cass Elliot record in Spring 1965.

Another resource is Erik Jacobsen's website which has online links to several of the 1964 recordings he made between The Big 3 and The Halifax Three and The Mugwumps: https://www.allabouterik.com/musical-journey/early-productions

Acknowledgments

This book is the fruit of four decades of researching, collecting, building friendships, and hearing lots of stories. Many people have played a part in bringing the stories of these lesser known groups to life. A great number of those who contributed have since passed away.

Owen Elliot-Kugell and I have traveled through almost half of our lives together as friends. It is a true blessing that our camaraderie goes beyond her mother's story and I'm so thankful for her support and our abiding friendship, along with that of her husband, my friend Jack Kugell. Over the years, my friends Denny Doherty and Michelle Phillips, have freely and readily given me time to clarify a memory or hear about a new discovery I made. I am grateful to them.

I appreciate Mackenzie Phillips, Jeffrey Phillips, and Chynna and Billy Baldwin's support and friendship as well as that of Jessica Doherty Woods, Emberly Doherty Bergeron, and John Doherty. Barbara Whelan Suchy was a lifeline

to John Phillips's earliest years. Mike Boran invited me to his home, bequeathed me with his Smoothies record and entertained my questions for hours. His widow Christine has taken up that mantle. My late friend, Paul Surratt was the catalyst for much that happened with The Mamas and The Papas legacy from the 1980's forward and he particularly championed The Journeymen's canon. During his life, Scott McKenzie spent time with me in Virginia and elsewhere listening to my questions. The surviving Journeyman Dick Weissman, has faithfully helped me understand much about that group's musical legacy. Pat LaCroix and Paul Ledoux have been trusted lifelines north of the border for decades. Myrna Galle Van Buren was a gem to share about Cass's early days in theater. Roy Silver, Tim Rose and Bob Bowers were always ready with an answer about The Big 3. I am especially indebted to my friend Jim Hendricks as the living veteran of The Big 3 and The Mugwumps. He has listened to me patiently on the phone and in person and shared his unparalleled knowledge graciously. I am blessed to have had conversations and heard the stories of Sheldon Harnick, Marshall Brickman, Gusti Hervey, Joe Cohen, Leah Kunkel, John Brown, Richard Brown, Chris Silver, Robert Embrey, Jr., Henry Diltz, Jerry Yester, Zal Yanovsky, John and Catherine Sebastian, Robert Morgan, Shelley Berman, Ruth Buzzi, Jim Butler, Chet Dowling, Erik Jacobsen, Bob Cavallo, Shel Wildes, Hallette Dawson, Linda Woodward, Hedy West, Jerry Haskew, Jim Butler, Jonathan Talbot, John Wesley Gardner, Doug Grean, Robin Green, Will Schwartau, Marilyn Moren, Mark Oropollo, Cathi Stevenson, Rita Perfater, James Hill, Skip Humphrey, John Eaton, Chris Andrews, Alan Lorber, Stephen Hirsch, Roxanna Rosel, Veyler Hildebrand, Vince Melamed, Bill Cleary, Bill DiCocco, Fred Wheary, Aleta Jenkins, Kevin Rogers, Jeff Foust, Eric Bray, Molly Hord, Daveen Saimo, Scott Petersen & Arthur, Bob Nelson, Homer Willis, Dawn Eden Goldstein, Molly Wiest, and Paul Winters. My editors David Johnson and especially Ryan Pinkard gave me insightful suggestions with much patience.

Clay Black, my dear friend of nearly 50 years, was creative consultant extraordinaire. My designer Adam Hay was the paragon of longsuffering but such a delight in creativity and encouragement.

I gratefully acknowledge the assistance of librarians and archivists in scores of universities and colleges and other institutions who helped me verify concert dates from over 50 and 60 years ago constituting a compilation of hundreds of appearances by the various groups: The Library of Congress Performing Arts Reading Room librarians, Cait Miller, Melissa Wertheimer and Stacey Jocoy; The Beaton Institute at Cape Breton University; Laurie Lounsberry, Alfred University; Matthew Lyons, Drexel University; Gabriella DiMeglio, Fordham University; Heidi Pettitt, Loras College; Fred Moratori, Cornell University; Catie Huggins, Northwestern University; Harrison Wick, Indiana State College; Adrian Broughman, Sweet Briar College; Jane LaBarbara, West Virginia University; Harland Eastman, Nasson College; April Armstrong, Princeton University; Leslie Nellis, American University; Robyn Lambert, Culver Stockton College; Kathy Renner, Westminster College; Jane Cowan, Cameron University; Elizabeth Scott, East Stroudsberg University; Prudence Doherty, University of Vermont; Olivia Garrison, Iowa State University; Steve Cox, Pittsburg State University; William Garvin, Drury University; Ariel Myers, Lynchburg College, Cliff Hight, Kansas State University; Melissa Mead, University of Rochester; Ray Butti, Brown University; Deanna Migdal, Na'amat; Stephanie Gardner, Bridgewater College; Germain Bienvenu and Barry Cowan, Louisiana State University; Patricia Threatt, McNeese University; Paul Haggett, St. Lawrence University; Joy Conwell, Iowa Wesleyan University; Ali Zawoyski and Kimberly Sims, The College of William & Mary; Rachel Gleiberman, Hartwick College. Thomas Raffleberger, Westfield State University Archives, as well as many others.

My colleagues who are mutual historians in responsibly documenting the history of The Mamas and The Papas and the period were a great encouragement to me: Karl Baker, Chris Campion, Richie Unterberger, Mark Opsasnik, Simon Wordsworth, Greg Russo and Eddie Fiegel. Fellow devotees Tony Sbriglia, Charles Corbett, Eran Edry, Kelly Ferrante, Kette, Jon Johnson and the late Sandy Granger heartened me with support in all of their individual ways.

And special thanks to my friends growing-up, Jack Cummings III and Jennifer Jenkins Wakefield who first introduced me to The Mamas and The Papas.

Finally, I thank my family for their support. My parents and my sister heard much of this music starting 40 years ago and have not just tolerated my avocation but embraced it. My daughters Libby, Clara and Alice have been more than patient with this endeavor, living with ever-present memorabilia and "Mamas and Papas stuff." Last but not least, I am deeply indebted to my beloved wife Karen, who has championed this book from the very start and loved me well in doing so. There have been many turns along this journey where I could have easily scotched the project. She has never wavered in her belief that the stories should be told and that I should tell them.

"And the singers and musicians all played as one to make one sound" 2 Chronicles 5:12-13

Photograph Credits

All photographs are from the author's personal archives and collection or used with express permission, including that of Barbara Nutwell Whelan Suchy, Molly Wiest & Jack Kugell, Christine Boran, Kette, Erik Jacobsen, Stephen Hirsch, Jonathan Talbot, Pat LaCroix, Paul Ledoux, Art, and Richard Brown, Simon Wordsworth, Tony Sbriglia, Marshall Brickman, Jeffrey Phillips and Fred Wheary.

Author

Richard Campbell serves as a Circuit Court Judge in Richmond, Virginia, and has been a judge and attorney in Virginia for nearly 30 years. Longer than that, he has been an avid collector of all things Mamas & Papas. "The Keeper of the Flame" as Michelle Phillips once dubbed him, Judge Campbell has been a consultant and/or expert for television programs such as *A & E Biography*, *Lifetime's Intimate Portrait*, *VH1's Behind the Music*, *Bravo TV* (Canada) and *E! True Hollywood Story*. He worked as a special consultant and contributor to Denny Doherty's theatrical production, *Dream a Little Dream – the Nearly True Story of the Mamas and the Papas* in Halifax, Toronto and New York –Off Broadway from 1999-2004. Together with Owen Elliot-Kugell, daughter of Cass Elliot, he created www.casselliot.

com, The Official Cass Elliot Website, over 25 years ago. Currently he is serving as an acting content adviser on an upcoming documentary on Cass Elliot, as well as an historical compilation of the complete discography of John Phillips compositions. He has penned and published more than 25 sets of liner notes for Mamas & Papas associated digital reissues and been quoted in domestic and international print and broadcast media. Additionally, he has taught a course on the History of Sixties Rock at The University of Richmond and Virginia Commonwealth University. Judge Campbell is a graduate of The College of William & Mary, and The University of Richmond School of Law and makes his home in Richmond with his wife and three daughters and their English Labrador Retriever.